Human Resources
in Research and Practice:
THE RQ READER

SOCIETY FOR HUMAN RESOURCE MANAGEMENT

Human Resources in Research and Practice: THE RQ READER

Society For Human Resource Management
Alexandria, Virginia
www.shrm.org

Strategic Human Resource Management India
Mumbai, India
www.shrmindia.org

Society For Human Resource Management
Haidian District Beijing, China
www.shrm.org/cn

The Society for Human Resource Management (SHRM) is the world's largest association devoted to human resource management. Representing more than 250,000 members in over 140 countries, the Society serves the needs of HR professionals and advances the interests of the HR profession. Founded in 1948, SHRM has more than 575 affiliated chapters within the United States and subsidiary offices in China and India. Visit SHRM Online at www.shrm.org.

Interior and Cover Design: James McGinnis

Library of Congress Cataloging-in-Publication Data

Human resources in research and practice : the RQ reader / Society for Human Resource Management.

p. cm.
Includes index.
ISBN 978-1-58644-207-1
1. Personnel management. 2. Human capital. I. Society for Human Resource Management (U.S.) II. Research quarterly (SHRM Research Dept.)
HF5549.H87185 2011
658.3--dc22
2010035100

10-0460

Contents

Preface

Human Resources in Research and Practice: The RQ Reader offers a broad spectrum of topics on human resource management (HRM) essential in today's global world. This book presents both research and a practical focus about key areas in people management. Each chapter includes perspectives and experiences of HR professionals in the field—with real-life scenarios—to illustrate the many challenges and opportunities encountered in HRM.

HR professionals, students, and professors all will value the richness of information and resources that provide a solid foundation of knowledge and opportunity for learning about the top issues of human resources. For the HR professional: This resource covers extensive ground, useful and important for everyone, in the HR field. For the student: Whether an undergraduate, in grad school or working on a dissertation for a Ph.D., the student will find a wide range of learning that can be directly applied in the classroom, citations for papers, and group study work. For the professor: Each chapter presents structures to serve as the basis for classroom discussion, supplemental reading, and/or project assignments.

Part I: *Strategic HR Management*
For sustainability in today's global marketplace, organizations must be strategic in their approach to human resource management. This section presents the critical areas of employee engagement, organization development, knowledge management, and change management. These topics are "must haves" for senior HR professionals—and for those learning about human resources on the journey to senior HR work.

Part II: *Staffing Management*
Staffing management has a wide-reaching impact on the workplace of today and tomorrow. No matter the economic environment, competition for talent is strong. HR professionals need to be knowledgeable about the many resources of talent—from the dynamic Millennial generation, the value of diversity in teams, innovation and customer service, to a solid and respectful understanding of cultural differences in the workplace.

Part III: *Employee Relations and Organizational Development*
Leadership. Motivation. Performance. Team work. Ethics. Fairness. What inspires employees to go beyond expectations, for themselves, their group and their organization? Developing leadership skills, working well in a team (local or global), being mentored or mentoring others, effective communication through technology: this section focuses on the important areas of employee relations and organizational development for effective communication, through corporate values, for strong performance.

Part IV: *The HR Professional*
What creates the impetus to learn? No matter one's level of experience in the HR profession, never underestimate the value of knowledge. This section showcases pathways to gain knowledge, be steeped in the value of people and management skills, and contribute to the success of the company's strategy, mission, and goals.

***

In closing, it is my sincere hope that the reader will use this book to go beyond his or her current knowledge base, find ways to make solid and meaningful contributions to his or her organization, and finally, to become the ultimate professional.

Nancy R. Lockwood, MA, SPHR, GPHR
Society for Human Resource Management

PART I

Strategic HR Management

Chapter 1

Leveraging Employee Engagement for Competitive Advantage: HR's Strategic Role

"The challenge today is not just retaining talented people, but fully engaging them, capturing their minds and hearts at each stage of their work lives." [1]

Employee engagement has emerged as a critical driver of business success in today's competitive marketplace. Further, employee engagement can be a deciding factor in organizational success. Not only does engagement have the potential to significantly affect employee retention, productivity and loyalty, it is also a key link to customer satisfaction, company reputation and overall stakeholder value. Thus, to gain a competitive edge, organizations are turning to HR to set the agenda for employee engagement and commitment.

Employee engagement is defined as "the extent to which employees commit to something or someone in their organization, how hard they work and how long they stay as a result of that commitment."[2] Research shows that the connection between an employee's job and organizational strategy, including understanding how important the job is to the firm's success, is the most important driver of employee engagement. In fact, employees with the highest levels of commitment perform 20 percent better and are 87 percent less likely to leave the organization, which indicates that engagement is linked to organizational performance.[3] In contrast, job satisfaction—a term sometimes used interchangeably with employee engagement—is defined as how an employee feels about his or her job, work environment, pay, benefits, etc.[4]

Employee engagement is a complex concept, with many issues influencing engagement levels. Consequently, there are many pathways to foster engagement, with no one "kit" that fits all organizations. While each company may define employee engagement differently, ultimately, the key to effective engagement will be rooted in the flexibility of approach most appropriate for each individual firm. For example, the company may consider a "best practice" and then determine the likely outcome of this practice in its workplace. This *Research Quarterly* is written to provide HR professionals and other business leaders with the knowledge and understanding of the many concepts and aspects of employee engagement as well as offer recommendations to foster engagement.

Trends in Employee Engagement

Today, society and business are witnessing unprecedented change in an increasingly global marketplace, with many companies competing for talent. As organizations move forward into a boundaryless environment, the ability to attract, engage, develop and retain talent will become increasingly important. In view of these changes, a number of trends, as identified in the *SHRM Special Expertise Panels 2006 Trends Report*, are likely to have a significant impact on employee engagement (see Table 1.1). For example, the increased demand for work/life balance and the changing relationship between employers and employees are driving the need for HR professionals and their organizations to truly understand what employees need and want and then determine how to meet those needs while at the same time developing and leveraging workplace talents at all levels.[5]

Table 1.1 Top Trends Lead to Focus on Employee Engagement

- Employee-employer relationship evolving/changing to partnerships.
- Increased demand for work/life balance.
- HR's greater role in promoting the link between employee performance and its impact on business goals.
- Increasing focus on selective retention for keeping mission-critical talent.
- Work intensification as employers increase productivity with fewer employees and resources.
- Acquiring and keeping key talent reemerging as top issues of concern.
- Decline in traditional communication methods and increase in cyber communication.
- Needs, wants and behaviors of the talent pool driving changes in attraction, selection and retention practices.

Source: Adapted from Society for Human Resource Management. (2006). *SHRM Special Expertise Panels 2006 Trends Report*. Alexandria, VA: Author.

In addition, trends in workforce readiness highlight the importance of organizational success. To ensure that new workforce entrants attain the essential skill levels needed in today's workplace, business leaders have the responsibility to partner with schools (e.g., high schools and two- and four-year colleges) and other organizations to provide learning opportunities, such as internships, summer jobs or job shadowing.[6] The continued acceleration of change, both domestically and globally, places greater emphasis on the role of HR to develop effective employee engagement strategies for the current and future workforce.

Engagement as a Driver for Organizational Success

Engaged employees work harder, are more loyal and are more likely to go the "extra mile" for the corporation. There are different levels of engagement (see Table 1.2), and understanding the types of engagement provides perspective into employee behaviors that can either positively or negatively affect organizational success. Employee engagement can be considered as cognitive, emotional and behavioral. Cognitive engagement refers to employees' beliefs about the company, its leaders and the workplace culture. The emotional aspect is how employees feel about the company, the leaders and their colleagues. The behavioral factor is the value-added component reflected in the amount of effort employees put into their work (e.g., brainpower, extra time and energy).[7]

Table 1.2 Levels of Employee Engagement

Engaged employees work with passion and feel a profound connection to their company. They drive innovation and move the organization forward.

Not engaged employees are essentially "checked out." They're sleepwalking through their work day, putting time–not energy or passion–into their work.

Actively disengaged employees aren't just unhappy at work: they're busy acting out their unhappiness. Every day, these workers undermine what their engaged co-workers accomplish.

Source: Adapted from "Engaged employees inspire company innovation." (2006, October 12). *Gallup Management Journal*, http://gmj.gallup.com

Employees who are highly involved in their work processes—such as conceiving, designing and implementing workplace and process changes—are more engaged. As highlighted in the literature, the link between high-involvement work practices and positive beliefs and attitudes—as associated with employee engagement and generating behaviors leading to enhanced performance—is an important driver for business success. For example, a recent study analyzed 132 U.S. manufacturing firms and found that companies utilizing high-performance work systems had significantly higher labor productivity than their competitors. When employees have the power to make decisions related to their performance, can access information about company costs and revenues, and have the necessary knowledge, training and development to do their jobs—***and*** are rewarded for their efforts—they are more productive.[8]

As highlighted in a recent report by the SHRM Foundation, employee engagement can be measured in dollars and can yield significant savings. For example, at the beverage company of MolsonCoors, it was found that engaged employees were five times less likely than nonengaged employees to have a safety incident and seven times less likely to have a lost-time safety incident. In fact, the average cost of a safety incident for an engaged employee was $63, compared with an average of $392 for a nonengaged employee. Consequently, through strengthening employee engagement, the company saved $1,721,760 in safety costs in 2002. In addition, savings were found in sales performance teams through engagement. In 2005, for example, low-engagement teams were seen falling behind engaged teams, with a difference in performance-related costs of low- versus high-engagement teams totaling $2,104,823.[9]

Related to productivity, employee health is a critical factor in employee engagement. Conditions that support health and psychological well-being are open communication, respect, trust, teamwork and positive work relationships. The Gallup Organization, a leader in employee engagement research, found that employee physical health and psychological well-being affect the quality and quantity of work. For example, 62 percent of engaged employees feel their work positively affects their physical health. Yet that number drops to 39 percent among nonengaged employees and to 22 percent among employees who are actively disengaged. In addition, 54 percent of disengaged employees say their work has a negative effect on their health and 51 percent see a negative effect on their well-being. The implication for HR and managers is that engaged employees are more likely to view the organization and job as a healthy environment and therefore more likely to support the organization.[10]

Research also shows that customer loyalty is closely related to employee engagement. In a recent empirical study, the relationship between the availability of organizational resources (i.e., training, technology, autonomy) and employee engagement in work units was found to have a positive effect on employee performance and customer loyalty. When employees feel more engaged in their work, the climate is better for service and the customer receives better-quality service, thus promoting customer loyalty. The practical implication is that the organization (e.g., service organizations, such as banks, hotels, restaurants, membership associations) must focus more on keeping employees engaged. HR leaders, as well as managers, have the mission to build and sustain a workplace environment that fosters engagement and is also attractive to potential employees.[11]

Levers for Employee Engagement

Employee engagement, as a work-related state of mind, can be characterized by vigor, dedication and absorption. Vigor means high levels of energy and mental resilience on the job, persistence in the face of difficulties and a willingness to invest effort in one's work. Dedication refers to a sense of inspiration, pride, significance, enthusiasm and challenge at work. Absorption is being happy, fully concentrated and deeply engrossed in one's work so that time passes quickly, with difficulty detaching from work.[12] Certain levers drive employee engagement (see Table 1.3) and reflect factors that promote vigor, dedication and absorption. Engagement is also strongly influenced by organizational characteristics, such as a reputation for integrity, good internal communication and a culture of innovation.[13] As HR works to establish meaningful programs and workplace practices to attract and retain talent, employee engagement levers are important to consider.

Table 1.3 Leveraging Employee Engagement

Business risks: Channel engagement efforts to those places in the organization where high engagement is critical to achieving business targets.

Key contributors: Expand the organization's understanding of "contribution" to include employees–beyond the high-potential population–who create significant value.

Engagement barriers (what gets in the way of high engagement): Be aware of the challenges in identifying 'what's really going on' in the organization.

Culture: Though often considered a "soft" concept, culture can yield compelling, hard business results. Organizations must provide employees with "three C's:" connection, contribution and credibility.

Source: Adapted from Corporate Leadership Council. (2004). *Driving performance and retention through employee engagement.* Washington, DC: Corporate Executive Board.

The employee's emotional commitment to the job and company is a key lever for engagement. Literally, the degree and quality of performance depend on heart over mind. The level of emotional commitment—the extent to which the employee derives enjoyment, meaning, pride or inspiration from something or someone in the organization—is a significant variable in engagement and thus in performance. Emotional commitment to the job, organization, team and manager has been found to determine stronger performance than rational commitment (the extent to which an employee feels that someone or something within the company provides developmental, financial or professional rewards in employee's best interests).[14]

In addition, work/life balance is increasingly important for engagement and affects retention. As emphasized in a recent study on generations and gender by the Families and Work Institute, Generations X and Y have different workplace expectations than do the baby boomers and mature workers.[15] By being aware of the unique needs of diverse groups, as well as by recognizing individual differences within these groups, HR can better understand the challenges of increased diversity in the organization's workforce (e.g., different generations, more females, more Hispanic employees in the United States) and work toward designing and implementing workplace policies and practices to engage diverse employee groups.

Finally, a holistic view of employee engagement can be helpful to determine what is working and what is not. Looking at predictors or "hot buttons" offers HR a way to better understand what practices and policies in their organization effectively promote employee motivation, attendance, retention and productivity. By using a matrix of engagement predictors (organizational process, values, management, role challenge, work/life balance, information, reward/recognition, work environment and products/services), HR can help the organization better manage engagement and ultimately foster motivation, productivity and retention.[16]

The Influence of Workplace Culture

Workplace culture sets the tone for employee engagement. Is the culture considered family-friendly, for example, or is the organization so focused on getting ahead that taking care of its employees is left out of the strategy? Or perhaps the nature of the workplace culture falls somewhere between those two possibilities. Research shows that organizations that provide a workplace culture with the psychological conditions of meaningfulness (job enrichment, work-role fit), safety (supportive manager and co-workers) and availability (resources available) are more likely to have engaged employees.[17] Consequently, organizations considered as an "employer of choice" are more likely to attract and retain the best talent and have higher levels of engagement. Beyond compensation and benefits, key retention factors include the mission and values of the company, treatment of people, learning and development opportunities, work/life balance policies and practices, and rewards to employees for their efforts.

In addition, employee loyalty must be earned through a culture of respect and integrity and learning and development.[18] A study on organizational respect and burnout in the human services profession, for example, emphasizes that respect plays a pivotal role in employee engagement levels. The study highlights that an organization that treats its employees with dignity and respect creates a workplace culture that fosters loyalty and engagement.[19] Such organizations often demonstrate proactive practices and best outcomes by weaving retention and engagement deeply into the fabric of the workplace culture.

The Power of Communication

Clear, consistent and honest communication is an important management tool for employee engagement. HR promotes thoughtful communication strategies that encourage employee engagement by keeping the workforce energized, focused and productive. Such strategies are critical to long-term organizational success. In addition, strategic and continuous communication lends credibility to the organization's leadership. (On the other hand, lack of communication or poorly communicated information can lead to distrust, dissatisfaction, skepticism, cynicism and unwanted turnover.) Branding, for example, is a type of communication strategy that can promote employee engagement by sending "the right message" about the company, its mission, values and products/services to the workforce and marketplace at large.

To recharge employee morale and support of the organization's objectives, HR can foster an environment for engagement by developing a targeted, proactive strategic communication plan. The communication strategy can provide focus on organizational goals and determine methods of communication and information points for different audiences (e.g., employees versus media). Key points for HR to consider are: (1) communicate from the top down to build employee confidence and buy-in; (2) involve employees whenever possible, such as through focus groups; (3) communicate and explain all aspects of change, negative and positive; (4) personalize communications to address the question "what's in it for me?"; and (5) track results and set milestones to evaluate the objectives of the communication plan.[20]

Commitment to the Organization

The number one factor that influences employee commitment is the manager-employee relationship. The manager creates the connection between the employee and the organization, and as a result, the manager-employee relationship is often the "deal breaker" in relation to retention. A recent study shows that employees who trust their managers appear to have more pride in the organization and are more likely to feel they are applying their individual talents for their own success and that of the organization. However, the findings show only 56 percent of employees feel their manager has good knowledge of what they do and promotes the use of their unique talents.[21]

Managers who demonstrate the following characteristics promote employee engagement: (1) show strong commitment to diversity; (2) take responsibility for successes and failures; (3) demonstrate honesty and integrity; (4) help find solutions to problems; (5) respect and care for employees as individuals; (6) set realistic performance expectations; (7) demonstrate passion for success; and (8) defend direct reports.[22] The organization will want to rethink keeping managers who foster disengaged employees and therefore lose valuable talent to other organizations.

In addition, HR practices can make the difference between effective engagement and valuable human capital joining the competition. For example, a study about the impact of HR practices and organizational commitment on the profitability of business units found a close relationship between HR practices, operating expenses and firm performance. In addition, employees were found to be more committed to the organization when managed with progressive HR practices. At a large food-service corporation with operations in the United States and Canada, the study results were put to practical use when the senior HR executive used the data in presentations to demonstrate the kind of performance the company might see as a result of developing and implementing proven HR practices. Going one step further, to assist business-unit leaders whose groups were not meeting performance goals, the company developed a portal to help identify key performance deficiencies and now offers information on HR practices to help increase performance.[23] As this study demonstrates, HR's role in promoting employee commitment—including coaching managers to be effective people managers—is a significant factor in employee engagement.

Barriers to Employee Engagement

Often in the form of rules, workplace culture and behaviors, barriers to engagement can be damaging to employees, customers and stakeholders—and ultimately, to the organization's financial success. In fact, by operating in a "black-and-white" world, even HR can act as a barrier—depending on how workplace policies and practices are implemented—rather than helping to motivate employees through innovative and proactive practices. Also, barriers can prevent efficiency, do not promote a positive and engaging work environment and may damage the ability of an organization to act quickly. Importantly, barriers can prevent customers from getting what they need.[24]

To be better positioned to address barriers to engagement, organizations must determine what is working and what is not. The Gallup Organization, for example, identified 12 indicators that link employee satisfaction with positive business outcomes and profitability. The initial study considered four key areas: customer satisfaction/loyalty, profitability, productivity and employee turnover. These indicators, known as the Q12, are based on employee involvement topics, such as attitude, feedback, recognition and measurement. Today, many employers base their employee attitude surveys on the Q12 (see Table 1.4).[25]

Table 1.4 Questions to Determine Employee Engagement (Q12)

1. Do you know what is expected of you at work?
2. Do you have the materials and equipment you need to do your work right?
3. At work, do you have the opportunity to do what you do best every day?
4. In the last seven days, have you received recognition or praise for doing good work?
5. Does your supervisor, or someone at work, seem to care about you as a person?
6. Is there someone at work who encourages your development?
7. At work, do your opinions seem to count?
8. Does the mission/purpose of your company make you feel your job is important?
9. Are your associates (fellow employees) committed to doing quality work?
10. Do you have a best friend at work?
11. In the last six months, has someone at work talked to you about your progress?
12. In the past year, have you had opportunities at work to learn and grow?

Source: Copyright © 1993 – 1998 The Gallup Organization, Washington, D.C. All rights reserved.

In addition, stress levels in the workplace have increased substantially due to the pressures of competition, technology that promotes the fast-paced 24/7 global economy and the blurring of boundaries between work and home life. For example, a 2004 study found that 27 percent of U.S. employees were overwhelmed by how much work they had to do and 29 percent often or very often did not have time to process or reflect on the work they did. Overworked employees make more mistakes and tend to have higher levels of stress and physical health problems, experience clinical depression and neglect caring for themselves.[26] The message for HR is that stressed employees are likely to be less engaged and less productive in the workplace.

Measuring Employee Engagement

Measuring employee engagement is a smart business strategy to improve productivity and attain business objectives. It allows the organization to track progress, or slippage, and determine what gaps exist in terms of organizational engagement, attendance and retention, motivation and aspirations. A recent article from the SHRM Foundation highlights common themes of how companies measure engagement (see Table 1.5).

Table 1.5 Ten Common Themes: How Companies Measure Engagement

1. Pride in employer.
2. Satisfaction with employer.
3. Job satisfaction.
4. Opportunity to perform well at challenging work.
5. Recognition and positive feedback for one's contributions.
6. Personal support from one's supervisor.
7. Effort above and beyond the minimum.
8. Understanding the link between one's job and the organization's mission.
9. Prospects for future growth with one's employer.
10. Intention to stay with one's employer.

Source: Vance, R. J. (2006). Effective practice guidelines: *Employee engagement and commitment.* Alexandria, VA: SHRM Foundation. (Reprinted with permission.)

The financial and competitive advantage of employee engagement efforts can be demonstrated by measuring engagement and commitment initiatives. The construction-equipment maker Caterpillar documented significant savings as a result of increasing employee engagement. For example, the company reaped an $8.8 million annual savings from decreased attrition, absenteeism and overtime at a European plant, had a 70 percent increase in output in less than four months at an Asian Pacific plant, and experienced a $2 million increase in profit and 34 percent increase in highly satisfied customers at a start-up plant.[27]

To effectively measure and manage predictors of employee engagement, it is best to use a combination of tools. Depending on the purpose, there are many measures from which to select. Examples of measures include predictive internal surveys and/or focus groups, detailed gap analyses by division, location, department, workplace, etc., and communication of prediction gaps and progress to the organization. Many companies use engagement surveys as a primary measurement tool to determine how well talent is being managed. Such surveys are often considered much more than a measure of employee satisfaction. Rather, engagement surveys also encompass other dimensions, such as intent to stay, employee trust and organizational commitment. Once engagement data are gathered, the next logical step would be to examine the relationship between the engagement measures and business results. By asking relevant questions about employee engagement, HR can learn information to better determine levels of motivation, trust/distrust and overall company spirit, help minimize the risk of potential key skill losses around concerns about rewards, recognition and career development, gain a measure of the effectiveness of management, and evaluate the effectiveness of HR strategies and systems, such as performance management.[28]

To get a sense of employee engagement levels or possible issues, research also suggests using pulse surveys or ad-hoc surveys with a structured questionnaire. For example, a recent empirical study in the banking sector indicated a relationship between job satisfaction, quality and productivity and customer service. The study found that three linked factors influenced employee empowerment and customer treatment: HR management practices (service training and service rewards), service systems practices and service leadership practices. This study provides HR and employers with food for thought regarding the relationship between job satisfaction, employee engagement, retention and financial results.[29]

In addition, organizations concerned with retention among new hires may use engagement surveys to track turnover during the first 30, 90 or 180 days or even the first year of employment. Specific measures for new-hire engagement might include (1) percentage of employees completing a comprehensive orientation process; (2) percentage completing an "entrance interview;" (3) percentage coached by a buddy or mentor; (4) percentage of new hires considered "outstanding performers;" and (5) first-year voluntary turnover rates. On the other hand, measures of sustained employee engagement may include (1) absenteeism rates; (2) performance/quality rates; (3) training hours per employee; (4) ratio of internal to external hires; (5) top-performer voluntary turnover rates; (6) overall voluntary turnover rate; and (7) percentage of employees completing individual development plans.[30] Ultimately, employee engagement measures provide employees with regular opportunities to give open and honest feedback. HR can use the data for strategic advantage to understand and work toward improving engagement, talent retention, positive company reputation and company growth.

Global Perspectives of Employee Engagement

Across the globe, critical factors for HR leaders are performance and retention. Due to the new employment contract in today's globally competitive and rapidly changing environment, retaining talent has become very challenging. As highlighted in the 2006 report on SHRM Special Expertise Panel trends, demographic changes are leading to increased diversity in the global labor market. The shift from mainstream and emerging markets to a multicultural majority is, in turn, leading to changes in HR business practices, such as the design of recruitment, benefits, training, motivation and rewards systems.[31] Trust and loyalty are also coming to the forefront in global firms as important issues that HR must address. In addition, among the global drivers for engagement are leadership, work/life balance, branding and opportunities to use employee talent. A study by Mercer, for example, found that companies with a high profile or good employer brand in China appeared to have more success attracting candidates.[32]

A recent global workforce study by Towers Perrin considered key success factors of employee engagement, job satisfaction and high performance. It surveyed 86,000 employees at all levels of the organization in mid-size and large companies in 16 countries across four continents about attitudes, needs, work ethic and personal commitment of people to their jobs and companies. The findings reveal that people tend to stay with organizations considered as "talent-friendly" and progressive—that is, organizations that have leading-edge work environments and people practices.[33]

However, while certain factors of engagement are considered to be universal, to effectively promote engagement, HR leaders will need to be aware of country, regional and cultural differences when designing employee engagement and commitment initiatives. To illustrate the myriad of different drivers in different countries, for example, consider these top attraction drivers: in Canada—competitive base pay, work/life balance and career advancement opportunities; in India—focus on the reputation of the organization as a good employer; in the United States—competitive health benefits; in Germany—the level of autonomy; in Japan—the caliber of co-workers; and in the Netherlands—the collaborative environment. These differences suggest that each country and/or culture has certain factors seen as important in the workplace.[34]

To retain top talent, research also shows that while compensation and promotions are important, employers need to pay more attention to "soft issues," such as job quality, flexibility and individual differences. A landmark study of global men and women executives—and the relationship between gender and career advancement—examined factors that enhanced and inhibited the success of these executives on the job and at home. The results found that while most executives (61 percent) were work-centric, a significant minority (32 percent) were dual-centric, giving equal weight to personal and work life. This latter group of executives was less stressed, felt more successful at work and more easily managed work and personal/family life demands. To promote engagement, advancement and retention of the upcoming generation of global leaders, global executives recommended these changes: improve career development and performance management systems for both genders, create an inclusive work environment and address work/life needs. In view of this study, global HR professionals will want to thoughtfully consider how to structure the work environment to foster the growth of employee commitment and increase levels of engagement for future global leaders (see Table 1.6).[35]

Table 1.6 Actions Recommended by Global Executives for the Next Generation of Leaders

Improve career development and performance management systems for both genders:

- Create objective and inclusive performance management systems.
- Provide key developmental experiences.
- Offer mentoring and networking opportunities.

Create an inclusive work environment:

- Provide equal opportunities.
- Educate the workforce about diversity and inclusion.
- Broaden the acceptable leadership styles for both women and men.
- Guard against reverse discrimination.

Address work/life needs:

- Reduce expectations of very long work hours.
- Provide role models.
- Rethink career paths.
- Support involvement in activities outside of work.

Source: Adapted from Galinksy, E., Salmond, K., Bond, J. T., Brumit Kropf, M., Moore, M., & Harrington, B. (2003). *Leaders in a global economy: A study of executive women and men.* New York: Families and Work Institute, Catalyst and The Center for Work & Family.

Studies on Employee Engagement

In recent years, a number of studies have focused on employee engagement and its link to company performance and sustainability. The following studies highlight the role of employee engagement in today's business environment. HR professionals who seek proactive practices that positively affect employee productivity will find this research pertinent to their work.

Feeling Good Matters in the Workplace[36]

According to this *Gallup Management Journal* study, supervisors play a critical role in worker well-being and engagement. The survey considers how employee perceptions of happiness and well-being affect job performance. Happy and engaged employees are better equipped to handle stress and change, are much more likely to have a positive relationship with their manager, feel more valued by their employer and are more satisfied with their lives. People with higher levels of engagement appear to substantially enjoy more positive interactions with co-workers than do their less-engaged counterparts. The study suggests that organizations can boost firm productivity if they recognize these issues and help employees improve their well-being.

Driving Performance and Retention through Employee Engagement[37]

In a global survey of the engagement levels of 50,000 employees in 27 countries, research by the Corporate Leadership Council emphasizes the link of engagement to business success and its direct impact on employee performance and retention. Organizations that have a highly engaged workforce were found to have almost 10 times as many committed, high-effort workers as those with a low-engaged workforce. The findings point to the manager as the most important enabler of employee commitment to the organization, job and work teams.

Employee Engagement Report 2006[38]

Building on research from 2004 and 2005, this study examines how employees in North America, Europe and Asia-Pacific feel about their organizations and jobs. The top reason people stay is for fulfilling work (44 percent). The findings also reveal that 35 percent of employees are likely at risk of leaving their organizations. Top reasons include career, the work itself and the manager. Interestingly, only 38 percent of employees had seen visible actions to increase employee engagement. More than 30 percent are considering leaving, and only 12 percent of employees intend to stay.

Recommendations

Determined by company mission and culture, proactive and best outcome practices around employee engagement vary for each organization. Below are recommended strategic actions for HR to strengthen engagement.

- Clearly and consistently communicate organizational goals and objectives.
- Establish policies and practices that promote a workplace culture that stimulates employee engagement.
- Align organizational goals to day-to-day work.

- Maintain an open dialogue among senior management, managers and employees.
- Reward managers whose behavior fosters employee engagement.
- Listen carefully to what employees want and need.
- Provide opportunities and challenges to leverage the respective talents of employees.
- Do a pulse check—are employees engaged? Find out what is working and what is not.
- Hold managers accountable for demonstrating organizational values, development of team members and results.
- Be sure that employees know how they can contribute.
- Genuinely thank employees for their contributions.

In Closing

The level of engagement determines whether people are productive and stay with the organization—or move to the competition. Research highlights that the employee connection to the organizational strategy and goals, acknowledgment for work well done, and a culture of learning and development foster high levels of engagement. Without a workplace environment for employee engagement, turnover will increase and efficiency will decline, leading to low customer loyalty and decreased stakeholder value. Ultimately, because the cost of poor employee engagement will be detrimental to organizational success, it is vital for HR to foster positive, effective people managers along with workplace policies and practices that focus on employee well-being, health and work/life balance.

Chapter 2

Organization Development: A Strategic HR Tool

To remain competitive in today's global marketplace, organizations must change. One of the most effective tools to promote successful change is organization development (OD). As HR increasingly focuses on building organizational learning, skills and workforce productivity, the effective use of OD to help achieve company business goals and strategies is becoming a broad HR competency as well as a key strategic HR tool.[1]

While there are variations regarding the definition of OD, the basic purpose of organization development is to increase an organization's effectiveness through planned interventions related to the organization's processes (often company-wide), resulting in improvements in productivity, return on investment and employee satisfaction.[2] Yet while OD and human resources may be viewed by some as competing disciplines, in fact, the overarching goal of these two fields is complementary: to promote and sustain organizational success. Further illustrating the link between OD and HR is the fact that organizational assessments typically fall under the responsibility of HR and the principles and value of OD correspond with many aspects of the HR mission. This article provides background on the complex field of OD and highlights how HR can use OD for the betterment of the organization.

The Evolving Field of Organization Development

As HR, in the role of strategic business partner, leads initiatives aimed at organizational design, process and performance, OD offers HR professionals a wealth of tools, models, theories and competencies invaluable for a competitive business environment. However, until recently, OD and human resources were considered distinct and separate entities. For example, OD has roots in social sciences and applied behavior, with values based in humanistic psychology, whereas the field of human resources is based in human capital theory, behaviorism and performance engineering.[3] Today, the division between OD and HR is less clear. In fact, the literature indicates that these two disciplines are melding together, with a growing collaboration and integration between OD and HR.[4]

From a historic perspective, the OD field began about 50 years ago. Changing and dynamic, organization development is a values-based interdisciplinary profession with a behavioral science approach, drawing from many fields: anthropology, business, counseling, economics, education, management, organization behavior, psychology, public administration and sociology. OD helps improve organizational effectiveness, with its major focus on both the total system and the interdependent parts of the company. OD professionals work to increase organizational effectiveness and performance, working closely with many stakeholders—from employees and management to customers, stockholders and the community at large.[5]

Over time, the OD profession has evolved and broadened in scope. In the late 1980s, leaders in the field suggested that organization development would better serve firms by becoming more strategic.[6] In 1988, researchers Jelinek and Litterer expanded OD by referring to it in terms such as team building, group decision, job design and helping teams cope with stress.[7] Today, HR leaders can use the collaborative approach of OD, through thoughtfully planned and long-range strategies, to address organizational challenges in today's dynamic business environment.

The Business Link Between OD and HR

Since OD helps identify and effect organizational process and design change, it is of immediate use to HR leaders. OD brings analytical skills and objective problem solving to the complex human system. As researchers Cummings and Worley point out, OD practices are of direct value regarding organizational workforce skills and learning, including goal setting through performance management, reward systems, career planning and workforce diversity.[8]

In fact, over the next five to 10 years, the demand for HR to effectively use OD in relation to organizational change will become even more critical. Changes in the marketplace already point in that direction. For example, as Generations X and Y move into key leadership positions, the workplace will become more diverse. Changes such as new advances in technology and people living and working longer contribute to the dynamics of organizational change. Even the emerging world economic powers, China and India, are already having an impact on the strategic goals of many organizations, which are now forced to rethink their profit centers and evaluate workforce skills.[9] Thus, the ability to successfully utilize and implement OD, in view of imminent and future workforce changes, is an advantage for HR leaders.

By using OD as part of its skill set, HR can broaden its depth of knowledge and skills regarding change and better support the organization. For example, a recent study points to the expectation of using change and innovation as a critical element for competitive advantage. According to the *IBM Global CEO Study 2006*, 65 percent of the world's top corporate CEOs plan to "radically change their companies in the next two years" due to pressures from competitive markets. The study, which polled more than 750 top CEOs worldwide, emphasizes that CEOs are increasingly focused on innovation through business models and operations as the key mechanism to drive change. In fact, 76 percent of CEOs rank business partner and customer collaboration as key sources for new ideas.[10] The implications of this study point to the importance of HR's role as a strategic partner in organizational change, locating the right talent and implementing organization-wide change effectively—and doing so in a strategically planned manner with clear direction and goals.

In addition, the effective use of strategic OD interventions promotes HR's agenda for organizational success (see Table 2.1). For example, knowledge management is an essential aspect of both OD and HR. In today's economy, the loss of organizational knowledge is a common result of downsizing. Whether these changes occur in the private or public sector, there are similar challenges for all organizations: the loss of individuals with organizational memory, a corresponding depleted supply of coaches and mentors and a decline in problem-solving ability. However, these changes also present an opportunity to reinvent the company mission and critical programs.[11] For example, HR can assess the work environment to identify strengths on which to build and areas where change and improvement are needed, develop systems to provide feedback on individual performance, create reward systems compatible with the organization's goals and coach senior executives on decisionmaking.[12] Thus, the use of OD processes to revisit the fundamental values of the organization, assist in the redesign of the company and develop and implement knowledge management initiatives is a strategic essential for HR to demonstrate not only its value to the organization but also its ability to be flexible and innovative.

Table 2.1 Strategic OD Interventions

- Organizational transformation
- Culture change
- Mergers and acquisitions
- Integrated strategic change
- Knowledge management
- Organizational learning
- Global strategic orientation
- Ethics change management
- Process improvement
- Organization design
- Whole system analysis

Source: Adapted from Yaeger, T., & Sorensen, P. (2006, Winter). Strategic organization development: Past to present. *Organization Development Journal*, 24(4), 10-17.

Finally, in view of the importance of sustainability in today's business world, HR professionals can use OD for strategic advantage in other key areas. Examples of interventions with broad, far-reaching effects are:[13]

- Creating a collaborative environment to help the organization be more effective and efficient.
- Designing a strategic plan for how the organization makes decisions about its future and how to achieve that future.
- Working with organizations immediately following a merger/acquisition to help develop a common culture by bringing personnel, policies and processes together.
- Working with organizational leaders to assist in the approach to move into other countries.

Principles and Values

As HR professionals gravitate toward organization development, it is helpful to have an understanding of its principles and values (see Table 2.2). Organization development is grounded in principles and core values, known as "interventions," to guide the OD professional in terms of behavior and actions. OD focuses on the whole organization as well as work groups, departments and individuals. Overall, OD is driven by humanistic values (respect, inclusion, authenticity, collaboration) and is an education-based discipline, with the goal to develop values, norms, attitudes and management practices, resulting in a healthy organizational climate that rewards healthy behaviors.[14]

Table 2.2 Key Values of Organization Development

- *Respect and inclusion:* Equally value the perspectives and opinions of everyone.
- *Collaboration:* Build win-win relationships in the organization.
- *Authenticity:* Help people behave congruent with their espoused values.
- *Self-awareness:* Commit to developing self-awareness and interpersonal skills within the organization.
- *Empowerment:* Focus on helping everyone in the client organization increase their individual level of autonomy and sense of personal power and courage to enhance productivity and elevate employee morale.
- *Democracy and social justice:* Believe that people will support the things that they have had a hand in shaping, that the human spirit is elevated by pursing democratic principles.

Source: Adapted from McLean, G. N. (2006). *Organizational development: Principles, processes, performance.* San Francisco: Berrett-Koehler Publishers, Inc.

Client-focused, OD is based in open-systems theory and approaches and uses action research to focus on process (the way things happen) and determine the best pathway and rationale for change. Planned interventions are based on results from active inquiry and assessment of both internal and external environments. For HR and OD professionals alike, to successfully effect cultural change in the company, change initiatives work best with a bottom-up approach.[15] For example, once the system components are evaluated, HR can use OD in short, quick, market-driven interventions as well as system-wide with numerous variables. At the same time, as HR leaders know, the value of organization development as a powerful catalyst for change is found when the entire company is engaged in the process. OD is particularly effective when supported by the CEO and senior management.[16]

Interestingly, based on the results of a recent survey that assessed the field of OD, the critical strong points noted in OD are directly of value to HR professionals. For example, OD promotes adaptive learning and knowledge management essential for organizational growth, creativity and innovation. Learning also promotes diversity of thought and experience in decision-making, key factors for leadership development.[17]

It is important to differentiate between OD and change management. While each has similar goals (e.g., promoting greater organizational effectiveness, productivity and return on investment), the underlying reason to use one process over the other is distinctly different. As researchers Beer and Nohria suggest, "O change" (the organization's human capability) is planned (e.g., usually long-term, system-wide planning), while "E change" (economic value) is market-driven and does not follow OD principles. In contrast to OD interventions (such as O change), change management (connected to E change) is often best used to make immediate decisions that require the ability to act swiftly.[18]

Mini-Case Study #1: Organizational Change in Health and Social Services[19]

Organization development initiatives are complex and require thoughtful planning and time, with periodic evaluations throughout the process. However, misunderstandings and resistance to change (e.g., by staff) can present significant challenges. The following mini-case study is an example of planned change that, despite good intentions, did not fully come to fruition.

A home care company serving 6,000 clients implemented an organizational change initiative, with the overall goal to move from a centralized allocation and control of services and resources to an empowered partnership approach to service delivery. To achieve this goal, organization leaders used a number of strategies, such as vision- and goal-setting exercises, recognition and rewards to promote commitment, the use of change champions, and train-the-trainer programs. Other venues included a comprehensive communication plan, media releases and brochures for clients. However, in the one-year follow-up, the findings indicated that while staff were making an effort to implement the partnering strategies, in fact, the long-standing service delivery behaviors, norms, expectations and goals had not changed significantly. The study results suggest that although much information was disseminated, it did not reach everyone at all levels to the same degree. Consequently, there was resistance to the projected change. At the client level, for example, there was deep skepticism and confusion about the processes. The misinterpretation and misunderstanding of the flexible client-driven care initiative further exacerbated resistance to change. Since providers tended to implement tasks and procedures in terms of their individual interpretations of the initiative, the partnering process—a critical aspect of the initiative—was often overlooked. The overall outcome was a transfer of work from higher to lower levels. Consequently, it was the clients who were expected to bear much of the burden regarding their own care. However, that intention, as part of the change initiative, was not well communicated to clients. Unfortunately, many were either unprepared or unable to proactively serve in the capacity of partner with their case worker. In addition, case workers found their decision- making authority diminished. Overall, the change initiative, as viewed by the organization, was unsuccessful.

As this mini-case study portrays, not all initiatives will be successful. This example highlights the importance of not only choosing appropriate change strategies for the intended result but also truly understanding and addressing what the change will mean to all involved. The change initiative may have been more effective had there been regular check points to evaluate the progress, thus providing an opportunity to redirect and/or refocus with alternative action plans to yield better results a year or so later.

OD Competencies

Much research has been done on organization development competencies. Critical competencies include the ability to remain neutral, have a "tough skin" and be courageous, naturally inquisitive, respectful, trustworthy and analytical with a commitment to application.[20] Researchers Worley and Feyerherm identified the core knowledge competencies for OD professionals: organization design, organization research, system dynamics, history of organization development and change, and theories and models of change. In addition, they determined six core skill competencies: managing the consulting process, analysis and diagnosis, designing and choosing appropriate interventions, facilitating and process consultation, developing client capability, and evaluating organizational change.[21] From an HR perspective, there are many opportunities to use these competencies on both individual and organizational levels:[22]

HR Professional

1. Using self-assessment tools (e.g., gap analysis) for success.
2. Developing a self-development plan.
3. Supporting performance reviews, mentoring, coaching and feedback sessions.
4. Determining targets for promotion or career development.

Organization

1. Focusing on the organization's priorities.
2. Assisting in budgeting for employee development.
3. Assisting in the development of succession planning.
4. Creating measures to evaluate the success of strategic initiative implementation.

Looking at the future of OD and how to best work with organizations, Dr. Saul Eisen developed 32 broad and long-reaching competencies for success in the 21st century (see Table 2.3). The overarching goal is to build high-performance organizations that are a great place to work, with focus on both performance and people to lead to a competitive advantage.[23] These competencies offer insight into development plans for HR leaders to expand the OD skills of their staff.

Table 2.3 Emerging and Future OD Competencies

- Ability to design and implement individual and organizational interventions that build capacity to think, make decisions and take action systematically: see the big picture.
- Ability to build effective feedback loops, recognize or anticipate and adjust for the unintended, delayed and counterintuitive long-term consequences.
- Ability to work ethically and courageously with inter-organization issues to create wider inclusive boundaries among stakeholders.
- Skill in bridge-building and alliance management, including developing trust across a wide range of diverse constituents.
- Expanded knowledge of systems thinking to include a global perspective, building strategic alliances and using large group methods when appropriate.
- Deep understanding of culture: how it influences behavior, how it can be changed and developed, and what is the connection between culture and performance.
- Skills for developing transformational leaders capable of championing change and transforming organizations.
- Ability to use and promote reflection, dialogue and exploration to understand issues, differences and values of paradoxes and not rush to find a single problem solution.

Source: Adapted from Eisen, S. (2002). *A Delphi study of global trends, implications for managers, emerging intervention strategies, and future competencies in OD.* Retrieved from www.sonoma.edu/programs/od/delphi/. [Material used with Permission from Saul Eisen, Ph.D.]

Organizational Context and Learning

Essential for the advancement of OD is a workplace environment that promotes learning. In addition, in view of the complexity of today's business world, the ability to do critical self-reflection thinking and learning is at the root of the organization review process. Peter Senge of the Massachusetts Institute of Technology Business School is one of the researchers known for the development of a learning organization model. This model promotes the development of openness and trust, finding new ways of reframing and thinking through issues and problems, team development through learning and the development of a shared set of values and vision for the organization. While not a guarantee, a strong culture of organizational learning can significantly contribute to the success of organization development.[24]

Learning not only promotes retention and career development but also supports the organization's ability to remain competitive. As HR professionals collaborate with management to promote learning, it is essential to be cognizant of core aspects and values of organizational learning (see Table 2.4). Thus, the ability to evaluate, design and implement organizational learning and development programs will likely become a key OD competency for HR professionals.

Table 2.4 Elements of the Learning Organization

- Provides continuous learning opportunities.
- Uses learning–individual and organization-wide–to achieve organizational goals.
- Links individual performance with overall organizational performance.
- Fosters inquiry and dialogue.
- Embraces creative tension as a source of energy and renewal.
- Encourages people to take risks (recognizing that sometimes risks result in failures).
- Encourages and facilitates the open sharing of experience.
- Ensures an active awareness of and interaction with the environment, both internal and external, in which the organization operates.

Source: Adapted from Rowden, R. W. (2001). The learning organization and strategic change. *SAM: Advanced Management Journal*, 66(3), 11-23.

Diagnostic Tools and OD Interventions

Many companies turn to professional development and training as a solution to organizational change. OD is a logical place to start to evaluate what problems contribute to a different outcome than desired and then determine the best solution. However, planned change requires a clear understanding of organizational issues. To do so, a number of diagnostic tools are available. For example, to understand the workings of the company, a well-known OD tool is the open-systems model that considers the relationships and behaviors of "systems"—such as organizations, groups, people.[25] However, prior to planning OD work, it is critical to know if the deficiency is in knowledge, skill or ability/aptitude.[26] For example, 85 percent of performance issues are not training-related (knowledge or skill). In addition, it is important for HR to have an in-depth understanding of how the organization is structured: the design may be a functional, divisional, matrix or process structure. Then, to determine appropriate actions, a detailed assessment is required. It is also essential to determine who in the organization would be involved and then make a selection of appropriate methods to collect data from those involved (e.g., questionnaires, interviews, observations, focus groups). While acknowledging that the use of diagnostic tools requires time due to complexity of some issues, the overall approach to OD interventions is that HR identifies the issue(s), collects and analyzes data, debriefs the results, develops the objectives for the appropriate action plan, implements the plan and then assesses the results.[27]

Once the issue has been identified, there are many OD interventions available. Some pertain strictly to working with individuals, such as self-assessment tools (e.g., Myers-Briggs Type Indicator® and DiSC®), as well as coaching and mentoring, reflection, multi-rater (360-degree) feedback, job design and responsibility charting. Interventions used with teams and groups include dialogue sessions, team building, brainstorming, conflict management and process consultation.[28]

Therefore, the key to planned change is methodical and thoughtful gathering and understanding of data and process evaluation. If an intervention is considered successful, it may then become part of how business is done. If not, discontinuation of new practices and/or procedures may be necessary. Either way, the process can be an important learning experience for both HR and the organization.

Evaluating OD Initiatives

Since evaluations can be difficult, they tend to be overlooked. To better ensure management support, it is important to know how well OD programs are working (see Table 2.5). For example, evaluations help determine if the OD intervention is aligned with business strategies or needs to be improved or changed. On the other hand, evaluations are also an excellent opportunity to reflect on the overall climate and health of the organization, as well as help keep employees motivated and productive.[29] According to the Organization Development Process Model, the decision about how and when to make evaluations is usually done during the start-up and action-planning process. Often, there is overlap during the intervention and evaluation phases. That is, evaluation is done on an ongoing basis (formative evaluation) as well as at the end of the process (summative evaluation). Some organizations conduct evaluations on a repeated basis well after the intervention has been completed (longitudinal evaluation).[30]

Table 2.5 Strategic OD Imperatives Related to Evaluation

- Tie every OD activity to the organization's strategy.
- Know what the client expects from OD: if the expectation is valid, deliver it; if invalid, help the client understand why and what is valid.
- Measure what is important to the client.
- Share the outcomes of effective OD widely within the organization.
- Foster learning within the OD group and steering team: what can we learn from this?
- Use triangulation: multiple measures that show the same outcomes will provide stronger evidence of the contributions OD has made.

Source: McLean, G. N. (2006). Organizational development: Principles, processes, performance. San Francisco: Berrett-Koehler Publishers, Inc.

The most commonly used evaluation approach is Kirkpatrick's four levels of evaluation. Often applied to training and development, this approach was first developed in the 1950s and updated in the 1990s and consists of four steps:

(1) reactions (usually measured by a short survey or focus groups); (2) learning (usually measured with a written test or a demonstration of performance); (3) behavior (based on observations of a supervisor, a third party or self-report); and (4) organizational impact. Kirkpatrick later added a fifth level of evaluation, return on investment. Today, this evaluation process continues to be widely used in the OD field.[31]

After completing an independent and objective evaluation, the next step is to create goals around the recommendations. These goals can be measurable (quantitative and/or qualitative) and monitored to determine value to the company. For example, turnover, promotions and diversity may be measured against specific staff training programs. While it can be difficult to determine exact cause-effect relationships, HR can present a solid case for future OD work by monitoring how things have changed to benefit the company.[32] Finally, by showing how OD contributes to the organization's success, HR is accountable to stakeholders, builds intellectual capital in the company and sets the stage for future investments in OD.[33]

Organization Development and Global HR

As the global economy expands, so do opportunities to use organization development in global human resource management. In addition, when changing political and economic environments create uncertainty, there are opportunities worldwide to use OD for effective change and transformation. At the same time, the practice of global OD requires the knowledge and understanding of cultural differences and regional/national cultural values. It is also important to keep in mind that the field of OD was developed in the United States and that U.S. management concepts do not always fit with the values of other cultures. For example, the traditional OD values of social equality, democracy and human dignity are not always accepted globally.[34] In addition, from analysis to implementation, building trust is critical in each phase of OD, but trust relationships require cultural etiquette. Therefore, as HR professionals use OD in global settings, it is important to be cognizant of cultural differences and avoid making assumptions about global workplaces.

Typical global OD interventions include global learning programs, expansion of cultural self-awareness, cross-cultural team building, virtual team building, expatriate job assignments, storytelling/sharing and organizational blending. However, to effectively implement OD initiatives in the global context—and increase the likelihood of success—it is important that OD professionals possess certain characteristics. For example, research strongly recommends that professionals be culturally aware of their own personal and national values, be knowledgeable, respectful and appreciative of the values and practices of other cultures, and have a global perspective and mindset. In addition, it is critical to have cultural empathy, flexibility, patience and a sense of humor.[35]

Further, having a basic knowledge of cultures will help avoid making mistakes that lead to unsuccessful organization development projects. The work of Hofstede, for example, provides a framework for cultural sensitivity. He developed four dimensions that differentiate national culture groups: power distance, uncertainty avoidance, individualism/collectivism and masculinity/femininity.[36] Understanding these cultural aspects, and their possible implications as related to human resource management processes, will help HR professionals design appropriate interventions for both global and local workplaces. It is equally important to consider how best to integrate different national cultures and values with others. Three issues are key: (1) the strength of the value set; (2) the presence of subcultures; and (3) value change—in other words, the degree to which most people accept values as desirable and legitimate, the presence of contradictory values within the general values set and the acknowledgement that value change is an evolving process, often slow to take hold.[37]

In addition, global OD has some unique challenges. For instance, language differences can be a major barrier. If the HR professional does not speak the native language, the situation may require that either host country individuals work in the HR professional's language or an interpreter be used. Either way, communication difficulties and misunderstandings can easily arise, and the OD progress may move forward slower than anticipated. Further, not all cultures have the same work ethic. In certain countries, for example, taking a long meal or mid-afternoon break may be an integral part of the culture, and the professional must "go with the flow" or otherwise risk alienating members of the host country. Also, the level of bureaucracy, and corresponding lack of flexibility, may differ from the types of organizations with which the HR professional is familiar. Finally, in some countries, corruption is taken for granted as a cost of doing business. The HR professional will have to come to terms with his or her own values regarding the feasibility of working in environments with vastly differing ethics and values.[38] All of these issues can have an impact on the degree of effectiveness of OD global initiatives and interventions.

Another area of caution for implementing OD in a global environment, according to researchers Cummings and Worley, is the country's level of economic development. Constraints, for example, may include (1) the level of employee and management skills; (2) the existence of motivational and reward systems, employee selection, placement and development practices; (3) decision-making and action-taking capabilities; (4) project planning experience; and (5) the availability of technology and information systems.[39] These issues are less likely to be encountered in more wealthy countries. In underdeveloped economies, where there may be little knowledge of contemporary management and business practices in the local workforce, OD may primarily be used to address community and/or social issues.[40] Finally, to be effective in global OD, HR professionals must know their own cultural orientation and blind spots, the value orientation of OD, and the value orientation of the culture, country and/or region within which they are working. By combining these values, HR professionals can determine the most appropriate OD interventions.[41]

Mini-Case Study #2: Employing OD Strategies in the Globalization of HR[42]

As discussed, OD in a global context can be challenging. However, with thoughtful planning and support from senior management, it is possible to effect positive change for the betterment of the organization and its workforce. The example below describes one company's experience using OD strategies to globalize its HR function. The goal was to develop global HR strategies to design programs and implement processes to manage the global workforce. As with all global OD interventions, the key to long-term success is balancing global standardization along with local autonomy.

This international real estate company had a vision to be the world's leading real estate services and investment management firm. To succeed, the organization needed to foster a high-performing work culture and attract and retain the best talent. To transform the company, the HR department developed a three-year plan that made it necessary for the company to move from a highly regionalized HR structure to an organization with shared best practices—a move that would increase interdependence across all regions. From employment to retirement, a consistent worldwide approach to HR management and the employee management life cycle was required. HR's intention was to integrate the new structure using three dimensions: people, process and systems. To provide a consistent framework, an overarching plan was developed around six phases: recruiting and selection, employee engagement, performance management, compensation and benefits, infrastructure (training and technology), and talent management. This framework was then used to develop organization-wide needs, as well as country- or region-specific actions that addressed local norms and cultures. To ensure successful onboarding and retention of new talent, the company designed a strong employer brand that communicated its identity and strategic goals. For example, assessment centers, using rigorous selection tools, were implemented in China to evaluate college graduates for local and multinational assignments. Finally, to ensure best practices throughout the company, the organization developed global councils to help implement and institutionalize these practices as well as define the new HR standards. The global councils were made up of regional and local subject matter experts dedicated to the successful execution of the new HR structure, in coordination with functional experts across the various regions. The global councils created that essential balance between worldwide and local HR practices and processes.

With the three-year plan successfully designed, the implementation stage was ready to go forward. To ensure success moving forward, HR will need to continue to evaluate and refocus its "people, process and systems" strategies. Using OD tools and evaluation processes, along with continued management support, HR is more likely to see the smooth transformation of the global HR function.

Conclusion

In domestic and global organizations alike, OD encourages broad ethical thinking, careful strategic planning and alliance management. Reflection, dialogue and bridge-building are skills that open doors to innovation and learning. As HR professionals explore the advantages of organization development—and hone their respective OD competencies—both the organization and the HR profession will benefit. OD is indeed a strategic HR tool and will become an integral part of HR in the future.

Chapter 3

Leveraging HR and Knowledge Management in a Challenging Economy

In an economic downturn, the collection of organizational knowledge and its application are likely to determine the next generation of industry superstars. Education and learning are cornerstones of the Obama administration, and President Obama strongly urges people of all ages to continue to learn. Each individual needs to grow intellectually and prepare to contribute to society and to his or her organization. In a global marketplace, successful companies focus on the education of their current workforce as well as the next generation.

Trust, relationships and dialogue are the foundation for building organizational knowledge sharing. As a strategic business partner, HR can forward organizational success—domestic and global—through the development, retention and transfer of organizational knowledge. With knowledge management (KM), business success is achieved in a culture of learning and workplace planning. This *Research Quarterly* presents key factors and solutions that HR can leverage, through knowledge management, for competitive advantage in a challenging economy.

Business Case

Historically, the world of work has evolved from manual labor to mechanical and technical expertise to a knowledge economy. Today, success requires agility and adaptability, largely dependent upon the quick assimilation and application of knowledge to develop and respond to new technologies, new products and new services that can lead to a competitive edge. While some firms may view knowledge management as "nice to have," proactive organizations see KM as a key component of an effective business plan. Developing a knowledge management strategy aligns with business viability and sustainability.

Knowledge begins with people. Retaining the right talent in today's tough economy presents a strategic opportunity to build a stronger organization. As a source of innovation and competitive advantage, KM is an important HR and managerial tool. However, for effective collaboration of knowledge in organizations, communication and trust are essential. How organizations treat their employees, particularly during difficult economic times, speaks to how organizations truly value their employees—and will either promote or deflate trust, performance and ethical behavior.[1]

As companies cope with the economy, HR can be instrumental in helping organizations leverage knowledge-based resources for business results. As highlighted in *Creating People Advantage*, critical HR challenges focus on three strategic categories, all related to knowledge management: (1) developing and retaining the best employees (talent, leadership development, work/life balance); (2) anticipating change (demographics, change, cultural transformation, globalization); and (3) enabling the organization (becoming a learning organization).[2] As indicated in a SHRM April 2009 poll of U.S.-based organizations and multinational companies, the primary focus of companies now is workforce planning. Although hiring expectations are low, talent management priorities remain high despite the economic downturn (see Figure 3.1).

Sustainability

Sustainability depends on effective knowledge management practices. From an organizational standpoint, sustainability refers to the business as a whole, including the employer brand, human capital, business ethics, social responsibility and financial well-being. At the SHRM 2008 Executive Roundtable Symposium on Sustainability and Human Resource Management Strategy, senior executives from around the world discussed the opportunity for HR to provide strategic leadership in sustainability. They emphasized that sustainability is a people issue—recruiting, developing and engaging employees for maximum performance and profitability.[3]

When considering research implications of knowledge measurement, one viewpoint is to use three related themes, as described by management author and researcher John W. Boudreau. First, measures focus on aggregated units of analysis (e.g., groups of individuals, such as profit centers, alliance partners and companies, to regions and economies). Second, measures aim to explain the link between knowledge and the strategic value of the organization: the value-chain context. Third, the focus is on the role of knowledge (such as in talent pools) and pivotal roles. The concept of pivotal roles refers to individuals whose performance has a positive impact on organizational value and competitiveness.[4]

Traditional benchmarking metrics are often used to identify KM effectiveness. Such measures include employee turnover, employee attitude, cost reductions/savings, number of communities of practice and customer satisfaction.[5] Linking cost-per-hire to revenue per FTE is an example of KM measurement. Because revenue per FTE measures employee productivity, selecting the most qualified person who can increase revenue is a critical success factor. However, enhanced selection strategies cost more. When HR is pressured to lower recruitment costs, caution is required to balance the need for targeted selection programs against their cost to ensure that appropriate candidates are hired to contribute to organizational revenue. SHRM data show that in 2008 high-tech organizations had an average cost-per-hire of $5,748 and revenue per FTE of $446,218.[6] When the economy turns in a positive direction, organizations that have the right talent will be better positioned for competitive advantage.

Fundamentals of Knowledge Management

As a management discipline, the field of knowledge management addresses human capital needs, policies, procedures, technology, incentives and organizational culture. There are various models put forth by researchers to describe the link between HR and KM. For example, researchers David P. Lepak and Scott A. Snell portray human capital management as a multilevel perspective for knowledge-based competition, with competencies and contributions at the individual, employee group and organizational levels.[7] The types of knowledge, a workplace culture of learning and the knowledge worker form the platform for KM.

Two Classes of Knowledge

Knowledge can be divided into two groups—explicit and tacit—both necessary for organizational success. Explicit knowledge is typically visible, definable and objective. In contrast, tacit knowledge lives within individuals and their behaviors. Tacit knowledge is context-rich, often subjective and not easily transferrable.[8] Explicit knowledge is organizational knowledge found in company documents, files, policies, training, patents, procedures, etc. Tacit knowledge is the shared learning and collective wisdom of an organization, such as how things are done on the job, internal and external work experiences related to the company and the overall collective organizational experience.[9]

Culture for Organizational Learning

In today's knowledge economy, KM is increasingly essential for organizational success. Cooperation, networking and collaboration are key in knowledge management. Two major workplace shifts make knowledge management both essential and challenging—the changing nature of work itself and the changing nature of the work environment becoming increasingly global and virtual. Critical aspects of KM help to ensure effectiveness of collaboration and sharing to build a knowledge organization (see Table 3.1).

Figure 3.1 | Changing Focus on Talent Management

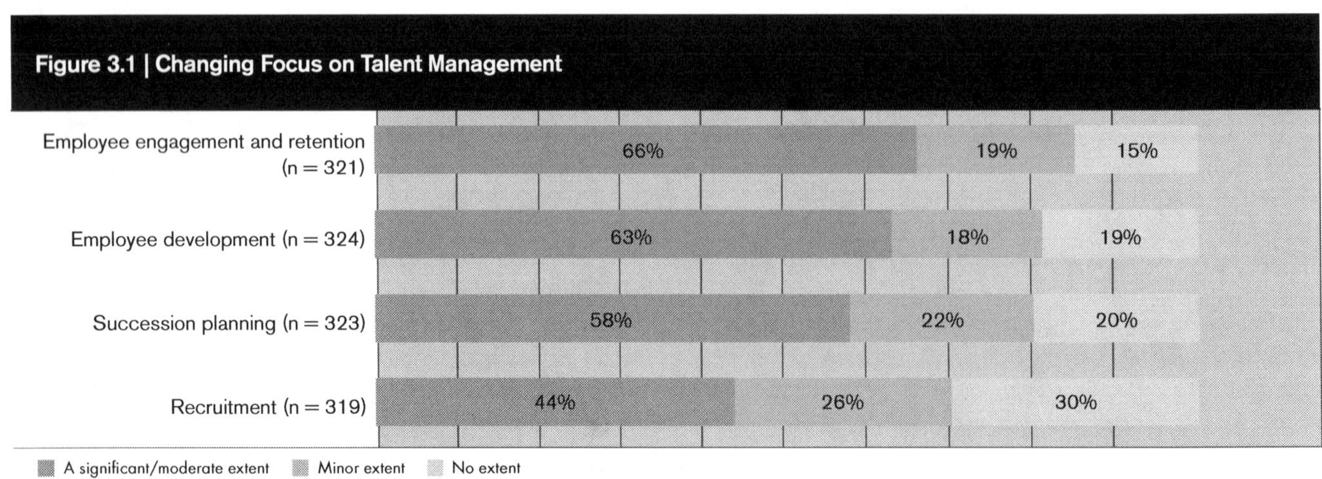

Note: Respondents who indicated "not applicable" were excluded from this figure.
Source: SHRM Poll: Programs and Practices to Confront the Workplace Effects of the Downturn in the Economy (SHRM, April 2009).

Table 3.1 The Four Sides of Knowledge Management

1. Culture–Encourages and supports employees to share their knowledge and collaborate with others.
2. Technology–Collaboration on products/projects requires the appropriate technology–hardware, software and connectivity.
3. Economic incentives–Bonus incentives can foster and promote collaboration and sharing of knowledge between employees.
4. Measurement–The development of indicators to gauge the success and effectiveness of knowledge management.

Source: Adapted from Lewison, J. (2001, October). *Knowledge management* [SHRM white paper]. Retrieved February 13, 2009, from www.shrm.org.

Organizational leaders shape the workplace environment for learning—for idea generation, innovation and ultimately for sustainability. It is within organizational culture that a learning environment is established, with the supportive dimensions of openness, continuous education, creativity and high value placed on learning.[10] A learning culture also involves risk-taking, with some tolerance for mistakes (the opposite of a "blame culture"). HR leadership of initiatives that foster knowledge development (such as career development and leadership training) emphasizes knowledge sharing and integration at the performance management level. Fundamental issues, such as adding value and increasing shareholder wealth, are important to consider when determining knowledge management pathways.[11]

By focusing on strategic learning capacities, HR can promote knowledge management as a strategic business objective. Examples include emphasizing training and development, focusing on professional development, and establishing policies and practices for employee talent retention through internal promotions, knowledge-sharing taskforces and an overall commitment to excellence. Although companies are now cutting training budgets, in a down economy HR can promote free professional development opportunities.

Research shows that many firms in nearly every industry sector now focus on knowledge management and organizational learning. A study by The Conference Board of 200 senior executives found that (1) 80 percent of companies are taking actions around KM, (2) 25 percent have a chief knowledge officer or chief learning officer, and (3) 21 percent have a communicated KM strategy. The findings reveal that senior management leadership is essential where learning is being inculcated into the corporate culture. Although technology is important for KM, it is informal employee networks and other workforce practices that develop effective action for KM. Ultimately, the implementation of organizational learning is a long-term investment for future success.[12]

The Knowledge Worker

As highlighted in an article "Learning to Compete in a Knowledge Economy," the effective management and retention of workers in a knowledge economy are crucial for success.[13] Knowledge workers often have organizational knowledge essential to the company. HR initiatives that connect employees, professional opportunities and accomplishments help retain knowledge workers. Participation in high-visibility projects and recognition for contributions are two examples of effective retention strategies. The working environment is also important for retention. Management practices that address a combination of personal growth, operational autonomy, task achievement and financial reward are supportive of knowledge workers.[14]

In a challenging economy, recognition for creative ideas is one KM initiative. Several organizations listed among "The 100 Best Companies to Work For" in a recent 2009 issue of *Fortune* reward knowledge and action. Qualcomm, a wireless-components designer in San Diego, Calif., keeps new ideas flowing through its award-winning recruitment program. At Whole Foods, a nationwide high-end food seller, employees are encouraged to come up with creative ideas to show off the company's merchandise—and the best ideas are shared with other Whole Foods stores. At Atlantic Health System, a hospital in Morristown, N.J., employees can receive $1,000 for a new idea.[15] In today's often frenetic pace, taking time to thoughtfully acknowledge work well done has a positive impact on talent retention.

The Right Behaviors

A 2008 SHRM survey indicates that the use of behavioral competencies is beneficial on many levels, such as increased job satisfaction, reduced turnover, increased productivity and a better pool of candidates for succession planning (see Figure 3.2). When it comes to knowledge work and knowledge integration, research suggests that HR can promote effective knowledge management by focusing on four tasks: (1) identifying behaviors needed for knowledge-based competition; (2) ensuring the workforce has the required competencies; (3) ensuring the workforce is motivated to engage in the required behaviors; and (4) providing opportunities for these behaviors in the workforce.[16]

Mini-case study #1 illustrates team behavior in engineering in a high-tech industry. While problem-solving is an essential part of engineering work, collaboration to achieve quality can be difficult with different expert opinions. A key learning from this study, for HR and managers, is a

Figure 3.2 | Outcomes of Using Behavioral Competencies in Organizations

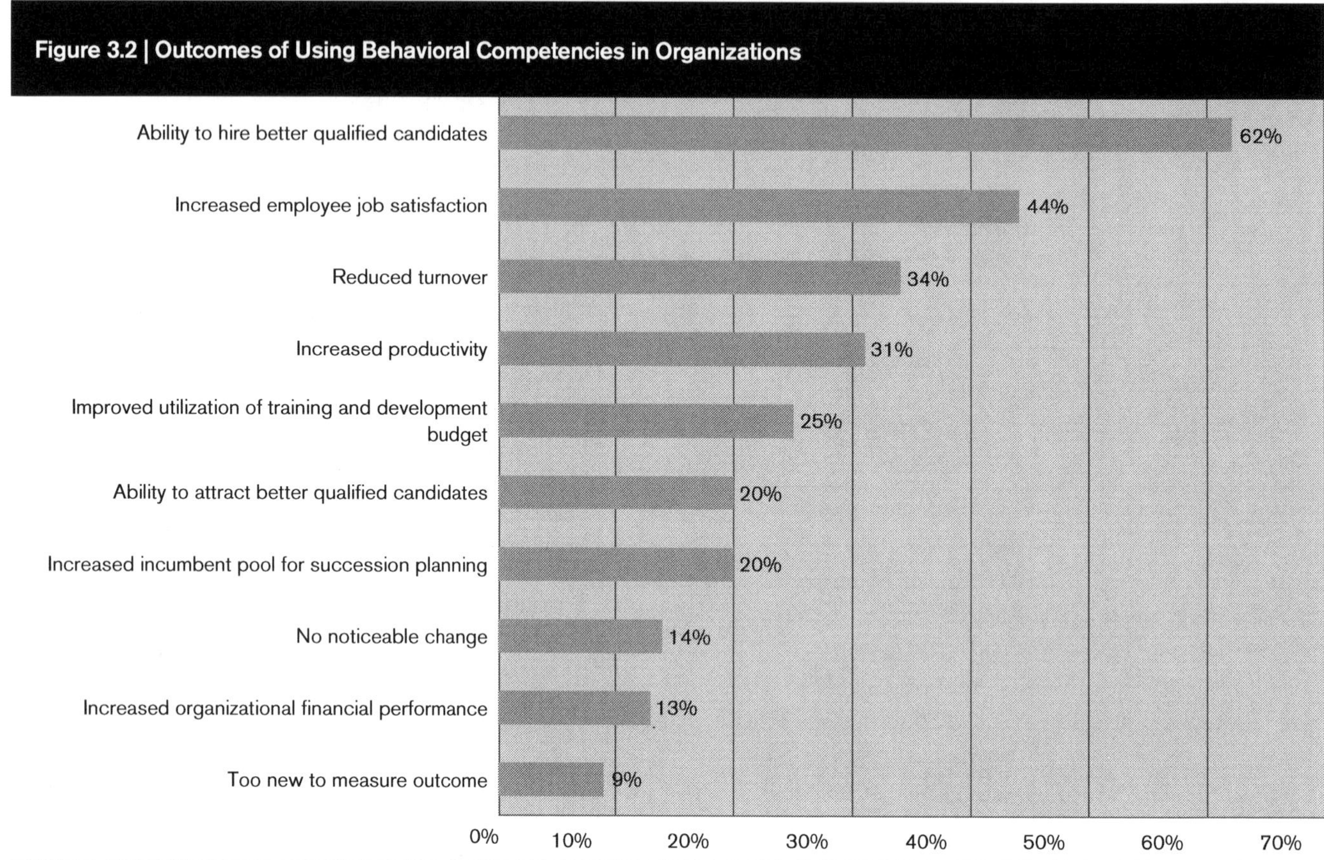

Note: Percentages do not total 100% as multiple response options were allowed. HR professionals whose organizations have not identified behavioral competencies were excluded from this analysis.
Source: SHRM Weekly Online Poll (January 2008)

heightened awareness of barriers to knowledge sharing and collaboration in situations where team boundaries can contribute to the difficulty of making informed decisions.

Mini-Case Study #1: Managing Knowledge Work: Specialization and Collaboration of Engineering Problem-Solving[17]

This study explored the tacit dimension of knowledge creation and knowledge sharing practices of three semiconductor manufacturers in Japan and Korea to examine the social processes of expert teams (design, process and process integration) and how they cooperate across team boundaries, with various viewpoints from team specialization. These teams were responsible for trouble management in the production of an integrated circuit semiconductor device. The study revealed that the primary challenges to the development of a successful knowledge management process were not the strategies for collecting and identifying the problem. Rather, the challenge was the management of the political process regarding the behaviors of different teams of engineers, each influenced by their respective areas of expertise.

Knowledge Management Tools for HR

The following four KM practices are tools that foster learning, knowledge sharing, retention and transfer: communities of practice, storytelling, knowledge retention practices and leadership development.

Communities of Practice (CoPs)

In today's economy, CoPs are instrumental in creating new business opportunities through staff with internal expertise who translate new insights into new services and products.[18] By bringing together groups that cross organizational boundaries (various teams, business units, divisions), HR can promote knowledge learning and sharing. Usually voluntary, what makes a CoP unique—if working well—is the sense of aliveness and engagement. Open dialogue, different levels of participation and a focus on value are three key factors for an effective CoP.

A recent study explored benchmarking the impact of CoPs. The results revealed that some companies take success stories of business benefits and translate them into measures for a "health check" for their CoPs. For example, the energy company ConocoPhillips measures the development of its CoPs ("networks of excellence"). Performance is calibrated against expectations with 10 critical success factors: clear business case, leadership/sponsorship, clear deliverables, adequate resources, development of trusted relationships, a transfer process, supporting technology, motivation, recognition/rewards, and network measurement. For transparency, progress toward goals is identified on the dashboard (an organizational scorecard process) with red, yellow and green indicators. The recommendations of the KM team are the outcome of the "health check."[19]

Storytelling

Storytelling teaches lessons, exchanges ideas, changes behaviors and builds community. Stories describe a journey, crisis, opportunity or choices with results and/or consequences. HR can use storytelling to illustrate corporate values and promote workplace behavior. The advantages are many: (1) people tend to listen to stories receptively, (2) stories are memorable, (3) stories can inspire heroic behavior, and (4) stories can forward change. In the business world, storytelling—in the form of business anecdotes—is a powerful corporate communication tool. It can promote organizational change in the workplace culture, deliver a message, capture and transfer tacit knowledge, and encourage innovation.[20]

Knowledge Retention Practices

Actions that demonstrate a positive organizational reputation have a direct impact on retention. SHRM research, titled "The Employer Brand: A Strategic Tool to Attract, Recruit and Retain Talent," found that candidates carefully consider a company's reputation for being ethical as a top reason to work for an organization. In fact, 74 percent of HR professionals cite the company reputation as critical for successful recruiting.[21] Organizations that take social responsibility seriously and give back to the community are viewed positively, especially by the Millennial Generation. As seen in *Fortune* magazine's 2009 "The 100 Best Companies to Work For" edition, several organizations emphasize social responsibility. For example, KPMG in New York City donated monies originally intended for staff holiday gifts to a local food bank. Salesforce.com in San Francisco provides its workforce with six paid days a year to volunteer. Such actions will likely increase in the future, in view of the stand by the Obama administration on the importance of volunteerism and giving back to the community.

Leadership Development

For both short- and long-term organizational success, building leadership capacity prepares the organization to rise above cyclical corrections. As noted in SHRM Foundation's report *Developing Leadership Talent*, a firm's performance depends on the development and management of knowledge, through and within its leaders.[22] SHRM found that in this difficult economy, 80 percent of companies are either initiating or expanding their strategies to develop a diverse generation of leaders from within a firm.[23] The 2008 Annual CHRO Survey by HR Policy Association shows that 80 percent of chief HR officers see leadership development and succession as a top HR challenge.[24] Yet, there remains a significant gap of internal leadership and an available pipeline for succession planning.

The Multigenerational Workforce

Few companies have begun to focus on knowledge transfer from older to younger workers. With projected skills shortages, appropriate measures must be in place to prevent knowledge loss in the coming years. However, due to the economic downturn, many Baby Boomers will remain in the workforce longer than planned. Some companies are now focusing on creative talent strategies to retain workers over the age of 50 for their knowledge and expertise. Older workers bring performance advantages needed in the global competitive environment, such as advanced skills, experience, and knowledge of the company, people and customer base. Programs such as innovative growth opportunities, health care benefits, flexible work and part-time employment help to retain talent of the multigenerational workforce.[25]

Older workers will eventually retire, taking with them valuable knowledge. The health care industry is an example of a sector facing a high loss of talent due to the aging workforce. A study explored the impact of corporate memory loss at health care institutes as the result of increasing retirement rates of senior executives. Interviews at diverse health care facilities revealed a loss of tacit knowledge compounded by insufficient managerial competencies for senior management positions.[26]

Effective cross-generational knowledge transfer requires awareness of the different styles of the four generations in the workplace. Generally, younger workers prefer interactive virtual learning, while older workers enjoy face-to-face learning.[27] Overall, understanding generational differences in terms of learning styles and communication preferences can aide in effective knowledge transfer. HR can educate the workforce about these differences, thereby improving design of knowledge transfer programs and processes. However, it is good to keep in mind that preferences of learning styles can change over time. Ultimately, it is important to carefully select the method based on learning objectives while also recognizing different learning styles and preferences.

Workforce Planning

Today, workforce planning is essential. A Watson Wyatt survey of North America-based organizations in a variety of industries found that four out of 10 companies now see workforce planning as important—reflecting economic changes—and nearly 31 percent of companies have begun activities on workplace planning. A majority of companies report that their CEOs (85 percent) and senior management (74 percent) are concerned about workforce planning issues. Actions employers are taking include (1) continuing to replace talent in all roles (50 percent); (2) restructuring (42 percent); (3) scaling back on replacing talent (33 percent); (4) only replacing talent for critical jobs (21 percent); and (5) not replacing talent (3 percent). Hiring freezes and layoffs are included in these workforce planning tactics.[28]

To learn about creative and proactive actions by HR and their organizations in this economic downturn, SHRM created an Economic Stimulus Prize. HR professionals identified best practices to avoid layoffs, keep talent, curb health-related costs and boost financial literacy. These three examples show how HR is working to safeguard the company and its workforce—and be better placed for the future economic turnaround.[29]

Career Development: Toyotestsu America, Inc. (a tier-one supplier for the auto industry in Somerset, Ky.)

The HR department devised a strategy to provide a program of career development training, with funds found by asking employees to "dig deep" and find new ways to cut costs.

Leadership Development: Noblis (a nonprofit organization for science/technology/strategy in Falls Church, Va.)

Talent is the primary source of the company's long-term reputation. Despite economic pressures, employee professional development was made the number one corporate priority. Participation in the formal leadership program has doubled.

Strategic Alignment: America Family Insurance (a *Fortune* 500 mutual insurance company in Madison, Wis.)

The company's goal is to be number one overall in customer satisfaction. To position itself for growth when the business climate improves, the 2009 HR business plan, titled "Mission: Alignment," includes eight initiatives: wellness, benefits, leadership, diversity, onboarding, technology, organizational design and social media.

Global HR/Knowledge Management and Knowledge Transfer

"The ability to transfer knowledge smoothly and efficiently across borders has become an important competitive differentiator," emphasizes Ernest Gundling, author of *Working GlobeSmart*.[30] While there are now fewer expat assignments, the manner in which companies are using assignments has been changing, as highlighted in a SHRM February 2009 article "Expats Still Essential But Recession Changes Their Roles." The 2008 GMAC Global Relocation Trends Survey found that over the past three to four years, the focus of expat assignments has shifted from filling skill gaps to building management experience for employees.[31] This shift in focus makes knowledge transfer even more important in global organizations.

In fact, research shows that global companies are increasingly working to break down boundaries that preclude knowledge from crossing cultural and national borders.[32] One study empirically explored the role of the expatriate assignment in knowledge transfer. The results suggest that temporary (short-term) assignments are more effective for knowledge transfer. At the same time, long-term assignments positively influence the willingness of expatriates to transfer knowledge across subsidiaries of multinational corporations, with greater autonomy and responsibility for employee performance.[33]

However, cultural differences can be a substantive barrier to knowledge transfer. As Aliza Dart-Scott, SPHR, director of HR in the Manufacturing Solutions Division at Oregon-based Autodesk, knows well, transferring critical knowledge depends on bridging the cultural chasm: "HR support is critical to ensure an effective cultural training and integration for the expat in his or her host country, the work environment—and for the family, too." How expatriates conduct themselves on assignment will, in part, influence their ability to share and transfer knowledge. As Lucinda B. Smith, GPHR, senior vice president of HR at AGCO, notes, "culture has a wide-reaching impact in knowledge management." Mini-case study #2 presents an example of a U.S. multinational company balancing cross-cultural relations to improve and increase knowledge transfer.

Mini-Case Study #2: Knowledge Transfer and Expat Exchange

Background: Founded in 1990, AGCO Corporation, "Your Agriculture Company" (NYSE: AG), offers a full product line of tractors, combines, hay tools, sprayers, forage, tillage equipment, implements and related replacement parts, distributed globally through more than 3,000 independent dealers and distributors in more than 140 countries worldwide. In 2008, AGCO had net sales of $8.4 billion (www.AGCOcorp.com). The company has plants throughout the world: Brazil, Finland, France, Italy and the United States.

Situation: The most active locations, from an expat perspective, are Brazil and the United States. Through several initiatives, the plants in Brazil and the United States have successfully exchanged and transferred knowledge. The exchange with Finland, however, has been quiet or nonexistent. Several years ago, the company sent a high-level U.S. expatriate to a plant in Finland. Interested in different cultures, he quickly learned about the Finnish culture and determined that the reason for the limited exchange to Finland may be partly due to cultural differences. He found the Finnish engineers to be top performers and suggested the company would benefit from an exchange of engineers from Finland. This expat has worked with HR to promote further exchange to and from the company's plants in Finland.

Learning: At the plants in Brazil, the engineers actively seek out assignments and trust the company to take care of them when on assignment. The U.S. engineers may not have sought expat assignments, but they are happy when offered and also content with the policy, including the compensation package. In contrast, the Finnish engineers who have been approached for expat assignments have been very focused on details. That is, they carefully assess the personal and economic risk associated with an assignment rather than approaching it as a personal and professional opportunity.

Actions: AGCO's international assignment manager will present assignment offers differently to potential Brazilian and Finnish assignees. The company is implementing cultural training for assignees as well as its business travelers. As a result, AGCO is now tapping into a new talent pool.

As highlighted by Kenneth J. Somers, SHRM Global Special Expertise Panel member, learning and accountability are essential for global knowledge transfer: "We all know that expatriate assignments are expensive in a 'normal' economic climate. When we have circumstances like those we are experiencing now, the focus on delivering tangible value becomes profound. In my experience and personal view, any expatriate—regardless of the duration of his or her assignment—must be held accountable for knowledge transfer. Having said that, the manner and effectiveness with which institutional knowledge or subject-matter expertise is transferred is subject to the influences of cross-cultural forces. In Japan, for example, it is customary that a new expatriate is granted position respect upon arrival. But he or she must quickly demonstrate competence to earn the personal respect needed to be successful in transmitting the knowledge associated with the expat's responsibilities. Owing to Japan's largely non-confrontational business culture, the real danger is that the expat to Japan may never understand why he or she is experiencing challenges in being effective."

"In contrast to Japan," Somers continues, "my experience in India taught me that an expat needs to earn personal and professional respect on an almost continuous basis. India's business culture is more assertive, and the expat will quickly know if he or she is respected. In both cases, HR needs to play the critical role of coaching the new expatriate for success by providing early and consistent feedback on how the expat is actually doing." Along with economic challenges, cross-cultural understanding is a key success factor for knowledge transfer in the global arena.

Overcoming Barriers

Most obstacles to knowledge management are internal. The lack of understanding about KM by company leaders, not having an organizational working definition of KM and a culture of hoarding knowledge are the top three factors that inhibit successful knowledge management. Functional silos also add to the difficulty of sharing knowledge. HR can be instrumental in educating senior management about the benefits of KM, such as better communication and knowledge flow. For example, companies can begin to overcome barriers by establishing a KM taskforce that includes a strategic business leader along with representatives from HR and IT. Through the use of tactics such as communications, education and performance management, organizations can leverage behaviors that promote knowledge sharing.[34]

Ethics in Knowledge Management

From the HR viewpoint, knowledge management is also about the ethical management of people. Knowledge sharing fosters creativity and innovation for competitive advantage. However, knowledge exchange cannot be at the detriment of the organization. At some point, HR may be involved in ethical investigations related to inappropriate knowledge sharing (e.g., confidential information, trade secrets, intellectual property). Keeping in mind factors such as those identified in Table 3.2 will help to frame the issue when evaluating situational ethics about KM. Rating these factors as yes, no or maybe can help HR and an ethics taskforce consider possible ramifications during an investigation.[35]

Table 3.2 Evaluation of Situational Ethics

Factor	Consideration
Involvement	Have all shareholder viewpoints been considered?
Fairness	If I were the shareholder, would I see this decision as fair?
Consequences	Have we considered all of the consequences of the decision?
Relevance	Have we gathered all information possible to make an informed decision?
Corporate Values	Does the decision uphold the organization's values?
Community	Would we want this decision to become a global law, applicable to all such situations?
Shame	If the details of this decision/action plans were disclosed to everyone, how would we feel?

Source: Adapted from Groff, T. R., & Jones, T. P. (2003). *Introduction to knowledge management: KM in business.* New York: Butterworth Heinemann.

In Closing

In today's economy, knowledge management is critical to ongoing organizational effectiveness, sustainability and profitability. Yet, KM does not occur in a vacuum and requires commitment on the part of HR and senior management to effectively utilize this strategic tool for competitive advantage. In the coming years, HR must focus on the management of knowledge workers to further knowledge integration and the resulting organizational benefits.

Chapter 4

Change Management: The HR Strategic Imperative as a Business Partner

To maintain a competitive advantage, organizations must be able to quickly change. Change is driven by economic, social and environmental factors as well as business trends (see Table 4.1). Many organizations strategically use change to improve organizational effectiveness. In fact, according to the *SHRM 2007 Change Management Survey Report*, 82 percent of HR professionals reported that their company had planned or implemented major organization change in the 24 months prior to the survey.[1]

Table 4.1 Ten Biggest Agents of Change

1. Merger or acquisition
2. New boss
3. Move to shared services
4. Outsourcing
5. Unwanted exposure
6. Downsizing
7. Going for growth
8. Under new management
9. New technology
10. Going public

Source: Kubiciek, M. (2006, July 5). 10 Biggest agents of change. *Personnel Today*, 17.

Change management—the formal process for organizational change—is the systematic approach and application of knowledge, tools and resources to leverage the benefits of change. Change management means defining and adopting corporate strategies, structures, procedures and technologies to deal with change stemming from internal and external conditions.[2] Increasingly, change management is seen as a permanent business function to improve productivity and profits by keeping organizations adaptable to the competitive marketplace.[3]

However, to create pervasive and sustainable change, there are often barriers to overcome. Typically, barriers develop as a result of the organization not closely addressing the essentials of change management—specifically, thoughtful planning, communication and collaboration, often across multiple organizational lines and cultures. To fulfill the role of strategic business partner, HR must be involved in change management from the moment the topic of change is brought forth. With an in-depth understanding of change—from the business imperatives to change management tools and techniques and employee reactions to change—HR fills an important role to foster successful organizational change.

Business Drivers for Change

In today's marketplace, change is a necessity. Business trends influence the decision of an organization to make changes, as do stakeholder expectations, environmental factors, demographic shifts, and social, global and political developments. Change initiatives are often broad in scope, with an impact on the entire workforce. For example, when a company decides to strengthen its brand to increase positive perception by its consumers—and thus increase profits—this process requires acceptance and agreement from all employees.[4]

Change initiatives can be placed in the following categories: (1) strategic change—looking at the organization as functional parts (e.g., mergers, acquisitions, consolidations); (2) leadership change—reconfiguring the organization's leadership (e.g., creating succession programs for availability of qualified leaders); (3) cultural change—programs that focus on human aspects (e.g., the relationship between managers and employees); (4) cost cutting—eliminating non-essential activities and operations; and (5) process change—focusing on how things get done (e.g., reengineering a benefits administration process).[5]

Change initiatives are complex (see Table 4.2), with success never a guarantee. A 2005 Conference Board study highlights that broad change initiatives often address the business process, organizational structure and/or organizational behavior simultaneously. The criteria most commonly factored into selecting a change strategy or model includes market demand (68 percent), availability of budget (52 percent), availability of other resources (47 percent), changes in leadership (41 percent), and

Table 4.2 Key Factors in Change Management

Dimensions of Change	Economically Driven	Organizational Development	Economic/Developmental Combined
Goals	Maximize shareholder value	Develop organizational capabilities	Embrace the paradox between economic value and organizational capability
Leadership	Manage change from the top	Encourage participation from the bottom up	Set direction from the top and engage the people below
Focus	Emphasize structure and systems	Build up corporate culture: employees' behavior and attitudes	Focus simultaneously on the hard (structures and systems) and the soft (corporate culture)
Process	Plan and establish programs	Experiment and evolve	Plan for spontaneity
Reward system	Motivate through financial incentives	Motivate through commitment; use pay as fair exchange	Use incentives to reinforce change but not to drive it
Use of consultants	Analyze problems and shape solutions	Support management in shaping their own solutions	Empower employees

Source: Adapted from Beer, M., & Nohria, N. (2000, May/June). Cracking the code of change. *Harvard Business Review*, 137.

employee satisfaction and turnover (37 percent).[6] Further, when an organization decides to implement a change initiative, the reason for the anticipated change often determines the timing. Timing is influenced by the type of change: anticipatory, reactive or crisis. For example, a company may be trying to keep ahead of the competition (anticipatory), making changes in response to business trends (reactive) or dealing with an unexpected crisis, such as a damaged organizational reputation or a natural disaster (crisis). Whatever the reason, HR should be prepared for any type of change by understanding the business drivers for the change as well as employees' potential reactions.[7]

HR's Role in Change Management

Through change management, HR has an opportunity to make a significant impact on—and contribution to—the organization. HR is best suited to identify and coach individuals in the company to lead change efforts. Also, by identifying and recommending change tools and techniques, as well as addressing barriers, HR's overall role is that of "change architect." As change agent, HR fills four primary roles:[8]

1. *Change champion:* HR publicly supports the change defined by the organization's top executives.
2. *Change facilitator:* HR enables change, such as providing insights regarding the company culture, history and political dynamics to external facilitators or developing programs for internal consultants.
3. *Change designer:* To help managers and employees better understand a change initiative and have a sense of ownership, HR redesigns the corresponding HR systems (e.g., total rewards, staff development, communication practices).
4. *Change demonstrator:* Within HR itself, HR manifests change and serves as an example of effective transformation.

The findings from the *SHRM 2007 Change Management Survey Report* reveal that HR involvement in major change is substantial. For example, 73 percent of HR respondents said they were involved prior to the change being introduced, 22 percent during implementation, and 5 percent after the change went into effect. Eighty-eight percent reported that the HR department was a point of contact for questions and concerns to assist employees in the transition, 76 percent coordinated meetings and communications, and 11 percent were responsible for calculating the post-implementation return on investment for major organizational change. In fact, 23 percent of companies had HR staff devoted full time to change management programs. The top three reported major planned or implemented changes were new and/or revised performance management and review processes (58 percent), facilities change (57 percent) and organizational culture change (54 percent). The findings also highlight key areas of HR involvement: (1) clearly communicating plans and goals regarding change initiatives; (2) hiring and developing effective leaders; (3) designing and implementing transparent reward systems; (4) giving people the opportunity to be involved in change processes; and (5) overall, making each interaction with internal clients a positive experience.[9]

Once it has been determined how effective change will be recognized, HR is often responsible for designing metrics to measure the progress and success of the change initiative, as well as communicating progress to employees. Surveys and scorecards are among the most commonly used metrics for change initiatives. These vehicles work best when tailored to focus on the most relevant factors of the change initiative or as a way to investigate issues of concern. Examples of key financial measures are revenue, costs and market share. Quality indicators may focus on components of the change process (e.g., training, communication) or desired outcomes.[10] HR demonstrates its role as strategic business partner through thoughtful and careful design of change initiatives and implementation that focuses on clear and open communication with appropriate time tables and metrics, as well as visible top management support.

Readiness for Change

Prior to considering a change initiative, it is imperative that an organization first determine its readiness and capacity for change. In reality, change is ongoing. Usually, small changes (e.g., reorganization of a department) are easier to manage and tend to have a better likelihood of success than broad changes (e.g., institutionalizing organizational values throughout the workforce). The possibility of successful change can also be hampered when change initiatives occur at the same time or when one initiative is implemented before others are completed. Further, multiple change processes can lead to change fatigue.

A 2005 study by The Conference Board explored factors of large-scale organizational change. The results showed that the degree of success depends in great part on how an organization develops its capacity to achieve change. Key success factors identified were balancing the need to implement change, maintaining daily operations and implementing short- and long-term change for the future. The top three challenges were people issues (e.g., employee engagement, staffing/talent problems and turnover), organizational resistance and communication weaknesses.[11] Yet, when organizations expect change on a regular basis, research suggests that change initiatives may be more likely to succeed. In their book, *Built to Change*, researchers Edward E. Lawler III and Christopher G. Worley point out that by coming from the perspective that change is normal, organizations are better placed to drive change by building practices that encourage change rather than hinder it. Intel, GE, Microsoft and PepsiCo are examples of organizations that have fostered the capability to manage change.[12]

To evaluate change readiness, a simple assessment can be made by taking the following steps: (1) develop a list of the major change activities currently taking place and identify which ones compete for budget, staff time and other resources; (2) estimate the level of effort required for each activity; and (3) compare this required effort to the change initiative being considered. These factors will provide information regarding the anticipated change and the organization's capacity to take on additional planned change.[13] A more structured assessment can be done by observing employee behavior to gauge possible reactions to change; auditing how the company communicates the why, when and how of change initiatives; documenting employee reactions to the change process through interviews and group discussions; and using structured survey methods to determine the organization's change readiness.[14]

A final key aspect of change readiness is the leadership/management factor. One of HR's roles is to be aware of the impact of poor management on workplace performance and turnover and managers' treatment of employees (e.g., level of respect). The company's leadership has a great deal to do with whether change will be effective or fail, depending on whether employees respect and have confidence in their leaders. While an organization may be known for its workplace-friendly policies and strong benefit and compensation reward systems, employee engagement and motivation can quickly deteriorate—along with company performance levels—as a result of just a few poor managers.[15]

Table 4.3 Twelve Steps to Build Support for Change

1. Identify the stakeholders and determine what you need as well as what support you are likely to get.
2. Make a case for change.
3. Determine strategies that will help you continue to make the case for change throughout the life of the project.
4. Determine who will lead and who will take part in planning the change.
5. Look for potential resistance.
6. Undertake all subsequent actions in a way that allows you to mitigate problems.
7. Create a vision that lets people know where you are headed.
8. Develop a plan for reaching the vision.
9. Create measures of success and timelines.
10. Keep the change alive.
11. Develop contingency plans.
12. Celebrate and learn from this change.

Source: Adapted from Maurer, R. (2006, Spring). Creating a shift. *The Journal for Quality and Participation, 29*(1), 21+.

Competencies to Manage Change

For today's HR professional, the ability to manage change is essential. For some HR practitioners, change management is a relatively new area and necessitates gaining a solid understanding and in-depth knowledge of the wide range of factors related to change (e.g., through on-the-job or formal training programs). The top three key competencies regarding change are building trust, communicating effectively and achieving collaboration.[16] In addition, the literature points to the importance of strategic flexibility, linked with two critical components: the ability to manage change regarding human capital in organizations and the ability of managers to develop organizational vision to become part of the strategic plan.[17]

There is a rising interest in the role of organizational trust in the change process. Trust can be a positive mediating force or a barrier. Trust takes time to build, and it can quickly vanish. Based on social exchange theory, a recent study on organizational change explored the role of trust in effective change in the workplace. Social exchange theory explains that trust emerges from the successful exchange of benefits between involved parties. While there is no formal contract, trust represents mutual support and an investment in the relationship. The study revealed that social relationships between employees and supervisors (e.g., organizational authorities) influenced the effectiveness of a change initiative: high levels of trust in the supervisor increased employee organizational commitment. Yet, a negative attitude toward change and toward the manager and organization at large reduced work satisfaction and productivity.[18] This study has important implications for HR professionals, as it provides evidence of the criticality of the employee-organization social relationship during change interventions.

Another key competency is that of creating/supporting the company's vision for change. In his book *The Fifth Dimension: The Art and Practice of the Learning Organization*, Peter Senge highlights that change and growth can result from effective, positive visions.[19] According to John Kotter, an expert in the field of change management, an effective vision describes a desirable future and is compelling, realistic, focused, flexible and easy to communicate. However, to achieve that vision, managers must be able not only to develop the vision but also to communicate it. Yet, not all managers have experience in establishing appropriate strategic and structural changes to make vision happen and be effective.[20] Researchers Zaccaro and Banks suggest that "leader visioning" is a critical competency to manage change. Leaders can effectively manage change through image and presence. For example, by using strategic representations of the change (e.g., carefully constructed images, statements and slogans), they can more steadily establish a vision for the future.[21]

Successful change is highly dependent on effective communication. HR leaders can help top management get employee buy-in by ensuring that communication about change is clear, continual and consistent. Communication largely determines how well change initiatives are received and supported. In fact, the *SHRM 2007 Change Management Survey Report* found that when HR was involved in change management communications, employee understanding improved (74 percent), communication between managerial and nonmanagerial employees improved (55 percent) and potential risks were identified and mitigated (32 percent).[22]

Yet, research suggests that real organizational change cannot be truly effective without a corresponding deep and lasting personal change (i.e., transformation) of each organizational leader at all levels of the company. Whether the change is about creating a more inclusive and innovative culture or a new program about stress management, creating a long-lasting organizational change depends on the individual mindset of leaders.[23]

Change Management Tools and Techniques

Within the literature on change management, there is no standard definition for change management models, tools or techniques. Often, these terms are used interchangeably, with much ambiguity. However, as one study points out, the most relevant issue is not what the tool is called but the importance of knowing its strengths and weaknesses, if it can be strategically useful over time (not a fad), if it is the best tool for the job—and the importance of adapting tools to fit the business system, not the other way around. SWOT, an analysis tool to evaluate weaknesses, strengths, opportunities and threats, is often used in change management.[24] A graphical representation, such as a flowchart, shows the specific steps of the change initiative and is an example of a tool that helps employees envision and understand the implementation of an upcoming change.[25]

One of the most important tools for building common understanding around change is organizational dialogue. Experience shows that the change process that combines physical representations of mental models of value creation with organizational dialogue enhances a company's capability to successfully conduct system-wide change initiatives. Value creation is best accomplished through (1) designing change processes that promote organizational dialogue between key stakeholders and organizational staff; and (2) discussing the organization's past, present and future value creation using a variety of forms (e.g., storytelling, metaphors, analogies, music) with physical models during the change process.[26]

Finally, it is important to mention enabling structures as a change management tool. While this article does not allow for an in-depth discussion, the five types of enabling structures are pilot programs, training programs, employee retention programs, outplacement programs and reward systems. For example, pilot programs allow HR to implement change initiatives on a small scale and get valuable feedback from managers and employees. A pilot program is an excellent vehicle to test new performance management programs before implementing them companywide.[27] Reward systems, for example, are appropriate for different stages of change initiatives. To encourage change readiness, performance-based plans, such as stock options and profit sharing, can help motivate employees. Additionally, during change implementation, awarding bonuses can be an effective way to celebrate milestones, such as when targets are achieved or when change is successful.[28]

Working with Change

Change can be uncomfortable, unsettling, intimidating and sometimes downright frightening. Depending on the individual, change in the workplace can be challenging, such as when job functions are changed, departments are reorganized or a new manager takes over. Adaptation to change has predictable psychological stages that resemble the grieving process and describe normal reactions to change. By understanding and being aware of these stages, HR professionals can better help managers and employees deal with change.[29] The psychological changes are:

1. *Shock:* People may feel threatened by an upcoming change, unsafe, unable to take risks and/or deny its existence. Generally, workplace production drops.
2. *Defensive retreat:* People often react to change and/or loss with anger and may try to hold onto the way life used to be. They may attempt to understand, yet feel conflicted. At this point, people do not feel safe to take risks.
3. *Acknowledgement:* Eventually, people don't deny the change. Psychologically, this stage includes both grief and a sense of liberation. People begin to consider the pros and cons of the new situation and are more willing to take risks.
4. *Acceptance and adaptation:* Most people will eventually internalize the change, do what is necessary to adapt and move on. People will have left behind the old situation, including confusion, pain or fear experienced earlier.

People move through each stage at their own individual pace. Sometimes, people get stuck in a stage, such as defense where they focus their energies on resistance. Pushing people through these stages is counter-productive. By being patient and understanding, demonstrating enthusiasm and commitment to long-term goals, as well as responding non-defensively when challenged, HR can help managers diffuse employee resistance to change. Importantly, HR can assist managers and employees alike by acknowledging the change and possible losses and focusing on the business reasons for the change and the advantages of the new future. HR and managers can also be a sounding board for employees to express opinions and views. In addition, should people be experiencing change from different directions, such as at work as well as on the home front (e.g., a merger and a divorce), the difficulty to adapt to change can quickly become magnified. Thus, some people may need additional support and time.

For HR and managers alike, recognizing the human side of change is a key factor in effective change management. In the business environment, this factor is not often sufficiently addressed. Beyond dialog in the workplace, people need to attend to their physical well-being and nourish their psyches. To better deal with change, HR and managers can support employees—as well as themselves—by encouraging them to follow some simple but important practices: get enough sleep, eat right, get regular exercise, relax with friends, engage in hobbies, indulge in something special (e.g., a trip, a movie, a massage) and practice relaxation disciplines (e.g., deep breathing, yoga). By focusing on emotional investments in areas outside the workplace, people can better achieve a sense of balance and control while going through change.[30]

William Bridges, in his book *Managing Transitions: Making the Most of Change*, points out that change is more likely to be successful when employees have a purpose, a plan for and a part in change.[31] HR can help overcome resistance and prepare for change by giving employees a chance to ask questions and provide feedback. To get on board with the change initiative, employees need to know the business reasons as well as the nature of the change (e.g., what kind of change, how this change will affect them, the scope of the change). Should there be possible negative ramifications, such as layoffs due to a merger, new reporting relationships or benefits changes, HR and management must be upfront with as much information as possible. The extent to which the organization is transparent in its communication regarding "bad news," such as layoffs, will greatly influence productivity and morale. To create stability during change, HR can also note what will not be changing, such as the organization's commitment to the corporate values.[32]

Finally, as pointed out by psychologists Robert Kriegel and David Brandt, certain personal characteristics promote change-readiness. For example, tolerance for ambiguity, optimism and adaptability allow individuals to have a positive view of the future while at the same time being better able to live with uncertainty and surprises. Characteristics such as being able to make the most of any situation (resourcefulness), being confident to handle difficult situations, being excited and willing to take risks (adventurousness) and being challenged by new experiences and possibilities (passion) lend themselves to the ability to handle change well.[33]

Barriers to Change Management

Failed change initiatives carry a high cost: the loss of credibility of leadership and employee resistance to future change, both at the individual and organizational level (see Table 4.4). According to the SHRM 2007 Change Management Survey Report, the two top obstacles encountered during major organizational change are communication breakdown and employee resistance. Other barriers include insufficient time devoted to training, staff turnover during transition, costs exceeding budget and insufficient timelines developed for effective change implementation. Interestingly, the findings reveal that only 32 percent of organizations conduct evaluations of major change initiatives after they have been implemented.[34] The empirical study below provides an example of successful change, despite potential barriers.

Table 4.4 Common Change Management Pitfalls

- Poor communication (e.g., of goals, motives, methods, commitment)
- Lack of understanding of the urgency of change
- Unclear rationale for change
- Mixed messages from top and middle management
- Too many initiatives at one time
- Underestimation of barriers; lack of due diligence
- Changed or diminished priorities; lack of focus
- Inadequate employee mobilization and engagement
- Cultural mismatch in mergers and acquisitions that seek to blend two contrasting cultures

Source: Adapted from Guy, G., & Beaman, K. (2005). *Effecting change in business enterprises: Current trends in change management.* New York: The Conference Board.

Mini-Case Study #1: Health Care Industry[35]

Resistance to change is a common barrier. Focusing on the experiences of the workforce of a large unionized hospital, this study explores whether discomfort with change is related to the individual or to the change itself.

In a single year, this organization underwent three major change initiatives: a structural change, a technological change and a relocation of the workplace. Conditions were positive for change, as senior leadership was committed and involved in the implementation of all three changes. The changes were also supported by the hospital's participatory philosophy, continuous communications and an organizational change specialist who had been involved with the change preparations for over a year. It should be noted, however, that these initiatives took place in a complex context that involved staffing shortages, budget constraints and the overall challenges of the health care sector (e.g., legislation, political pressures). Thus, there were a number of potential barriers that could derail any one—or more—of these three critical changes.

The study findings revealed that on an individual basis, few people experienced discomfort about change in general. However, the results also showed that no matter the occupational group (e.g., surgery, medicine, emergency response), discomfort levels increased in relation to a specific change. The two groups that experienced the highest discomfort level were the administrative and clinical managers. Since these groups were closer to the change events and were well-informed about them, it could be that these employees were better able to distinguish their responses to the specific changes. This study suggests that discomfort with change can vary more as a response to the change itself (situational), as compared to individual reaction to change.

The lessons learned from this mini-case study are twofold: (1) the communication to the hospital's workforce regarding these changes was clearly appropriate and effective in that it negated possible barriers; and (2) because employees had an opportunity to talk about their reactions to the change (supported by the organization's participatory philosophy), they were therefore less likely to experience high stress levels in relation to the change.

In addition, this study is representative of the growing interest in the human factor in organizational change. The results suggest that HR professionals need to be sensitive to the reactions of the workforce regarding change while at the same time acknowledging that change can be challenging. The study also illustrates that when significant and numerous change initiatives occur within the same time frame, having appropriate support from top management and establishing an environment that encourages employee participation will support positive results during and after implementation.

Change Management in the Global Environment

Change in global organizations can be complicated by factors such as national and regional cultural mores, cross-cultural communication (often in different languages), different employment legislation and different time zones. In addition, the global workplace is often virtual, and thus, opportunities for face-to-face communications regarding change may be rare. Further, the cultural impact of change and how it is communicated influence the likelihood of change effectiveness. Typical global change management projects include corporate workplace culture changes, strategic realignment, work and process design, and staff relocation around the globe. While this article does not allow for an in-depth discussion of global change management, below are examples that illustrate issues that HR professionals may encounter.

Today's business environment requires speed in decision-making and implementation. Clearly, global companies that are agile and can adapt to change quickly are at a competitive advantage. Yet, not all cultures are easily oriented toward change. In their book, *The Global Challenge*, Evans, Pucik and Barsoux point to the reality of tensions in multinational enterprises as a result of change. For example, in consensus cultures, such as the Japanese culture with its heritage of life employment, careful attention to fairness and process is required. As consensus cultures are not typically flexible, change can create enormous tension. HR professionals working in the global environment need to be cognizant of, and sensitive to, cultural differences that can hinder or slow change initiatives.[36]

In addition, to expand globally, companies often use change management to restructure and/or change business processes. For example, some organizations are taking advantage of the availability of business process outsourcing (BPO) to help integrate complex workflows and data on a global technology platform. Recently, Starbucks signed a contract with a provider of HR business process services, with the goal to help build a single global platform for HR services to support its global expansion. This massive change initiative will require specialized and regionalized service.[37] As globalization and technology become more complex, such outsourcing contracts may become the norm.

Mergers and acquisitions present significant dilemmas in change management. For example, only 30 percent to 50 percent of international M&As create shareholder value, the high end of success rates of M&As is around 67 percent, and 80 percent of risks are related to poorly managed cultural integrations. These statistics reflect failures often due to cultural differences. Thus, when global corporations do not carefully consider the impact of culture-based differences on organization performance, the possibility of successful change in M&As is low.[38]

Overall, change in the global business environment requires thoughtful planning, communication and employee acceptance. The study below provides an example of a global change initiative in which HR played a significant role.

Mini-Case Study #2: Communications Industry[39]

BT Global Services is a global service provider helping multi-site organizations master the complexity of business communication in today's digitally networked economy. To improve its business effectiveness, the organization began a major global transformation, called the "Connected World," that was designed to bring its various change agendas, involving more than 33,000 staff and service to 156 countries, under one program. The initiative was led by BT's president of people and organizational change, with the purpose to transform the firm from a product-oriented organization—with growth through acquisitions—to a service company, under one global model. The HR team played a key role, addressing four critical success factors: (1) establishment of a new management team; (2) employee relations; (3) engagement and communications; and (4) systems and processes.

Several major elements supported the success of this change initiative. First, HR was involved in the organization design change from the beginning. Second, HR coached management to manage the process independent of the HR team. Third, HR ensured that the process was clearly communicated at every stage to everyone involved. With employees located in 50 countries, along with five new acquisitions, the engagement and communications process was a challenge. The process focused on high-level communication programs to convey key messages in a series of events, with many led by the CEO (e.g., global conference calls, e-mail updates, Web chats). In addition, each business unit was supported by its respective communication plan. Certain processes were found to be particularly useful: (1) a communications representative and organization development consultant were appointed for each business area; and (2) a pulse survey was used to track impact over time and provide feedback. The 10-question survey ran every two weeks over a 10-week period, each time surveying 20 percent of the workforce. Results were used to determine effectiveness and make adjustments as appropriate.

Due to the leadership and critical detail provided by the HR team, this initiative significantly contributed to the company's turnaround. The company now makes decisions more quickly, moves skills and capabilities across the business with speed and agility, and delivers greater consistency to customers worldwide. BT Global Services has become known as a leader in its industry. While not all global change programs are successful, this initiative is a good example of how HR strategically implemented effective change globally.

In Closing

Whether in a domestic or global context, communication is the number one factor for success—or failure—of change initiatives. Research shows that HR is the critical link to successful organizational change. To ensure agreement of stakeholders at all levels of the company, HR fosters effective change management through the organization's vision for change, carefully designed initiatives, communication updates at all stages of the program and engagement of both top management and employees throughout the process.

Chapter 5

Maximizing Human Capital: Demonstrating HR Value with Key Performance Indicators

"In order to fully value human capital, we must go beyond the view of human effort as purely individual. We, humans, affect each other profoundly, and it is the way we affect each other that determines our value to our organizations. And, it is the way that strategic human resource professionals bring this understanding to the fore of their organizations that determines HR's value at the senior management table." [1]

In 1995, the seminal study by management guru Mark Huselid linked high-performance work practices with company performance and revealed that workforce practices had an economic effect on employee outcomes such as turnover and productivity, as well as on short- and long-term measures of corporate financial performance.[2] This study marked a new era of measuring the influence of HR to promote effective organizational performance, sustainability and financial success.

As HR positions itself as a strategic business partner, one of the most effective ways to do so is to support the strategic business goals through *key performance indicators.* Key performance indicators (also known as KPIs) are defined as quantifiable, specific measures of an organization's performance in certain areas of its business. The purpose of KPIs is to provide the company with quantifiable measurements of what is determined to be important to the organization's critical success factors and long-term business goals. Once uncovered and properly analyzed, KPIs can be used to understand and improve organizational performance and overall success.[3]

Why Measure Human Capital?

The primary motivation to measure human capital is to improve the bottom line. To design better KPIs, it is essential for HR to understand what is important to the business and what key business measures exist. In addition, the drive to measure human capital reflects the change of role of human resources from administrative to that of a strategic business partner. In general, human capital measurement is a measure of effective human resource management.

Broadly stated, HR metrics measure efficiency (time and cost) and the effectiveness of certain activities. Yet mastering human capital measures can be a very complex undertaking. Today, HR professionals are expanding the "traditional" metrics, such as head count, time-to-fill and turnover, to KPIs that align with corporate objectives and create greater stakeholder value. However, KPIs often demand large amounts of data and technological support. In addition, the trial-and-error required to set appropriate and meaningful measures comes into play, as well as patience and education of those involved. Yet despite these challenges, 84 percent of companies expect to increase the application of human capital measures in the next few years.[4]

With a clear line of sight on workforce and organizational performance, effective use of KPIs also illustrates HR's in-depth understanding of the links to business success. KPIs help build the credibility of the HR department, demonstrate HR value and foster respect and partnership with senior management and the C-suite. For example, when an HR professional not only shows that a new recruiting program resulted in a lower time to fill positions in the organization, but can also demonstrate that the program yielded an additional amount of revenue because billable staff were able to start at client sites more quickly, he or she builds HR credibility. Credibility is increased because HR is able to link HR activities to firm performance and communicate it in financial/business terms. Additional critical reasons to measure human capital include steering human capital resource allocation, winning business cases for human capital investment, tracking human capital activities to develop human capital predictions, linking variable compensation to human capital best practices, delivering human capital information required by law and providing investors with information on human capital performance. Some firms even use KPIs to enhance their company image as a progressive employer of choice.[5]

Further, with many HR functions increasingly being outsourced, credibility is earned through activities and outcomes that result in "deliverables" that promote and lead to organizational success.[6] Consequently, it is important to select KPIs that are most meaningful to the organization. For example, logical KPIs to select are those that reflect drivers for human capital measurement, such as financial outcome measures (e.g., revenue growth and cost reduction) and performance drivers (e.g., customer satisfaction, process technology innovation, product technology innovation, globalization). Within that framework, the most common categories of people measures include turnover, productivity (revenue, profit per employee), employee satisfaction/employee engagement, recruitment, diversity, remuneration, competencies/training, leadership, and health and safety. Most frequently measured are turnover, voluntary resignation, average compensation, average workforce age, diversity and compensation/total cost. Such KPIs will help HR professionals predict what they need to know to act in a timely and effective manner and identify ideas and areas where HR can develop new initiatives, or revisit others, to obtain stronger results.[7] Clearly, KPIs are the wave of the future for HR.

Culture, Stakeholders and KPIs

As the saying goes, "what gets measured gets managed." The company culture and corresponding values define what is measured. Therefore, when HR considers important KPIs, the first place to look is at corporate culture and what is most valued within that culture. In addition, stakeholders (both internal and external) go hand-in-hand with company culture. A stakeholder is an individual or entity with a stake in how the organization performs and/or conducts itself. Internal stakeholders are employees, line managers, senior management, C-suite and the board of directors. External stakeholders include shareholders, customers, vendors, the community and the government.

Working closely with internal stakeholders is beneficial for HR to (1) prioritize capabilities and create action plans to deliver them; (2) focus on deliverables rather than doables; (3) build relationships of trust; and (4) help resolve misconceptions of HR.[8] Different stakeholders have different criteria. The key priority is to give business partners the information they need to manage the company. For example, senior management values performance measures that predict and lead to future organizational financial success and sustainability. On the other hand, while one employee considers the availability of upward career mobility very important, another employee stays for health care benefits. As a result, training to promote opportunities to move up in the organization and informational sessions about employee benefits packages may be important. Overall, most important are KPIs that track key business indicators of human capital issues. HR must focus on KPIs that best illustrate stakeholder values that will lead to organizational success.

KPIs–A Strategic Management Tool

To think strategically about measurement and how best to use KPIs as a strategic management tool, it is essential to understand the meaning of the measurements and their purpose. This approach will not only be beneficial to help better manage the HR function, but also will naturally lead to aligning HR's goals and objectives with those of the organization.[9]

According to a recent national longitudinal study on the assessment of human resource organizations, strategy is the top high-value add for HR. However, in only 60 percent of companies did the HR executive see HR as a "full partner." In addition, 24 percent of executives outside of human resources viewed their HR counterparts as working at lower levels of strategic involvement, compared with 40 percent of HR executives. The study suggests that activities related to strategy provide the most high-end impact for HR to demonstrate its value (see Table 5.1). In addition, the relationship between business strategy activities and HR's strategic role points to areas where HR can contribute: growth, the core business, quality and speed, information-based strategies, knowledge-based strategies, and organizational performance. The study data also reveal key strategic HR activities that link business emphases with the organization's strategic focus: (1) having a data-based talent strategy; (2) partnering with line managers to develop business strategy; (3) providing analytic support for business decision-making; 4) providing HR data to support change management; (5) driving change management; and (6) making rigorous data-based decisions about human capital management.[10] From these HR strategy activities, key performance indicators can be developed.

Table 5.1 HR Value-Added Strategic Activities

- Help identify or design strategy options.
- Help decide among the best strategy options.
- Help plan the implementation of a strategy.
- Help design the criteria for strategic success.
- Help identify new business opportunities.
- Assess the organization's readiness to implement strategies.
- Help design the organizational structure to implement a strategy.
- Assess possible merger, acquisition or divestiture strategies.
- Work with the corporate board on business strategy.
- Recruit and develop talent.

Source: Adapted from Lawler III, E. E., Boudreau, J. W., & Mohrman, S. A. (2006). *Achieving strategic excellence: An assessment of human resource organizations*. Palo Alto, CA: Stanford University Press.

At the same time, when determining strategic KPIs, it is essential to consider who designs human capital measures and how they are created. Research by The Conference Board reveals key contributors to these metrics. Overall, HR designs 94 percent of human capital measures, often basing them on measures in the company scorecard. To create human capital measures, 77 percent of HR professionals meet with company business managers. For example, finance, strategic planning, outside consulting experts, business managers and IT contribute to HR measurement design. However, if HR lacks expertise with metrics, it is helpful to partner with groups such as marketing that have considerable expertise in measure design and analysis.[11]

Alignment of people metrics with organizational strategy is still at an early stage in many firms. To move human capital investments forward, several key points will assist HR to better strategically align with organizational goals and garner support for human capital programs: (1) involve HR in the development of overall business strategy; (2) enlist leaders outside of HR to help develop and back KPIs; (3) collaborate with business managers to ensure KPIs link to business unit strategic goals; (4) focus more attention on links between people measures and intermediate performance drivers (e.g., customer satisfaction, innovation, engagement); (5) increase manager acceptance through training programs and concrete action plans; and (6) work with HR to simplify metric and automate data collection.[12]

In addition, benchmarking can make human capital metrics more valuable. When used wisely, benchmarking data can protect programs that are performing well, create support for organizational change and help executives in HR and other disciplines make strategic decisions that affect their organizations.[13] By focusing on internal benchmarks, customized measures may help improve the alignment of activities to HR strategy. However, caution should be used with external benchmarks due to mixing "apples and oranges"—that is, different industry sectors and underlying issues in benchmarking measures. Also, external benchmarks tend to emphasize results rather than processes. Because an external benchmark does not explain what part of the process can lead to better results, the use of external measures may not always be appropriate for internal use. In the rapid expansion of highly advanced e-learning programs, for example, different programs may deliver the same content at the same low cost, but the quality of the programs is not revealed in the benchmark itself.[14]

Overall, the top KPIs for human capital and HR effectiveness can be used by all companies, regardless of size or industry. For example, the Hay Group found that the most admired companies had effective business practices in the following areas: organizational culture, strategy implementation, attraction and retention of talent, leadership development, fostering innovation, and performance management. Successful companies assess performance by balancing profit measures with measures of shareholder value, customer satisfaction and employee satisfaction.[15] Keeping this research in the forefront will help HR develop effective and strategic KPIs for their organizations.

The Importance of Lagging and Leading Indicators

The purpose of measuring KPIs and determining what leads and what lags is to help the business make predictions. To demonstrate HR value with KPIs, it is imperative that HR has a working knowledge of lagging and leading indicators. These terms describe data regarding outcomes and/or events that affect organizational performance. Lagging and leading indicators offer a way to understand and/or predict various aspects of firm performance. However, to identify and quantify these relationships, it is essential to know more than HR is a leading variable and customer satisfaction is a lagging variable.[16] To accurately gauge the relationship between lagging and leading indicators, a sense of the magnitude of the time lag between changes in the leading indicator and subsequent changes in the lagging indicator is required. (See Figure 5.1 for an example of lagging and leading indicators, with turnover as the lagging indicator in response to selection and supervisory training, the leading indicators.)

To be more specific, a lagging indicator represents information that is the result of change or an event. Lagging indicators, for example, are measures of profits, sales and service levels. They reveal various aspects regarding the success or failure of a firm. Lagging indicators are particularly useful for shareholders, creditors and government agencies. Lagging indicators do not, however, help a company react quickly, show what specifically went wrong or right, or indicate exactly what needs to be done to improve. In general, lagging indicators are not useful in managing on a day-to-day basis.[17] In contrast, a leading indicator precedes, anticipates, predicts or affects the future. For example, higher employee turnover can precede outcomes such as lower customer service scores. Of the two indicators, the leading indicator is more useful for investments or predictions. The state of the major stock markets, for example, is a leading economic indicator for the global economy. Figuring out how to measure events, practices, initiatives or outcomes helps to determine the most valuable leading indicators—that is, those indicators that may lead to clear outcomes.[18] However, part of the difficulty is clearly proving what indicators lead and with what degree of influence. For example, while the availability of talent is generally thought of as a leading indicator—as one can measure the quality of hire from it (the larger the talent pool, the more likely you are to hire more qualified

Figure 5.1 | The Effects of Selection and Supervisor Training on Turnover

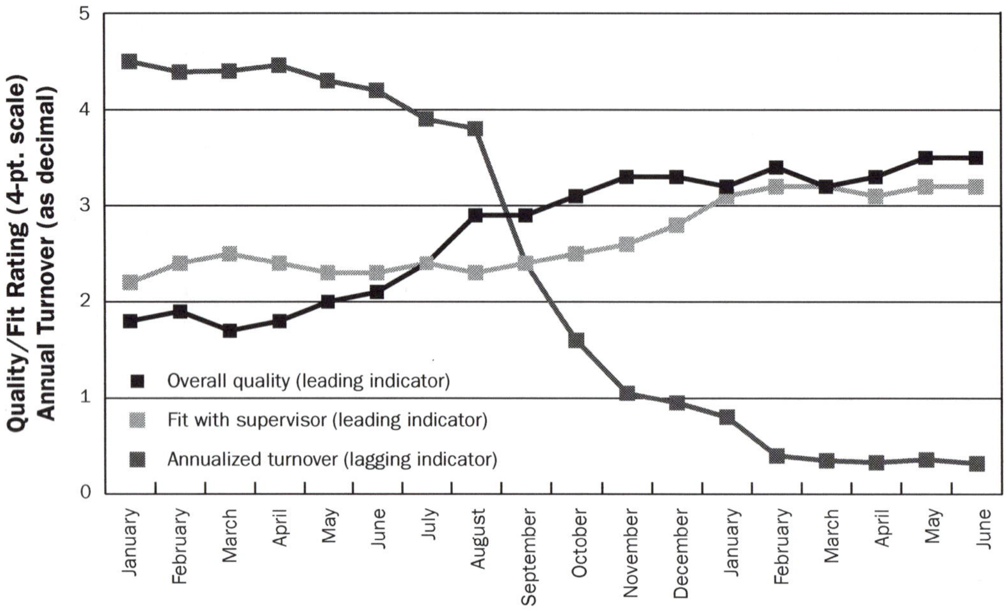

Note: Percentages do not total 100% as multiple response options were allowed. HR professionals whose organizations have not identified behavioral competencies were excluded from this analysis.
Source: SHRM Weekly Online Poll (January 2008)

people)—it is also a lagging indicator in comparison to certain political decisions. For example, consider how changes in a local taxation rate, perception of crime and ratings of school quality affect people's desire to move to a city and become part of the talent pool. Here, political decisions lead and talent availability lags. In general, the most useful measures are leading indicators, as they may predict future firm performance.

Scorecards and Dashboards

In recent years, HR scorecards and dashboards have gained popularity as a management tool. Documenting and tracking defined metrics validates human capital investments. For example, firms are increasingly tracking employee movement as a metric. Cisco Systems, Inc., the California-based communications giant, views building talent as a priority and has added to its dashboard of people measures a metric to track how many people move and the reason why, including revenue per employee. This KPI allows Cisco executives to quickly identify divisions that are creating new talent. Another firm, Valero Energy Corp. in San Antonio, developed a recruitment model using human capital metrics based on applying the supply-chain business process to labor. Scorecards help the company track the labor sources that provide the most productive employees. Using a detailed analysis of these metrics, the company can accurately forecast the demand for talent by division and title three years in advance.[19] The HR scorecard, based on the format of the balanced scorecard, is a key management tool to strengthen HR's strategic influence in the organization. The scorecard has four perspectives—strategic, operational, financial and customer—that help organize and track areas where HR adds value: (1) the strategic perspective focuses on measurements of effectiveness of major strategy-linked people goals; (2) the operational perspective reflects the effectiveness of HR processes; (3) the financial perspective relates to financial measures of HR value to the organization; and (4) the customer perspective focuses on the effectiveness of HR from the internal customer viewpoint. Depending on the organization's business goals, these perspectives also help determine KPIs that best demonstrate HR value (see Table 5.2).[20] Additional key benefits of the HR scorecard are (1) reinforcement of the distinction between HR "doables" and HR "deliverables" (i.e., a policy implementation is a doable and becomes a deliverable when it creates employee behaviors that drive strategy); (2) HR's ability to control cost and create value; (3) measurement of leading indicators; (4) assessment of HR's contribution to strategy implementation and to the bottom line; (5) support of HR to manage its strategic responsibility; and (6) encouragement of flexibility and change.[21]

Table 5.2 Examples of Key Performance Indicators for the HR Scorecard	
Strategic Perspective	Organizational culture survey
	HR budget/actual
	Employee skills/competency levels
	Change management capability of the organization
Operational Perspective	Training cost per employee
	Attrition rate
	Time to fill vacancies
	Average employee tenure in the company
Financial Perspective	Compensation and benefits per employee
	Turnover cost
	Sales per employee
	Profit per employee
Customer Perspective	Employee perspective of human resource management
	Employee perspective of the company as an employer

Source: Adapted from Becker, B. E., Huselid, M. A., & Ulrich, D. (2001). *The HR scorecard: Linking people, strategy and performance.* Boston: Harvard Business School Press.

KPIs and Employee Engagement

Employee engagement is quickly becoming a critical success factor for competitive advantage. Using KPIs, HR can demonstrate organizational success as well as gain support for initiatives related to employee engagement. Research studies offer evidence that employee engagement is key to organizational success. In the *SHRM 2006 Job Satisfaction Survey Report*, employees identified four key aspects of job satisfaction directly linked to employee engagement: meaningfulness of job, contribution of employee's work to the firm's business goals, the work itself and variety of work.[22] Watson Wyatt's research, *The Human Capital ROI Study*, reinforces the link between employee engagement, reward systems and retaining valuable human capital.[23] A Carlson/Gallup study on employee engagement and business success shows that employees who are extremely satisfied at work are four times more likely than dissatisfied employees to have a formal measurement process in place as well as receive regular recognition. Further, 82 percent said recognition motivated them to improve job performance.[24] Thus, as these studies highlight, employee engagement—whether through job satisfaction indicators, reward systems, effective communication programs or succession planning initiatives—has the power not only to clearly demonstrate HR value, but more importantly, to propel human capital investment to the forefront of the C-suite agenda.

KPIs for Organizations with Small HR Departments—Mini Case Study No. 1

Not all organizations have the luxury of a dedicated HR staff to develop, track and analyze HR metrics. When an HR staff of a small organization has limited time to track all possible HR KPIs, careful choices must be made about which KPIs best serve HR's needs. This mini case study illustrates the types of KPIs selected and tracked by a small HR staff supporting a workforce of 400 employees of a firm that sells and leases health care equipment to hospitals. With only an HR director and HR assistant, this tiny HR department tracks human capital measures that reflect the state of the organization, selecting KPIs based on metrics that best reflect the company's culture and strategic goals.

In this company, certain KPIs are tracked throughout the year, while others (e.g., absenteeism) are reviewed on a quarterly basis. Overall, the HR department benchmarks progress against prior years, with the goal that the employee cost tracks favorably against revenue and profit. The primary metrics tracked are employee cost over sales revenue, employee cost over net income before taxes, turnover of full-time and part-time staff, absenteeism, time-to-fill for critical positions, and HR performance ratings. Of these metrics, four are lagging indicators: employee cost over sales revenue, employee cost over net income before taxes, turnover and performance ratings. The other two metrics—absenteeism and time-to-fill—are leading indicators. The turnover of full-time staff, for example, was 11 percent in 2004 and 16 percent in 2005, the difference reflecting the recent retirement of several long-time employees. As a result of analyzing the turnover increase, HR developed a knowledge management transfer program for employees close to retirement. Finally, to anticipate the possible effect on the next year's budget, HR reviews any changes in benefits programs against the cost of benefits per employee.

The Value of Qualitative KPIs—Mini Case Study No. 2

KPIs—as a simple tabulation of numerical indicators—do not necessarily provide management with useful information. Moving from "bean counting" to strategic HR, a more qualitative type of key performance indicator becomes essential. As this mini case study illustrates, turnover rate, as a leading indicator, is an excellent example. In a mid-size manufacturing company with 650 employees, HR, using a qualitative assessment process, asked questions to explore the true reason behind the high turnover rate of 30 percent. First, what was the value of the employees who left the organization? Since the turnover rate was high, for example, were the employees who left a drag on performance? If yes, then the hiring process was the next step to examine. Second, was the high turnover among valuable employees? If yes, then the next step was to examine the nature of the employee-organization interaction.

To begin, HR went back to its performance assessment process and considered people who left in each of the four categories: 4—exceeds expectations, 3—meets expectations, 2—needs improvement to meet expectations and 1—not performing even to minimal expectations. They looked at high turnover among the 3s and 4s, which represented a loss of high performers who, assuming the performance assessment was valid, were more valuable to the organization. They also considered high turnover among the 1s and 2s, a possible indication that supervisors were doing a good job of weeding out those who could not perform. Looking at turnover rates over time, HR found a need for supervisor training as well as the need to improve pre-hiring screening and the overall selection process. After tracking turnover for a year following the supervisor training initiative and improvements in the hiring process, the end result was that the savings in reduced turnover far outweighed the cost of the pre-hire assessment and supervisor training.

Role of Technology and KPIs

Today, the increasing demand for HR technology runs parallel with the growing use of workforce analytics and KPIs. HR technology systems are fast proving to be a critical vehicle for HR to contribute value to their organizations. While initially used primarily by large organizations, more small and mid-size companies now use software products to both effectively measure human capital investment and track a wide range of HR metrics. Further, there is growing evidence of cost savings in organizations that effectively use HR technology. Consequently, HR in companies of all sizes will increasingly use technology to better showcase the effects of human capital initiatives.[25]

Research by management gurus Boudreau, Lawler and Mohrman points to the critical role of technology and the corresponding strong relationship between HR and IT. Two key findings reveal that, due to technology, completely integrated HR IT systems lead to the highest level of HR effectiveness, and the effectiveness of the HR IT system is strongly related to the overall effectiveness of the HR organization. Further, the *SHRM 2005 HR Technology Survey Report* emphasizes the importance of return on investment (ROI) to build a business case to incorporate HR technology systems in the firm. The top five successes of HR technology systems are: increased accuracy of employee information; decreased cycle time for processing employee information transactions; less time spent by HR staff on administrative work; greater access by managers to employee information; and the HR department's ability to manage the workforce with the same number of HR staff. Yet, few organizations document the advantages of HR technology systems:[26]

- 65 percent of organizations are not measuring the ROI for HR technology systems.
- Of those that do measure the ROI, 68 percent measure it by determining cost savings and losses and 31 percent consider HR headcount.
- 10 percent of HR professionals do not know how the ROI is measured.

Recent Studies: Human Capital Practices Drive Performance

Increasingly, research finds that best practices around human capital can help companies successfully compete with their peer organizations. The following studies highlight the importance of human capital practices to drive organizational performance. Correspondingly, KPIs that measure these practices both validate the value of HR and advance the profession at all levels.

Achieving Strategic Excellence: An Assessment of Human Resource Organizations[27]

This national study, the fourth in a series on the HR function in large corporations, focuses on measuring whether the HR function is changing to become more effective and, more specifically, whether HR is changing to become an effective strategic partner. The key findings show a "strong relationship between what is happening in the HR function and a company's strategic focuses." The degree to which the firm has knowledge and performance strategies is the degree to which HR is viewed as a strategic business partner. Overall, with the importance placed on talent management, the emphasis on human capital, knowledge and competencies creates a favorable environment for the HR function.

SHRM 2006 Human Capital Benchmarking Study[28]

This executive summary provides HR professionals with key human capital measures from nearly 600 organizations on HR departments and their expenses, employment, health care, compensation, and organizational revenue and size. The key findings reveal changes and trends in the workplace. For example, of the 57 percent of firms that expected their HR department expenses to increase, 11 percent were in durable goods manufacturing. For all industries, the median for HR expense per full-time employee was $1,072. And in 2005, organizations also increased their hiring by more than 50 percent from the previous year. Telecommunications, services (profit) and biotechnology industries had the top three highest medians for percentages of positions filled in 2005.

2006 *Fortune* Most Admired Companies: The Effectiveness of Managing Globally[29]

This study of 74 companies worldwide found that successful global organizations exploit unique knowledge and capabilities. They then effectively diffuse and adopt them worldwide to their strategic objectives, contributing to competitive differentiation. Successful global leaders, for example, take a hands-on approach to develop talent management and provide ongoing coaching to their workforce. Most admired companies have a better understanding of their talent, and consequently, positions can be filled more quickly based on required skills and career objectives.

Maximizing the Return on Your Human Capital Investment: The 2005 Watson Wyatt Human Capital Index Report[30]

This study of 147 organizations representing all major North American industries illustrates that companies with superior human capital practices can create more shareholder value that substantially surpasses companies with average human capital practices. Excellent human capital practices—such as recruiting excellence, employee development, total rewards, turnover management and communication—make a difference, no matter the state of the economy. Key findings, for example, show that companies that filled vacancies faster reduced disruption and lost productivity from turnover. Organizations that filled positions quickly (in about two weeks) outperformed those that took longer (around seven weeks) by 48 percent (59 percent three-year total returns to shareholders versus 11 percent).

Using KPIs in the Global HR Function

The value of global HR is assessed by how well global HR strategy, policies and practices link with, support and forward organizational strategy (see Table 5.3). In addition, global HR is often assessed by its effectiveness to deliver major organizational change. HR is often called upon, for example, to help in the design of high-level projects for major global business initiatives (e.g., talent management for expansion into new regions, a global communications program regarding new organizational values).

Recommendations

Selecting practical KPIs requires thoughtful consideration of the message behind measures and their corresponding effect on the organization. The real-life examples below—starting at the idea stage and ending at results with meaningful measures—demonstrate HR value through KPIs.

1. Qualitative measurement is one path to assess qualitative characteristics of the workforce, such as engagement.

Example: A public agency was experiencing high customer complaints and low staff morale. A combination of open-ended survey and focus group outputs was analyzed, and leading indicators were identified. Training was specifically designed to target the key areas, and as a result, customer complaints fell as morale improved.

2. Employee feedback provides useful perspectives on HR efficiency.

Example: Health care costs were unusually high and customer service was very poor for the last fiscal year. Six months after a new health care provider was chosen, costs were down by 20 percent. The organization's HR manager developed a survey for employees to provide feedback about the new program relative to the previous one and learned that employee perception of the new program was extremely favorable.

3. Whenever possible, the impact of recruiting is best described in terms of financial gains.

Example: An organization wanted to know the effect of its new recruiting program. The program was able to reduce time-to-fill by an average of seven days, which meant new employees could start billing sooner to client sites. Since the average daily bill rate per person was $900, the recruiting program was able to increase the firm's revenue by $6,300 per new billable employee hired.

4. Retaining older workers for future leadership roles depends on what they most value.

Example: A survey by a multinational corporation of its older worker population in North America and Europe revealed the following top three key values: (1) support from managers; (2) ability to make one's own job-related decisions; and (3) opportunities for advancement. Leadership development programs were created to retain key talent from this group. Over a two-year period, tracking of performance, mentoring and promotions of older workers in the leadership development program found that turnover rates for older workers decreased by 28 percent.

Table 5.3 Examples of Key Performance Indicators for Global HR Effectiveness

- Design and implementation of an international HR information system.
- Development of global leadership through cross-cultural assignments.
- Development of a global mindset for all employees through training and development.
- Cost reduction of expatriate assignments.
- Implementation of formal systems that improve worldwide communications.

Source: Adapted from Sparrow, P., Brewster, C., & Harris, H. (2004). *Globalizing human resource management*. London: Routledge.

Yet measuring the contribution of HR on an international level becomes ever more complicated due to factors such as complexities of scope, authority level, and political, cultural and legislative barriers that directly affect the link between organizational performance and HR. Two approaches are recommended: identifying and proving the link between organizational performance and people management, and using methods of evaluation of the global HR function's contribution. The measure of the global HR function also often rests on "perceptions of effectiveness" from key stakeholders—that is, the company's worldwide employees and managers. Therefore, the ability to market HR globally as a source of competitive and strategic advantage is fundamental to measuring the contribution of the corporate global HR function.[31]

Measuring the value of international assignments, for example, is a critical success factor for global HR. Companies measure the ROI of international assignments through cost estimating, tracking and comparison. A recent global relocation trends survey, for example, found that 70 percent of companies required a statement of assignment objectives prior to funding assignments. In addition, to minimize expatriate turnover—a global HR KPI—64 percent of companies found opportunities to use international experience, with 50 percent of firms offering a greater choice of positions upon return and 43 percent offering repatriation career support.[32] However, as highlighted in an SHRM case study on repatriation, different assignments have different measures of success and, consequently, different results. A common KPI is the retention rate of expatriates following repatriation for one and/or two years. Other measures may also reflect "softer" results, such as managerial approach shifts or cultural changes. The concept behind using a variety of measures is to create a "report card" that can provide a broad view of the assignment overall.[33]

In Closing

Becoming more facile with metrics in general is a goal of many HR professionals. Further, as more HR professionals become immersed in human capital measurement, they can more effectively use key performance indicators to illustrate the value of human capital investments through successful organizational performance at many levels. These important steps will increasingly demonstrate the high value-add required by the C-suite to be a true strategic business partner.

PART II

Staffing Management

Chapter 6

Talent Management: Driver for Organizational Success

"It is nearly unanimous that HR can and should add more value to corporations. The best way to do this is by being a business partner—by directly improving the performance of the business. This can be accomplished by effective talent management, helping with change management, influencing strategy and a host of other value-added activities that impact effectiveness." [1]

In a competitive marketplace, talent management is a primary driver for organizational success. Broadly defined, talent management is the implementation of integrated strategies or systems designed to increase workplace productivity by developing improved processes for attracting, developing, retaining and utilizing people with the required skills and aptitude to meet current and future business needs.[2] A recent study shows that 85 percent of HR executives state that the "single greatest challenge in workforce management is creating or maintaining their companies' ability to compete for talent."[3] Without question, effective talent management provides one of the most critical points of strategic leverage today.

Offering enormous business value, talent management is complex and continually evolving. Influenced by external factors such as the economy, global expansion and mergers and acquisitions, critical success factors for effective talent management include alignment with strategic goals, active CEO participation and HR management. Over time, common themes around talent management are emerging, such as the role of line leaders in the development of talent (see Table 6.1). Overall, the main recurring themes are CEO involvement, culture, management, processes and accountability.[4]

Research shows that organizations increasingly focus on talent management. Moving from reactive to proactive, companies are working hard to harness talent. According to SHRM's *2006 Talent Management Survey Report*, 53 percent of organizations have specific talent management initiatives in place. Of these companies, 76 percent consider talent management a top priority. In addition, 85 percent of HR professionals in these companies work directly with management to implement talent management strategies.[5]

Table 6.1 Common Principles of the Talent Management Agenda

1. Expectations regarding the differentiation of talent.
2. The role of line leaders in the development of people.
3. Philosophy regarding the movement of people across businesses and functions.
4. The role of diversity in staffing strategy.
5. Beliefs about hiring for potential versus hiring for position.

Source: Why the leadership bench never gets deeper: Ten insights about executive talent development. (2002). HR. *Human Resource Planning.*

Yet different companies may not define talent the same way. The belief in talent and its impact on the bottom line are at the heart of talent management. To be effective, the talent mindset must be embedded throughout the organization, starting with the CEO. Going beyond succession planning for top leadership positions, companies that value talent have a deep appreciation for the contribution of individuals at all levels, now and for the future. In essence, talent is the vehicle to move the organization where it wants to be.[6]

Drivers for Talent Management

To gain competitive advantage, the demand for human capital drives talent management. Talent management strategies focus on five primary areas: attracting, selecting, engaging, developing and retaining employees. Although pay and benefits initially attract employees, top-tier leadership organizations focus on retaining and developing talent (see Table 6.2).[7]

Workforce trends drive talent management strategies. Factors such as an increasingly global and virtual workforce, different generations working together, longer life expectancies and an empowered and autonomous workforce have forever changed the workplace. Due to demographic changes, the workforce is also increasingly diverse—from age, gender and ethnicity to lifestyles, migration patterns and cultural norms. Organizations are already taking advantage of these workplace trends. For example, The Home Depot, Inc., the home improvement giant, focuses its staffing initiatives on older workers and partners with AARP for referrals; 15 percent of its workforce is over 50.[8] Talent management strategies also provide the context for diversity and inclusion. Procter and Gamble, for example, feels that getting the right mix of people is a major part of talent management and hires many of its leaders as university recruits.[9]

Table 6.2 Seven Hallmarks of Distinction of Top-Tier Leadership Organizations

1. Senior executive commitment to development.
2. Organizational reinforcement of development (through manager incentives and recognition).
3. Hiring for organizational compatibility.
4. Culture of meritocracy.
5. Offering rising executives a full exposure to the business.
6. Selecting successors based on leadership ability.
7. A succession management system focused on skills scarce in the labor market and emphasizing position fit above general skill development.

Source: Corporate Leadership Council. (2003). *High-impact succession management: From succession planning to strategic executive talent management.* Retrieved from www.executiveboard.com

Talent management is also driven by the anticipated skills shortage in the coming years. While not all organizations, industries and professions will experience a lack of skills, organizations are already competing for talent. For example, customer service, health care, computer support and technology repair are areas where there is an anticipated acute talent shortage.[10] In addition, as noted in SHRM's *2005 Future of the U.S. Labor Pool Survey Report*, the anticipated loss of talent in the next decade will vary by organization size, sector and industry. For example, large organizations—as compared with small and medium companies—are more concerned about loss of talent from the retirement of the baby boom generation, and public and government organizations are more concerned about the loss of potential talent than private companies.[11]

Finally, key business strategies also drive talent management. For example, with the growing need for global technical expertise, Ford Motor Company links competency development to its organizational strategic goals. Corporate branding, a key organizational strategy, is another business strategy that drives talent management. Increasingly, firms are linking their brand to employees and corporate behavior. At JPMorganChase, for example, the concept of leadership for all employees is part of its corporate branding: "One Firm, One Team, Be a Leader."[12]

Ownership of Talent Management

Supported by the CEO and the board of directors, talent management is headed by human resources, usually the head of the HR organization (e.g., vice president of HR, chief human resource officer). While responsibility for talent management is shared throughout the organization—from the CEO to the line manager—the role of HR is to identify and deploy optimal strategies to engage employees by driving satisfaction, loyalty and retention. Commitment to talent management requires HR to be a strategic business partner. A 2005 study on global human capital found that chief HR officers (CHROs), as "chief talent architects," played a central role as strategic business advisors by leveraging human capital to improve organizational performance and workforce effectiveness. Based on CEO priorities, the top seven CHRO initiatives were organization transformation, people development, talent management, HR transformation, leadership development, recruitment initiatives and rewards.[13]

Moving talent management initiatives forward, however, requires organizational buy-in. That is, all levels of management must be on board with the importance of talent management strategies. When the board is involved, the value of talent management is apparent and has high visibility. Yet to be successful, the value must be understood throughout the organization. In high-performing companies, for example, senior management also is responsible for the success of talent management. At the same time, for talent management initiatives to be effective, organizations need formal processes, with many people involved and with strong links between leadership and talent to translate into specific organizational value-based behaviors.[14]

Ownership of talent management is also reflected in dedicated resources. A formal budget for talent management initiatives, for example, is evidence of organizational commitment. As noted in SHRM's *2006 Talent Management Survey Report*, firms with talent management initiatives are more likely than organizations without such initiatives to have formal recruitment budgets (72 percent compared with 39 percent, respectively).[15]

Further, it is important that HR educate top management on the link between the talent management cycle and the cost of turnover. For example, an employee's decision to stay or leave is related to career possibilities in the company as well as how he or she can become better prepared to move to other opportunities. To keep a valued employee, the easy answer is not merely compensation. Employee loyalty tends to be more directed to his or her professional skills rather than to the organization.[16] Thus, to best attract, engage, develop and retain talent, those who have responsibility for talent management must understand what is important to employees.

The Role of HR

As a primary owner of talent management, HR has many roles—one of the most important is that of facilitator of the talent mindset. HR leads the way for the organization to own, as an entity, the role of talent management for organizational success. In the role of business partner, HR works closely with the board, the CEO and senior management to ensure that they are committed to talent management work. As talent management facilitator, HR also pays close attention to how the organization's culture supports talent. Broadly speaking, HR's role encompasses communicating the talent management philosophy companywide and knowing the industry competition. In addition, HR needs to develop an integrated and proactive strategic approach to talent management—the big picture—as well as managing critical information, such as tracking turnover and knowing what factors contribute to retention (see Table 6.3).

Table 6.3 Seven Keys to Effective Talent Management

1. Develop an integrated, proactive talent management strategy: View "employer of choice" status as an outcome of coherent corporate culture rather than ad-hoc programs.
2. Balance grassroots involvement in talent attraction and retention with management accountability.
3. Know the company's business environment and plans–the competitive climate: Know plans for growth, merger, divestiture, new products or technologies and project their impact on immediate and longer-term talent needs.
4. Know what factors contribute to difficulties in attraction and retention: Base initiatives on the real concerns of employees. Raw numbers on turnover can show where retention problems are but not what they are.
5. Keep various retention factors in balance, especially the mix of compensation and nonfinancial motivators.
6. Track turnover: Know its costs and where they are the greatest and convey them to management to support the business case for retention.
7. Market the company and its brand to current employees as vigorously as to the outside talent pool.

Source: Dell, D., & Hickey, J. (2002). *Sustaining the talent quest.* New York: The Conference Board.

To integrate talent management into all areas of the company, HR also plays a role of change management agent. To drive this change, HR addresses four diverse talent management activities: recruitment, performance management, leadership development and organizational strategy. In this role, HR manages four major risks to the business: (1) vacancy risk (to safeguard key business capabilities, focus on scarce skills and fit to position); (2) readiness risk (to accelerate leadership development, provide full business exposure to rising stars); (3) transition risk (to avoid loss of key talent, select successors with leadership ability and hire for organization capability); and (4) portfolio risk (to maximize strategic talent leverage, focus on senior management's commitment to development and performance standards).[17]

Finally, proactive HR leaders take a holistic approach to talent management. It is important to establish clear expectations and communicate openly about the talent management process. By HR explaining to management and employees why talent management is important, how it works and what the benefits are to the organization and participants, talent management strategies are more likely to be seen as a fair process.[18]

Employee Engagement and Its Relationship to Talent Management

Effective talent management policies and practices that demonstrate commitment to human capital result in more engaged employees and lower turnover. Consequently, employee engagement has a substantial impact on employee productivity and talent retention. Employee engagement, in fact, can make or break the bottom line. Employees who are most committed perform 20 percent better and are 87 percent less likely to resign. In addition, the foundation for an engaged workforce is established by the quality, depth and authenticity of communication by HR and senior management to employees, as well as the quality of supervision. The role of the manager as the most important enabler of employee commitment to the job, organization and teams cannot be overemphasized. Furthermore, when done well, practices that support talent management also support employee engagement (e.g., work-life balance programs—flex time, telecommuting, compressed workweeks, reward programs, performance management systems).[19]

Rewards and recognition also help both to retain talent and to improve performance. A Carlson/Gallup study on employee engagement and business success showed that employees who were extremely satisfied at work were four times more likely than dissatisfied employees to have a formal measurement process in place as well as receive regular recognition. Further, 82 percent said recognition motivated them to improve job performance.[20] Increasingly, organizations are putting formal and informal reward programs in place. For example, according to *SHRM's 2005 Reward Programs and Incentive Compensation Survey Report*, 84 percent of companies offer some form of monetary and/or nonmonetary reward programs to employees. To be most effective, however, organizations must regularly communicate to employees about reward programs. Discussing reward programs as early as during the interview process demonstrates that the organization values its employees.[21]

The process of building employee engagement is ongoing. Beyond compensation and benefits, employee engagement is best fostered through a meaningful and emotionally enriching work experience. Effective employee engagement—a mixture of tangible and intangible factors—fosters an environment of stimulation, development, learning, support, contribution and recognition. However, a recent study found that less than one-fifth of employees were highly engaged, one-fifth of the workforce was disengaged and about two-thirds were moderately engaged. The impact of employee dissatisfaction varies, depending on work experience (e.g., overwhelming workloads, distant and noncommunicative senior leadership, few developmental opportunities). The risk is that moderately engaged employees may move toward being disengaged. The opportunity and challenge for HR, working with senior management, is to increase the strength of employee engagement. Focus on engagement demands strong leadership, a sense of shared destiny, autonomy, accountability and opportunities for development and advancement. To better engage workers, companies must work harder to inspire people and provide a sense of passion, pride and mission.[22] Ultimately, it is organizational culture that determines employee engagement and retention of talent.

Finding the Right People

In the war for talent, organizational success depends on effective recruitment and retention. To accomplish this goal, HR can provide value by focusing on five key areas: ensuring organizational stability, emphasizing employer brand and reputation, developing integrated talent strategies, supporting multilevel accountability, getting involved in talent management initiatives and offering opportunities for career and personal development.[23]

Regarding recruitment and retention, HR has a number of challenges to address. According to *SHRM's 2006 Talent Management Survey Report*, the top areas in need of improvement regarding talent management practices and strategies are (1) building a deeper reservoir of successors at every level; (2) creating a culture that makes employees want to stay with the organization; (3) identifying gaps in current employee and candidate competency levels; and (4) creating policies that encourage career growth and development opportunities.[24]

To attract and retain talent, hiring for compatibility—the "fit" between employer and employee—is critical. In addition, companies with excellent reputations and strong brands are well positioned to attract top talent. Yahoo! Inc. exemplifies the organization that effectively links organizational culture and company values in its recruiting initiatives to determine the best candidates. This process, however, takes time. For example, in the first six months of 2004, Yahoo! spent 6,000 hours interviewing candidates to fill 500 positions—an average of 12 hours per new hire.[25]

Another effective recruiting strategy is tapping into specific labor pools. By assessing the organization's areas of strength in its workplace programs and policies, HR may identify possible segments of the labor force to target. For example, women who have either not yet begun their careers or are reentering the labor market from childbearing years represent a sizeable talent pool. With a workplace environment supportive of women's career development, Whirlpool Corporation, a top U.S. home appliance maker, targets women in recruiting and promotion. Some organizations focus on workers with disabilities, an excellent source of talent. For example, at IBM, 42 percent of the organization's disabled workers possess key skills such as marketing, IT architecture and software engineering.[26] By carefully assessing the organization's current and future talent needs, HR can develop recruiting and retention strategies that align with the company business goals, thus promoting organizational growth and sustainability.

Succession Planning Management

Investment in human capital requires careful planning. Under the talent management umbrella, succession planning and leadership development are important organizational business strategies to develop and retain talent. As noted in the *2005 Human Capital Index Report*, succession planning is also one of the key strategies to reduce turnover costs.[27] While in the past succession plans were primarily focused on key leadership roles, organizations are now establishing leadership development and succession planning initiatives early in the process of employee career development. In addition, according to SHRM's *2006 Succession Planning Survey Report*, 58 percent of organizations have either a formal (29 percent) or informal (29 percent) succession plan and 26 percent plan to develop one. The survey findings note that large organizations (500 or more employees) and publicly or privately owned for-profit organizations are more likely to have formal succession plans. The responsibility for implementing succession planning varies, starting with HR and followed by senior management, the president/CEO and the chief operating officer. However, not all organizations are jumping on the bandwagon to develop succession plans; 16 percent do not intend to do so. The reasons vary, with companies saying more immediate needs take precedence, some companies have too small a staff size, while others have not yet considered it, and still others have no support from senior management.[28]

At the same time, organizations grapple with how to best utilize succession planning—and the corresponding leadership development initiatives—to manage, develop and retain talent. For those considering leadership development as part of their talent management agenda, it is important to (1) determine whether the parts of the program, when combined, enable the organization to be more competitive; (2) assess if the leadership development system reinforces perceptions about the company that the organization wants others to have; and (3) evaluate whether employees view the leadership programs as legitimate. For example, do they take them seriously? Do these initiatives really affect business decisions?[29]

Increasingly, organizations are putting structured processes in place for leadership development (see Figure 6.1). As highlighted in SHRM's *2006 Talent Management Survey Report*, organizations anticipate that their employee development budgets will increase in the next three years (according to 60 percent of organizations with talent initiatives and 58 percent of those without talent initiatives).[30] Clearly, employee development is seen as important for organizational stability and growth. S.C. Johnson & Son, the consumer products company, is a good example of a company that uses its performance appraisal program to identify rising stars for management and technical positions. High performers are evaluated through 360-degree feedback to evaluate promotion readiness. The company has processes to identify ready replacements for crucial jobs. Due to the organization's carefully-honed talent development strategies, nine out of 10 positions are filled internally.[31] As HR leaders work to support their organizations, leadership development and succession planning are areas that provide substantial business value.

Figure 6.1 | Structured Process to Develop, Track and Evaluate Employees

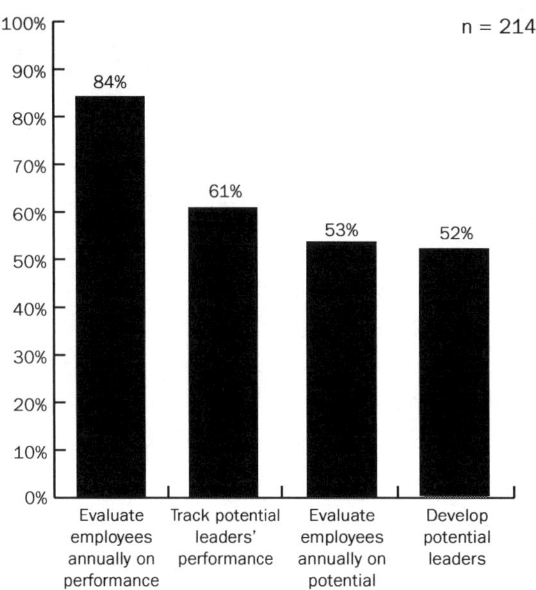

Note: Excludes respondents who indicated that their organizations did not have formal or informal succession plans.
Source: SHRM *2006 Succession Planning Survey Report*

Measuring Business Impact

Talent management metrics link human capital investment to financial performance. According to management gurus Huselid, Becker and Beatty, there are three critical challenges to successful workforce measurement and management. First, there is "the perspective challenge"—meaning, do all managers really understand how workforce behaviors and capabilities drive strategy execution? Second, there is "the metrics challenge"—that is, are the right measures of workforce success identified (e.g., workforce culture, mindset, leadership, competencies and behaviors)? The third challenge is "the execution challenge"—specifically, in order to monitor progress and communicate the strategic intent of talent management initiatives, are managers motivated to use these data and do they have access and capability to do so?[32]

Talent management metrics are evolving. As organizations increasingly focus on talent management strategies, they seek ways to validate these initiatives and measure their business impact. Many firms are beginning to include talent management in their dashboards or scorecards. For example, HSBC, a banking and financial services institution, uses the Balanced Scorecard™, with talent management listed under learning and growth. Scorecards provide a clear "line of sight" to organizational strategic goals by linking talent management to objectives and performance appraisals. Measures may include factors such as employee survey results, turnover (e.g., talent pools) and the number of employees on secondments (temporary assignments).[33]

Companies also create their own measurements to fit their organizational cultures. Pfizer, for example, developed three primary talent management objectives—strength of leadership team and pipeline, robustness of talent management processes, and development of talent mindset and values—with corresponding drivers and metrics. One metric used to evaluate the robustness of talent management processes is the percentage of key position holders with individual development plans.[34] Avon, a global cosmetics company, is an example of a company that transformed its talent management system by shifting how it looks at talent and consequently how it utilizes technology. This transformation was necessary to be able to answer four key questions: (1) is there the necessary bench strength to staff the organization's growth and transformation initiatives; (2) is world-class talent in key roles; (3) how can the talent "hit rate" be increased; and (4) when and where does the company make or buy talent? The core of this transformation was the change from a "referral of talent" mode (e.g., a manager recommends an employee for a position) to a more objective and formal approach to talent management. This shift resulted in talent being assessed objectively through a leadership model to better determine suitability for various roles. To be able to identify where talent in the organization is located, a database now houses employee profiles, which can be routinely updated. As a result, the organization can make more data-driven decisions regarding talent.[35]

Increasingly, talent management technology to house and track talent management strategies is becoming available. Databases with all relevant data in one location can result in significant time savings for staffing, such as the ability to quickly identify talent for open positions. Organizations are recommended, however, to carefully evaluate which talent management technology program best fits their current and future needs. Some vendors include talent management solutions in their HR suites. Strategic talent management software may help manage workforce skills and capabilities (hourly, salaried and contingent), demographics, career planning, employee retention initiatives, workforce and succession planning, and performance and learning management. Although few vendors offer all of these options in one package, it is important to know if the software can be integrated with other systems.[36] Opinions vary, however, on the value of technology systems regarding talent management.

Challenges of Global Talent Management

Global competition for skilled workers is keen; worldwide, many employers are experiencing a talent shortage. A survey of nearly 33,000 employers in 23 countries reveals that 40 percent are struggling to locate qualified candidates.[37] With the liberation of trade policies, transnational companies moving production to low-cost areas and the corresponding growth of global supply chains, increased globalization has resulted in socio-economic and cultural challenges. Further, talent now takes many forms, from migrants crossing borders (temporarily or seeking new homes), students gaining degrees and expatriates on assignment to tourists, refugees and business travelers. Consequently, the demand for skills has countries working hard to develop policies that will attract talent with human and technological skills to support economic growth, retain talent and even reverse talent migration. In a "reverse brain drain" effect, China and India, for example, encourage their educated nationals to return and fill jobs at home.[38]

Thus, the need for talent creates movement between countries. The United States relies on foreign talent, particularly in certain fields. U.S. universities, for example, are not graduating enough U.S. students in science and engineering, and by 2010, 25 percent of the nation's scientists and engineers will reach retirement age. Reflecting this shift, in 2000, 22 percent of all U.S. science and engineering positions were held by foreign-born professionals, up from 14 percent in 1990.[39] In contrast, countries such as China and India have a wealth of talent in science, engineering and technology. Each year, China produces 350,000 graduate engineers and India 120,000, compared with 63,000 in the United States.[40] In addition, the demand for foreign-born talent is further demonstrated by the fact that the total cap on the number of available H-1B visas under U.S. immigration policies is regularly reached months in advance of the application deadline. Clearly, the ability to attract and retain talent is increasingly important to long-term growth.

Managing global talent has challenges and significant implications for sustainability and growth. A recent study of global companies, for example, states that companies are concerned about the development of future leaders capable of navigating the global business environment. Key findings show that the most important determinant of global talent management (GTM) success is the degree of involvement by the CEO, the board of directors and the GTM leader in talent management activities. On average, for example, CEOs spend 16 percent of their time speaking publicly about GTM, mentoring high potentials, participating in talent reviews and approving the succession plans. Board members in 46 percent of companies provide input into assessment of key employees and 39 percent meet with high potentials during the year.[41]

In sync with the trend to develop global HR policies and practices, organizations are creating global talent management processes. For example, at Intel Corporation, a global chip maker, HR utilizes a talent management program and works with management to assess workforce needs.[42] Research shows organizations value having global frameworks, specifically around a common language and structure in areas such as performance management, leadership development for high potentials and professional development. There is less agreement, however, about developing common frameworks for recruitment.[43]

Recent Studies on Talent Management

Studies on talent management reveal a number of common themes. First, the focus on talent management forces companies to become aware of—and assess—their workforce talent and current and future talent needs. Second, organizations that understand the business case for talent management successfully link talent management and organizational strategy, reaping benefits in increased workplace performance. Third, organizations are seeking effective ways to measure talent and determine bottom line impact.

2005 Talent Management Strategies Survey[44]

According to this study, 43 percent of companies see retention of key talent as the issue that will have the most impact on their business. Further, 72 percent of organizations are concerned about the negative effect on the bottom line due to inadequate skills of incoming workers. The study emphasizes that as baby boomers turn 62 in 2008 and skills gaps widen, the impending talent crisis will quickly become a global, cross-industry threat. For example, 33 percent of companies state that 11 percent of their workforce may retire in the next two or three years. For 31 percent of companies, the issue of retirement and impending skills shortages is being discussed at the board level. However, only 50 percent of organizations have a defined list of critical skills for the future.

The High-Performance Workforce Study 2004[45]

Executives in six countries spanning more than 15 industries were surveyed. The findings reveal six practices that dramatically improve workforce performance, yielding strong contributions to business performance. The number one practice is a formal process for talent management, supported by technologies, that enables an organization to objectively assess employee skills and capabilities and quickly identify the best candidates for open positions.

Survey of Global Talent Management Practices[46]

This survey explores global talent management practices among multinational companies (MNCs), focusing on global-scale processes to identify and develop leaders. According to the study findings, the most effective processes for identifying talent and increasing visibility of high potential candidates are assessment processes with open and frank discussions. Yet not all MNCs consider these discussions at the same level; 80 percent of American companies see talent review meetings as open and frank, compared with 55 percent of European companies. Many MNCs explicitly seek and encourage diversity in their talent pools. Within development planning, the most critical experiences are those that provide high potentials with a broad organizational view, visibility and experience outside of their comfort zones (e.g., participation on global task forces, two- to three-year international assignments, inclusion in critical meetings).

How Leading Organizations Manage Talent[47]

From in-depth interviews with HR leaders of large employers in a variety of industries, this study reveals that leading companies make attracting, engaging and retaining employees a strategic business priority. Senior leadership focuses on clearly communicating the business strategy to the workforce as well as defining the role people play to execute that strategy. Effective leaders have a clear understanding of what drives value in their organizations, what motivates their customers and how to achieve growth in the future. Many companies have developed talent management metrics to support business and financial measures, with metrics built into the balanced scorecard. Through the performance management system, managers are held accountable for employee retention and creating opportunities for high-potential employees.

Looking to the Future

Anticipated workforce changes and cost-effective ways to access talent are key to the next generation of talent management. Predictive workforce monitoring will lead to effective strategic talent decision-making. Factors such as flexible talent sourcing, customized and personalized rewards, distributed and influential leadership, and unified and compassionate workplace cultures will be important for successful talent management. Companies will increasingly utilize different types of employment relationships, and nonstandard employment models will continue to evolve. Free agency employment relationships—contracting for the best talent on an as-needed basis—will become more common. To benefit from the knowledge, skills and corporate memory of mature workers, phased retirement will become prevalent. Keeping workers engaged—particularly the next generations—may call for HR to redesign the workweek, benefits packages and reward programs.[48] Scenario planning and talent-match databases will become essential planning tools.

In closing, to sustain outstanding business results in a global economy, organizations will rethink and reinvent their approaches to talent management. Effective talent management calls for strong participatory leadership, organizational buy-in, employee engagement and workplace scorecards with talent management metrics. Companies that master talent management will be well-positioned for long-term growth in workforce performance for years to come.

Chapter 7

Workplace Diversity: Leveraging the Power of Difference for Competitive Advantage

"Diversity represents a company's fundamental attitude that it not only respects and values the individuality of its employees but also understands how to tap the potentially significant contributions inherent in diversity." [1]

Alexandra Groess
Allianz Group's International Diversity Project

Workplace Diversity–An Evolution

From compliance to inclusion, the concept of workplace diversity is evolving. Coming from an organizational viewpoint, this article explores the changing perception of workplace diversity, elements of an inclusive corporate culture, the business case and HR's leadership role to maximize the benefits of a diverse workforce in a changing marketplace. While a broad range of issues is covered, it should be noted that "one size does not fit all," as organizations are in different stages of development regarding workplace diversity. In addition, workplace diversity is not strictly a U.S. concept: a brief discussion on the drivers of workplace diversity in the European Union is presented.

Diversity Defined Today

As predicted in the landmark study Workforce 2020, rapid technological change, globalization, the demand for skills and education, an aging workforce and greater ethnic diversification in the labor market have forever changed the employment landscape.[2] The definition of diversity extends well beyond the traditional view that once focused primarily on gender and race and reflects the broader perspective of workplace diversity today.

"A broad definition of diversity ranges from personality and work style to all of the visible dimensions such as race, age, ethnicity or gender, to secondary influences such as religion, socioeconomics and education, to work diversities such as management and union, functional level and classification or proximity/distance to headquarters." [3]

Integration and Learning: A New Paradigm for Managing Diversity

Diversity in the United States has evolved since the 1960s. As illustrated in Table 7.1, diversity was first based on the assimilation approach, with everyone being part of the "melting pot." Compliance (e.g., affirmative action, equal employment opportunity) is important in diversity, and key legislation has been an effective tool for change (e.g., Title VII of the Civil Rights Act of 1964, Age Discrimination in Employment Act of 1967, Americans with Disabilities Act of 1990). Today, however, the impetus behind workplace diversity is that of inclusion and the business case: embracing and leveraging differences for the benefit of the organization. The collaboration of cultures, ideas and different perspectives is now considered an organizational asset—bringing forth greater creativity and innovation—with the result that many companies are increasingly focusing on corporate diversity initiatives to improve organizational performance.[4]

Diversity initiatives do not always meet expectations. The traditional schools of thought behind many diversity interventions are: (1) assimilation, based on the idea that "we're all the same" (promoting equal opportunity); and (2) differentiation, from the philosophy "we celebrate differences." Today, groundbreaking research goes beyond the historical framework of workplace diversity. The emerging paradigm is integration and learning. That is, companies promote equal opportunity and value cultural differences, using the talents of all employees to gain diverse work perspectives. To achieve this

Table 7.1 Evolution of Approaches to Workplace Diversity

Approach:	assimilation	→	legal	→	valuing diversity	→	managing diversity
Basis:	melting pot myth	→	EEO/AA	→	difference as assets	→	multicultural corporate cultures

Source: *Carr-Ruffino, N. (1999).* Diversity success strategies. *Boston: Butterworth-Heinemann.*

level of diversity management, however, organizational leaders must have a clear understanding of how they define diversity as well as what exactly the organization does with the experiences of being a diverse workforce.[5]

An Inclusive Corporate Culture

The concept of inclusion is increasingly important in the discussion of workplace diversity. In many ways, this evolution reflects societal values in the workplace. For example, two beliefs commonly held by Americans are that everyone deserves a chance (equal opportunity, sometimes referred to as the "level playing field") and that all people should be treated with dignity and respect.[6] The values of equality, respect and opportunity for all represent the cornerstone of workplace diversity. Inclusiveness is thus a win-win dynamic: it generates opportunities for growth, flexibility and adaptation in the marketplace for both the employee and the organization.

The Business Case for Workplace Diversity

Increasingly, the case for workplace diversity as a business imperative is gaining recognition by leaders in the business world. At a symposium sponsored by The Conference Board regarding diversity in the workplace, for example, 400 executives agreed that "diversity programs help to ensure the creation, management, valuing and leveraging of a diverse workforce that will lead to organizational effectiveness and sustained competitiveness."[7]

One of the major drivers behind the business case is the demographic changes that directly affect the labor pool and available talent (see Table 7.2). These changes are significant. In an organization, human capital and workforce relationships are the backbone of success. The flow of information between colleagues, work teams, customers and suppliers, for example, depends on the quality of relationships and talent in the workplace.[8] Consequently, workplace diversity is increasingly viewed as an essential success factor to be competitive in today's marketplace.

Table 7.2 Demographic Trends Transforming the Workforce

- **Greater diversity in the labor pool:** By 2008, women and minorities will represent 70 percent of the new labor force entrants, and by 2010, 34 percent of the U.S. workforce will be non-Caucasian.
- **An aging workforce:** By 2010, the U.S. workforce will have an increase of 29 percent in the 45-64 age group, a 14 percent increase in the 65+ age group and a 1 percent decline in the 18-44 age group.
- **Globalization:** In the next decade, 75 percent of new workers will likely be from Asia, while North America and Europe will have 3 percent of the world's new labor force.

Source: Hewitt Associates. (2004, February). *Preparing the workforce of tomorrow.* Retrieved March 21, 2005, from www.hewitt.com.

Advantages

Six key reasons to tie workplace diversity to organizational strategic goals and objectives are: (1) greater adaptability and flexibility in a rapidly changing marketplace; (2) attracting and retaining the best talent; (3) reducing costs associated with turnover, absenteeism and low productivity; (4) return on investment (ROI) from various initiatives, policies and practices; (5) gaining and keeping greater/new market share (locally and globally) with an expanded diverse customer base; and (6) increased sales and profits. Workplace diversity can be viewed as having both direct and indirect links to the bottom line. In business, the preferred equation for success is a single action that directly impacts financial performance. Workplace diversity, however, is a complex phenomenon. Consequently, the link of workplace diversity to financial success is not always immediately apparent, nor is it always linear. Two examples below illustrate scenarios with direct and indirect links of workplace diversity to organizational performance.[9]

> *Direct link:* Organizations that expand their customer base most effectively do so with a workforce that is reflective of their clients. DuPont, for example, considers diversity a business imperative vital to ongoing renewal and competitiveness in the 21st century. This philosophy was illustrated when the company learned how one small change could directly translate into significant profits. At DuPont Merck, the sales of an anticoagulant drug in the Hispanic markets were low. When a Hispanic manager noticed that the drug was only labeled in English and consequently translated the instructions into Spanish, sales improved significantly. Now, educational materials for the drug are translated into 15 languages and bring in millions of dollars in new business.[10]
>
> *Indirect link:* Having access to and retaining talent from a worldwide diverse labor pool is key to gaining a competitive edge in the global marketplace. To expand and keep their market share, Nortel views lost revenue due to turnover as a reason to support diversity. With the cost of replacing an employee at $55,000 and turnover at 7 percent (compared to 17 percent in the information technology industry), the overall turnover cost is still quite high. For example, 7 percent attrition for 80,000 employees translates to replacing 5,600 people. Thus, when 5,600 (people) is multiplied by $55,000 (the cost of replacing one employee), turnover cost is $30.8 million! Thus, at Nortel, attracting and keeping talent—a key aspect of workplace diversity—has a significant impact on the bottom line.[11]

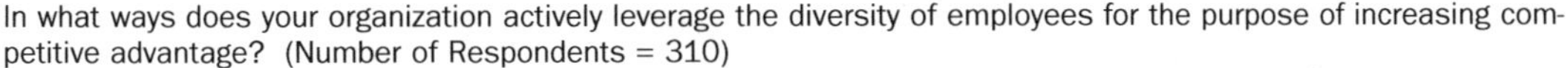

In what ways does your organization actively leverage the diversity of employees for the purpose of increasing competitive advantage? (Number of Respondents = 310)

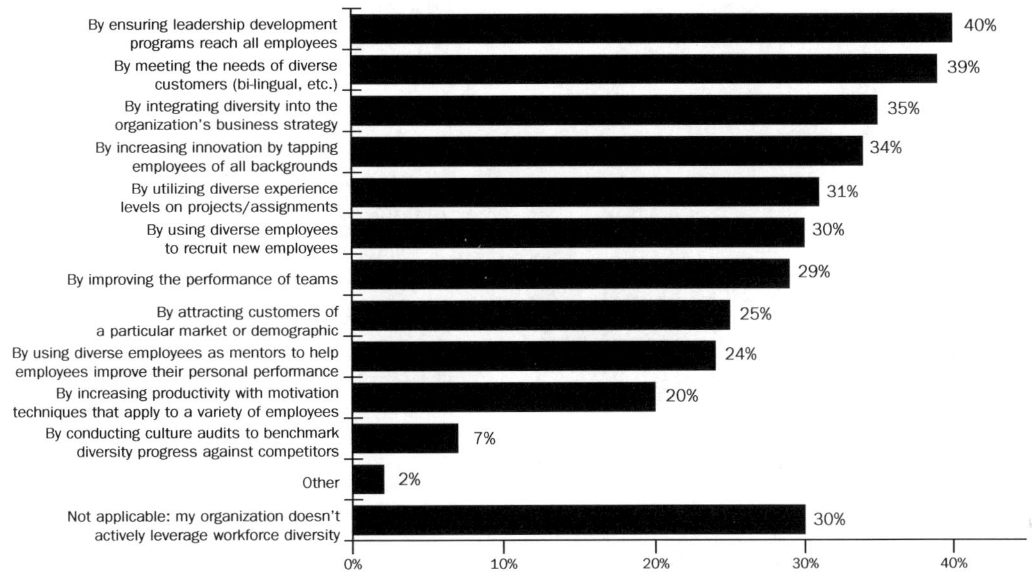

Source: Society for Human Resource Management. (2004, August 3). SHRM/Fortune Diversity Weekly Survey. *Retrieved March 25, 2005, from www.shrm.org.*

Source: Society for Human Resource Management. (2004, August 3). SHRM/Fortune Diversity Weekly Survey. Retrieved March 25, 2005, from www.shrm.org.

Firms are increasingly aware of the impact of diversity initiatives on organizational effectiveness. For example, factors that affect organizational profits are highlighted in a study by the Society for Human Resource Management on the impact of diversity on the bottom line. HR professionals from companies on *Fortune's* list of Top 100 Companies to Work For state that diversity initiatives provide organizations with a competitive advantage by positive improvements in corporate culture, employee morale, retention and recruitment (Figure 7.1). For example, 40 percent of companies ensure leadership development programs are available to all employees, 34 percent increase innovation by tapping talent of employees of all backgrounds, and 31 percent utilize diverse experiences for special projects and assignments.[12]

The importance of positive community relations also illustrates the link between workplace diversity and the business case. When organizations develop external partnerships with minority communities and suppliers, for example, this can lead to good will and a reputation as an "employer of choice."[13] When employees are proud of their organization for its contributions and connections to the community, they are more loyal to their employer and more likely to boast about their company to family and friends. The result is lower turnover and a positive employer brand that better attracts the best talent in the marketplace.[14] A prime example of diversity partnerships is that of Pitney Bowes, the No. 1 company on the 2004 DiversityInc Top 50 Companies for Diversity list, with recruitment initiatives and partnerships developed with organizations such as the National Urban League and the National Society of Hispanic MBAs. Another example is that of Ford Motor Co., the No. 1 company on the 2003 DiversityInc Top 50 list, that made community relations a priority: Ford spent six percent of its total procurement budget ($3.2 billion) with its first-tier diversity suppliers.[15]

Money Talks

The shift in purchasing power in the United States provides further evidence for the business case for workplace diversity. According to the Selig Center for Economic Growth, the purchasing power of minorities in the United States will quickly outpace that of whites in the next five years. In 2009, for example, the combined buying power of African-Americans, Hispanics, Asian-Americans and Native Americans is expected to exceed $1.5 trillion, more than triple the 1990 level by a gain of $1.1 trillion or 242 percent. In contrast, the buying power of whites will increase by 140 percent.[16]

Thus, in order to ensure that the company's sales and marketing teams reach the minority groups with funds to purchase its products and services, one of the most effective avenues is to utilize the knowledge of minority employees who can relate to different groups in the marketplace. Verizon Communications, for example, utilizes its African-American spokespeople, such as the actor James Earl Jones, to attract African-American consumers.[17] Fannie Mae, a leading mortgage lending firm, wanted to reach the many minorities who did not yet own homes; in the United States, only 46 percent of African-Americans and Hispanics own homes, compared with 72 percent of whites. The company utilized diversity training as a strategic business initiative to reach a segment of the population that could profit from their service.[18]

Finally, the SHRM 2004–2005 Workplace Forecast notes that one of the top economic trends is expansion into the global marketplace.[19] Organizations can better capture, keep and serve their international customer base when their own workforce—such as sales, marketing and customer service—understands the needs of other cultural and ethnic groups.

Metrics—the ROI of Diversity

As with all business initiatives, measuring the return on investment of diversity makes good business sense. Measurement of diversity management can be considered in a number of areas, such as organizational culture, demographics, accountability, productivity, growth and profitability. For example, measuring diversity leadership commitment may involve many individual factors, such as the development of diversity vision/mission statements by a specific date, the number of times diversity is mentioned as a strategy in executive presentations, the percentage of board representation by group, the percentage of diverse employees who were promoted due to mentorship and the percentage of diversity strategy plans implemented.[20]

To determine the return on investment, hard and soft data must be converted to monetary values. There are five basic steps: (1) identify a unit of measure that represents a unit of improvement; (2) determine the value of each unit; (3) calculate the change in performance data; (4) determine an annual amount for the change; and (5) calculate the total value of the improvement.[21]

The diversity return on investment (DROI) is calculated by using the diversity initiative cost and benefits to get the benefit/cost ratio (BCR). BCR = diversity initiative benefits ÷ diversity initiative costs. This ratio is also referred to as a cost-to-benefit ratio. Specifically, the DROI calculation is the net benefit of the diversity initiative divided by the initiative costs: DROI percent = (net diversity initiative benefits ÷ initiative costs) x 100. This formula is the same basic formula used to evaluate other investments in which the ROI is reported as earnings divided by the investment.[22] For example, the initial cost of a diversity awareness program may be $50,000. The measurable value of the program is determined to be three years. During a three-year period, the program will have a net savings of $30,000 ($10,000 per year). Since the average book value is approximately half the cost, the average investment in this case is $25,000 ($50,000 ÷ 2). The average ROI = annual savings ÷ average investment: $10,000 ÷ $25,000 = 40 percent.

Short- or Long-Term Investment

The business advantage for workplace diversity is clear. Yet companies often expect short-term results. The challenge is to demonstrate measurable impact on financial success as well as realistically manage expectations. Rather than a quick fix, the business case for workplace diversity is a long-term investment and offers sustainability in a competitive marketplace.

Senior Management's Role

Visibility, communication and accountability are key to achieving a competitive diverse workforce. A recent study on what makes and breaks diversity initiatives found three critical points of leadership: (1) accountability; (2) a passion for diversity; and (3) sustained involvement. Visible commitment throughout the organization is important: adding diversity on the agenda at executive meetings and company conferences, appointing diversity candidates to top positions, and assigning clear roles and responsibilities to the senior management team regarding diversity management. Accountability creates sustained involvement—that is, holding managers accountable to deliver diversity results. Participation in diversity councils is recommended as a development path for senior leadership.[23]

However, simply placing women and/or minorities in high-profile positions, for example, is insufficient. Rather, the more effective approach is to hold management accountable for results. Consequently, to get middle management and employee buy-in, top management must establish clear implementation and reporting requirements. At DuPont, for example, senior management ensures accountability for diversity management by integrating diversity into the overall business performance evaluation process, including developing cost and profit objectives as well as how compensation is determined. The company also uses targeted career development initiatives to help diverse people fill key work assignments, thus supporting advancement and addressing glass ceiling issues. The Quaker Oats Company aims to keep diversity management simple by using two key tools: (1) the diversity progress menu; and (2) the diversity accountability guidelines. The company's goal is to supply managers with a best practices list that offers flexibility tied to individual business cultures as well as performance.[24] Nine of the top 50 companies on the 2004 DiversityInc Top 50 Companies for Diversity list tie diversity to managers' compensation. For example, CitiGroup measures its managers' attempts to attract talent and develop a diverse workforce. At Verizon Communications, five percent of bonuses for directors and above are related to diversity.[25] Simple daily actions also communicate commitment to workplace diversity: the CEO greets employees in their native language, and the supervisor takes time to understand direct reports with different cultural values and viewpoints.[26]

Diversity Management and the Board of Directors

Increasingly, the business case for diversity focuses on the board of directors. The impetus to change the board composition is a direct result of the trend toward corporate governance and diversity of the workforce, customer base and other stakeholders. Organizations want a wider range of leadership skills, work styles, perspectives and expertise, as well as increased representation of women and minorities among board directors.[27] There is positive evidence of change. For example, in the Fortune 500 in 2003, women held 14 percent of board seats (up from 10 percent in 1995), and 54 companies had 25 percent or more women on boards of directors (up from 11 percent in 1995).[28] Finally, change in board composition is also occurring at an international level, as global organizations expand the cultural diversity of their boards with expertise in international business from other countries.[29]

Managing Diversity: HR Challenges and Opportunities

With the changing marketplace and an increasingly diverse labor pool, HR leaders are dealing with a myriad of factors regarding diversity management. Broadly speaking, workplace diversity challenges can be considered within three interrelated categories: attracting and retaining talent, greater diversity among employees and training.

Attracting and Retaining Talent

Competition for talent is growing—from competition abroad, lower education levels of U.S. workers compared with other countries, U.S. immigration challenges and fear of terrorism in the United States.[30] Further, with the retirement of the baby boom generation (those born from 1944 to 1960) in the next 10 years, a key concern is retention of older workers. Organizations are in different stages of preparation regarding this likely loss of talent. As of 2003, 35 percent were just becoming aware of the issue, 35 percent did not know if their organizations were ready, 23 percent were beginning to examine policies, and four percent had proposed specific changes. Many HR leaders are looking for ways to attract and retain older workers. Benefits and workplace programs, such as reward initiatives and flexible work arrangements (e.g., part-time work, phased retirement), are key tools that offer attractive options to older workers.[31]

The skill shortage, however, will hit some industries harder and sooner than others. The nuclear power industry, for example, faces replacing as much as 50 percent of its workforce. The talent crunch will also strike the expanding service industry: sales positions in the United States, for example, are expected to increase by 25 percent, yet many in today's sales force are aged 55 or older.[32]

A recent study notes most firms are not paying close attention to retention and promotion strategies. For example, top minority talent is seeking leadership opportunities; yet companies indicate they have difficulty attracting talent for executive leadership (42 percent) and professional and technical skills (42 percent).[33] In corporate America, the "revolving door syndrome" is particularly evident for women and minorities. To retain women and minorities, HR professionals should re-evaluate their organization regarding talent, mentoring, career development and succession planning. Strategic initiatives, such as mentoring, on-boarding and "listening" forums, are additional tactics to address minority retention.[34]

Greater Diversity Among Employees

The term "diversity" has typically referred to women and minorities. Today, however, employers are beginning to formally acknowledge other employees as well (e.g., ethnic groups, people with disabilities and self-identified gay, lesbian and bisexual persons). Some firms encourage a welcoming and inclusive environment for all employees by creating diversity network groups. Kraft Foods uses employee councils to build employee development. Through nine employee councils (African-American Council, Hispanic Council, Asian-American Council, Rainbow Council, Women in Sales Council, Black Sales Council, Hispanic/Asian Sales Council, Women in Operations and African-Americans in Operations), Kraft takes an active role in mentoring and supporting its diverse workforce. For example, the company builds relationships with universities to bring in talent through internships and internally sponsors career days focusing on leadership competencies.[35]

Different groups have different needs, and they want their needs recognized and met. Acknowledgment of different needs yields greater employee satisfaction, employer loyalty and, in turn, lower turnover and greater productivity. As a result, more organizations offer programs to address issues such as work/life balance and demands for more flexibility with telecommuting, adoption support, flexible health and dependent care spending accounts, elder care and domestic partner benefits.[36]

Within workplace diversity, one of the least discussed minority groups is people with disabilities. This group is a source of under-represented talent in the workplace. One study reveals that in the majority of companies, individuals with disabilities comprise less than 10 percent of their total workforce. The study recommends top management lead by example and hire qualified individuals with disabilities on their staff. Through training and focus groups, HR leaders can improve sensitivity toward employees with disabilities.[37]

Training

Within the context of workplace diversity, training plays a key role in retaining talent. The role of training is to promote workplace harmony, learn about others' values, improve cross-cultural communication and develop leadership skills. Awareness training raises understanding of diversity concerns by uncovering hidden assumptions and biases, heightening sensitivity to diversity in the workplace and fostering individual and group sharing. Skill-based diversity training improves morale, productivity and creativity through effective intercultural communication.[38] Leadership development, team building and mentoring programs are also examples of organizational training that promotes growth and collaboration. An overlooked area regarding retention is cross-cultural competence within the organization, often a missed opportunity to address minority retention concerns.[39]

Finally, working in a diverse organization requires diversity competencies for everyone, including HR (see Table 7.3). Yet not all HR professionals are experts in diversity. A survey notes that only about one-third of companies think their HR staff has the skills to serve a diverse U.S. workforce and only 22 percent believe HR has the skills to serve a global workforce.[40] HR professionals best qualified to deal with workplace diversity have experience in areas such as team building, change management, conflict resolution and cross-cultural communication.

Table 7.3 HR Competencies for Diversity Management

- Active/nonjudgmental listening.
- Willingness to challenge one's own concepts about diversity.
- Collaboration skills.
- Experience with conflict resolution and change management.
- Sensitivity toward terms labeling groups regarding diversity.
- Ability to identify diversity issues and understand related tensions.
- Intercultural team building.
- Ability to express respect and appreciation.
- Openness to learning about others who are different.
- Ability to educate others on how to build diverse people skills.
- Ability to provide appropriate responses.

Source: Adapted from Carr-Ruffino, N. (1999). *Diversity success strategies.* Boston: Butterworth-Heinemann.

Aligning the Diversity Process with Strategic Business Goals

The organization that best utilizes the full potential of all employees intentionally and thoughtfully aligns workplace diversity with strategic business goals by following these steps:

Define diversity. Clarify the role of workplace diversity in the organization, including leadership roles and expectations for diversity initiatives. In vision and mission statements, highlight the importance of diversity (for example, is the organization's philosophy on inclusion clearly stated?). Place the vision and mission statements on the company Web site as a public statement of the organization's commitment to workplace diversity. Communicate commitment by allocating the necessary resources—staff, budgets and time—to move the diversity process forward.[41]

Establish accountability. With senior management, HR diversity leaders should develop challenging yet realistic goals for diversity interventions. Demonstrate organizational commitment: (1) appoint senior executives to diversity task forces for succession planning, education and training initiatives; (2) recruit diversity candidates for senior leadership positions; and (3) establish diversity goals and objectives for all leadership levels in the performance management process and reward programs. Demonstrate commitment to workplace diversity by developing solutions when problems are identified through employee attitude surveys, focus groups, etc.[42]

Develop a diversity scorecard. Often overlooked, the scorecard is an important tool to manage diversity. The scorecard includes financial and nonfinancial recognition of diversity ROI initiatives as well as relevant feedback (e.g., change management lessons). When developing the diversity scorecard, include measures aligned with the organization's strategic business goals. When determining measures, keep in mind four themes: (1) key deliverables that leverage the role of diversity in the organization's overall strategy; (2) utilization of diversity in the development of a high-performance work environment; (3) ways in which the corporate culture is aligned with the organization's strategy; and (4) the efficiency of the diversity deliverables.

Studies on Workplace Diversity and the Bottom Line

Several studies link workplace diversity and company performance. The study results run the gamut from identifying critical success factors for diversity initiatives that impact organizational effectiveness to connecting gender and diversity with financial performance.

The "Makes and Breaks" of Diversity Initiatives[43]

This study found that successful initiatives that leverage diversity to enhance organizational effectiveness share certain characteristics and approaches. Specifically, successful workplace diversity initiatives hinge on committed leadership, goals/targets of measures of effectiveness, strong diversity professionals, employee involvement and ties to performance evaluation, as well as data to identify, quantify and communicate progress and challenges.

Diversity Practices That Work[44]

Companies with diversity practices collectively generated 18 percent greater productivity than the U.S. economy overall. The results of this study suggest that, at a minimum, diversity progress may enhance productivity through effective good leadership and management practices. Key factors that had the greatest impact on overall perceived effectiveness of diversity initiatives were: (1) a track record of recruiting diverse people; (2) management that is accountable for diversity progress and holds others accountable; (3) leaders who demonstrate commitment to diversity; (4) rewarding people who contribute in the area of diversity; and (5) training and education to increase awareness and help employees understand how diversity can impact business results.

The Effects of Diversity on Business Performance[45]

This study looks at the effects of racial and gender diversity on organizational performance. A key finding reveals that racial diversity has a positive effect on overall performance in companies that use diversity as a resource for innovation and learning. Further, the study results suggest that the best performance outcomes occur when diversity is found across entire organizational units.

Connecting Corporate Performance and Gender Diversity[46]

Based on an examination of 353 Fortune 500 companies, this study connects gender diversity and financial performance. (The study does not, however, demonstrate causation.) The key findings show that the group of companies with the highest representation of women on their top management teams experienced better financial performance than the group with the lowest women's representation: that is, 35 percent higher return on equity and 34 percent higher total return to shareholders. The study results suggest there is a business case for gender diversity (e.g., recruiting, developing and advancing women)—specifically, organizations that focus on diversity are in a stronger position to tap the educated and skilled talent in the marketplace. This is important because women comprise 47 percent of the U.S. paid labor force and hold 46 percent of management positions. In addition, women earn more than half of all bachelor's and master's degrees in the United States (57 percent and 59 percent, respectively) and nearly half of all doctorates and law degrees (45 percent and 47 percent, respectively).

Global Diversity–The European Union

Focus on gender equality and anti-discrimination by the European Union (EU) offers a unique example of workplace diversity outside of the United States. With the addition of 10 member states in May 2004, the European Union—with 25 member states in 2005 and nearly 500 million people—is one of the largest economic forces in the world. Through legislation (called Directives) under the Social Policy Agenda, the EU is establishing significant social, economic and political change. The goal is to be "the most competitive and dynamic knowledge-based economy in the world capable of sustainable economic growth with more and better jobs and greater social cohesion." To achieve the necessary economic and social renewal, the Commission of the European Communities developed a five-year action plan (2000-2005) that focused on investing in people and combating social exclusion.[47] In 2000, with the introduction of the EU Article 13 Race and Employment Directives (to be effective by 2006), the EU put in place measures designed to enforce the right to be treated equally.[48]

1. The Racial Equality Directive 2000/43/EC prohibits discrimination on the grounds of a personal racial or ethnic origin.

2. The Employment Equality Directive 2000/78/EC prohibits discrimination on the grounds of religion or belief, disability, age or sexual orientation.

However, the establishment of a Directive does not guarantee immediate results or even substantial progress. While EU Directives require member states to meet the minimum legislative standards, more work is needed to achieve workforce diversity. For example, a recent report notes that while gender employment and education gaps are closing, the gender gap in the EU remains almost unchanged.[49]

Drivers and Benefits of Diversity in Europe

In Europe, there is a growing recognition of the benefits of workplace diversity for both the society and the economy. To remain competitive, however, there are a host of issues to address, from racial and ethnic diversity and new roles of women to work/life balance and an aging population coupled with declining birthrates. A recent study notes that a third of the top European companies are gaining competitive advantage from diversity management. These progressive organizations, rather than seeing diversity as a regulatory response that requires anti-discrimination and equal opportunity policies, view diversity management as a vehicle to develop an engaged, motivated and heterogeneous workforce to develop creative business solutions in the global marketplace.[50]

Another study notes the three most often mentioned benefits of workplace diversity by European companies are: (1) improved team effectiveness and cooperation; (2) improved productivity; and (3) improved customer markets with broader access to labor markets. Other drivers considered moderately beneficial are improved employer image, more openness to change, improved morale and commitment, ease of entry into new markets and enhanced effectiveness of complex organization. Overall, the most important shifts in workplace diversity are in the areas of gender and ethnic diversity. For example, as women obtain higher professional degrees and qualifications and earn more money in the marketplace, they are increasingly viewed as important in the workplace. Ethnic minorities are seen as a growing workforce as well as customer base.[51]

Enhancing Competitive Advantage through Diversity Management: Recommendations for HR

Assess

Conduct a top-to-bottom critical assessment of all company policies and programs. Determine if there are biases that create potential challenges for diverse employees. Review diversity initiative results (e.g., recruitment of top talent, retention strategies, succession planning, career development goals) to determine if the workplace is structured to exclude certain employee groups. Determine where changes in organizational culture, policies and programs need to be made.

Capitalize

Promote diversity initiatives to the top agendas of senior management by capitalizing on reputation as a diversity management consultant.

Dialogue

Develop and maintain continuous dialogue with the CEO and senior management regarding diversity as a business strategy.

Discover

Through focus groups, confidential employee surveys and exit interviews, determine how diversity initiatives are viewed and gather feedback for improvement.

Network

Network with other HR professionals to learn different approaches to diversity management, challenges encountered and recommended best practices.

Learn

To best utilize a diverse workforce, profit from lessons learned.

In Closing

There is no "best way" to manage diversity. The identification, selection and purpose of diversity initiatives and their development and implementation differ from company to company. The likelihood of success is dependent on business needs and workforce issues as well as situational factors, such as the organizational culture and workplace environment. Ultimately, the strength of commitment by the CEO, senior management and HR leadership will determine whether the organization successfully leverages workplace diversity for competitive advantage.

Chapter 8

Selected Cross-Cultural Factors in Human Resource Management

As a concept and as a reality, culture is broad and multifaceted. On a daily basis, culture influences who we are—as individuals, families, communities, professions, industries, organizations and nations—and how we interact with each other within and across regional and national borders. Defined as a set of values and beliefs with learned behaviors shared within a particular society, culture provides a sense of identity and belonging.[1] From language, communication styles, history and religion to norms, values, symbolism and ways of being, "culture" is everywhere.

> Human resource management is the formal structure within an organization responsible for all decisions, strategies, factors, principles, operations, practices, functions, activities and methods related to the management of people.[2]

In domestic and global workplace settings, people in organizations reflect their respective cultures. As shifting demographics bring together people of many cultural backgrounds, human resource management (HRM) must be thoughtfully examined—and sometimes altered—to support organizational goals. SHRM Special Expertise Panel members point out that for sustainability, organizational leaders must expand their perspectives from a local to a worldly view.[3] SHRM's 2008 *Workplace Forecast* highlights several trends in culture that will likely have a major impact on the workplace: (1) heightened awareness of cultural differences in domestic and global workplaces; (2) greater need for cross-cultural understanding/savvy in business settings; (3) managing talent globally; (4) greater emphasis on global leadership competencies; and (5) increased use of virtual global teams.[4]

Thus, HR professionals experienced in workplace diversity and cross-cultural communication are well-positioned to develop and implement culturally appropriate HRM strategies, policies and practices. While not exhaustive, this *Research Quarterly* focuses on selected cross-cultural factors in HRM in today's workplace and provides insights for HR to better serve the needs of the organization.

Business Case for Cross-Cultural HRM

With the advent of globalization, research on cross-cultural organizational behavior has become a pathway to understand the dynamics of multicultural domestic and international workplaces.[5] In fact, successful organizations of the 21st century require leaders who understand culturally diverse work environments and can work effectively with different cultures that have varying work ethics, norms and business protocols. Yet, diverse cultures create HRM challenges. As Lisbeth Claus, Ph.D., SPHR, GPHR, associate professor of global HR at Willamette University, points out, "the HRM challenges lie between the various types of cultures—the cultures of emerging and developed countries and the growing heterogeneity of the workforce in terms of multiculturalism."

Gaining cross-cultural competence takes time, education, experience, openness and sensitivity. When people lack intercultural skills, miscommunications can damage business relationships, deadlines can be missed, projects may fail and talented people will go to the competition. Key HR responsibilities are to understand how cross-cultural factors interact with HRM, be the conduit for organizational learning for cross-cultural intelligence and foster cross-cultural communication throughout the organization.

Cultural Value Dimensions

Cross-cultural intelligence is the ability to switch ethnic and/or national contexts and quickly learn new patterns of social interaction with appropriate behavioral responses. This competence is essential to work effectively in multicultural environments. Thus, linking future career paths and global business success with cultural competence is important for HR to emphasize, with the goal that managers are motivated to acquire new behaviors and skills and understand the benefits of learning from different cultures.[6]

To become culturally competent, the first step is to have a solid understanding of one's own values and how they shape cultural identity. Within this process, it is also important to realize that different cultures often exhibit different values. Cross-cultural management researchers and theorists (i.e., Edward Hall, Geert Hofstede and Fons Trompenaars) have developed cultural value dimensions, often within the realm of comparing national cultures (see Table 8.1). Today, many of these terms are used to explain cross-cultural differences in the workplace.

Table 8.1 Cultural Value Dimensions

Edward Hall (1966)[7]	Geert Hofstede (1980)[8]	Fons Trompenaars (1993)[9]
▪ High- and low-context cultures ▪ Concept of time	▪ Power distance ▪ Individualism ▪ Masculinity ▪ Uncertainty avoidance ▪ Long-term orientation	▪ Universalism vs. particularism ▪ Individualism vs. collectivism ▪ Neutral or emotional ▪ Specific vs. diffuse ▪ Achievement vs. ascription ▪ Passage of time ▪ Relationship to the environment

For the purpose of discussion in this article, several major cultural value dimensions are defined below:[10]

1. *High power distance* indicates that hierarchy is important.
2. *Uncertainty avoidance* is achieved by behavior that results in fewer unforeseen consequences.
3. *High-context cultures* rely upon an internalized social context and/or physical environment (such as body language) and face-to-face communication for all or a large part of the message (e.g., indirect, subtle, ambiguous), whereas *low-context cultures* rely on direct messages (e.g., clear, stated in words, with emphasis on time management, punctuality and deadlines).
4. *Collectivism* refers to societies in which the group is valued over the individual and the individual's responsibility to the group overrides the individual's rights; *individualism* refers to societies that emphasize individual achievements and rights.
5. *Long-term orientation* indicates that cultural values are future-looking, including thrift, perseverance, humility/shame, and observe hierarchical relationships, whereas *short-term orientation* values look to the past, such as respecting tradition.

The concept of "face" is yet another term essential for understanding cross-cultural communication. Face is a sense of self-respect in an interaction and may be related to social status, a projected identity and/or a communication phenomenon. Facework strategies include verbal and nonverbal cues, acts of self-preservation and management impression interaction.[11] In Chinese society, for example, the concept of guanxi is that of personal relationships, trust and returning favors to support a network of influence.

Through cultural value dimensions, HR will gain a greater awareness of miscommunication or cultural conflict that may occur in the multicultural workplace. Should these concepts be new to the reader, the cultural factors outlined in Table 8.2 offer another way to consider key cultural differences.

Table 8.2 Factors in Cultural Differences

Communication	Verbal and nonverbal
Concepts of time	Adherence to schedule
Group dependence	Importance of group over the individual
Hierarchy/authority	Perception of rank in relationship to others
Openness to diversity	Country of origin, religion, race, gender, language
Physical space	Space and privacy needed for personal comfort
Relationships	Importance for business interactions
Status attainment	Perceived level of "success"
Tolerance of change	Perception of control over one's destiny

Source: Adapted from Henson, R. (2002). Culture and the workforce. In K. Beaman, (Ed.), *Boundaryless HR: Human capital management in the global economy* (pp. 121-141). Austin, TX: Rector Duncan & Associates, Inc.

Corporate and Organizational Cultures

The culture of an organization's headquarters may highly influence the overall organizational culture. Specific factors determine the shape of corporate culture: (1) the relationship between employees and the company; (2) the hierarchical system of authority; and (3) the overall view of employees about the company's future, including its mission and goals, and their respective roles in the organization.[12] According to cross-cultural researchers and management consultants Fons Trompenaars and Charles Hampden-Turner, there is a link between corporate and national cultures. Organizations can be classified into four different ideal-types of corporate culture, based on their focus on tasks/relationship and the extent of hierarchy: (1) the family; (2) the Eiffel Tower; (3) the guided missile; and (4) the incubator.[13] These models of corporate culture provide insights as to why HRM policies and programs differ.

In the family model, a high-context culture, the leaders set the tone. This model gives high priority to doing the right things rather than doing things right. Pleasing one's superior, for example, is considered a reward in itself. Within this corporate model, some HRM policies, such as pay for performance, are viewed as threatening to family bonds. Countries that often use the family model include Japan, Italy, France and Spain. The Eiffel Tower model—contrary to the family model, where relationships are most important—is based on prescribed roles and functions within a rigid system (e.g., Germany). In this model, people are viewed as capital and cash resources. Typical HRM strategies in the Eiffel Tower culture include workforce planning and performance appraisal systems.[14]

The guided missile model is egalitarian, impersonal and task-oriented (e.g., United States, United Kingdom). The focus is on achieving the end goal ("do whatever it takes"), and the value of employees is in how they perform and to what extent they contribute to the overall outcome. For example, teams serve as vehicles to accomplish goals and are disbanded once the goal is reached. HRM strategies focus on management by objective and pay for performance.[15] At the other end of the spectrum, the incubator model has a different philosophy, wherein the fulfillment of individuals is more important than the organization. The structure is egalitarian, personal and individualistic, such as entrepreneurial firms in Silicon Valley in California and many Scandinavian companies, where the goal is innovative products or services. HRM strategies focus on rewards for innovation.[16]

As illustrated through these four corporate culture models, approaches to work, authority, problem solving and relationship building differ. This information provides HR with additional insight when working with companies of different corporate cultures.

Building Business Relationships

Building optimal business relationships requires global fluency. Global fluency—defined as "facility with cultural behaviors that help an organization thrive in an ever-changing global business environment"—is a competitive advantage to establish and maintain good business relationships.[17] To promote people working effectively with those of other cultures, cross-cultural training assists employees in becoming knowledgeable about cross-cultural communication in terms of their own cultural values, behaviors and assumptions, and those of other cultures. Cross-cultural communication also includes global business etiquette—from greeting behaviors, exchanging business cards and toasting at business dinners to work attitudes, appropriate work attire and nonverbal communication. To not cause offense, it is helpful to be aware of differences in greetings, such as the handshake.[18] Another differing communication style is the use of silence, a form of nonverbal communication. In high-context cultures, such as in Asian countries, silence indicates thoughtfulness in decision-making. In contrast, people in low-context cultures, such as the dominant culture in the United States, are uncomfortable with silence and tend to fill the void with "small talk," such as comments about the weather.[19]

People establish rapport in accordance with their cultural values. Based on social capital theory and the importance of social networks, a recent study explored intercultural communication strategies for business relationship building through interviews with business executives in China, India, New Zealand and South Africa. The findings indicate that building a business relationship is defined within the sociocultural and economic contexts of the respective cultures and that depending on the culture, different strategies are used to build and maintain business relationships. The following mini-case study demonstrates a success story from the viewpoint of the Indian culture.[20]

Mini-Case Study #1: "The Indian Story"[21]

A senior manager works at an Indian company that sells a broad array of products (groceries, liquor, durable goods) and describes his philosophy about relationship building with an example from his company:

"To successfully achieve our business goals, establishing and maintaining relationships with distributors is an essential strategy. Some of our customers are large firms, managed by graduates from the elite university I attended. This link creates strong networking opportunities. Once this *jan pehchan* (connection) is made, it is critical to invest time in this relationship, and I always counsel my subordinates on the importance of relationship building. One employee in particular is very good at maintaining relationships. He works hard to do so, even going to the airport or train station without prior arrangement to meet clients upon their arrival, once at 5 a.m.! This effort shows that he is sincere and demonstrates how far he will go to maintain this valuable relationship. This personalized service adds to our commitment to nurture a long-term business relationship."

Effective cross-cultural communication is necessary to build and maintain business relationships. To support their organizations, HR professionals can develop HRM practices and policies that promote cross-cultural training and reward managers for their part in educating employees on effective cross-cultural communication.

The Role of Language

Today, communicating in the global marketplace requires new perspectives and new communication skills. In fact, the appropriate use of language in cross-cultural settings often depends on the situation. Thus, when developing HRM policies, practices and initiatives, it is important to consider the role of language in cross-cultural environments. For example, to roll out new initiatives worldwide, it may be necessary (and often required by law) to translate HRM policies and programs into other languages. Colgate-Palmolive Company is an example of an organization that has effectively communicated key HRM programs to its global workforce. Keeping in mind the different languages spoken in the firm, two critical HRM core value initiatives, ***Valuing Colgate People*** and ***Managing with Respect***, were translated into 10 languages. ***Valuing Colgate People*** includes a section on the company's business ethics, code of conduct and business practice guidelines. These initiatives set the stage for the organization's strategy to become a best place to work.[22]

When working with people from different cultures and/or countries, organizational leaders must know how to "read" body language, a key communication factor in high-context cultures. Misunderstanding body language can lead to inaccurate expectations. With many Western companies now doing business with India, a good example of a common cross-cultural difference is one of the head gestures by Indians. As cross-cultural trainer and management consultant Craig Storti explains, the Indian head gesture for "yes" appears similar to how Westerners shake their head to indicate "no." When seeing this gesture, Westerners may think that the Indian has disagreed, when that is not necessarily so.[23] Taking time to understand communication through body language can make the difference in a positive or negative outcome. These various points are representative of the many scenarios that require flexibility and knowledge about language and cross-cultural communication.

Finally, although the international language of business is English, not everyone speaks English fluently. When non-native English speakers come in contact with native English speakers, the result is often miscommunication. ***International English***, a relatively new term, describes a mode of communication increasingly used in international business where non-native English speakers speak English with native English speakers. International English requires the avoidance of culturally laden language, such as cultural shortcuts, metaphors, jargon, slang and idiomatic phrases. U.S. Americans, for example, often use metaphors with sports terms, such as "all the bases are covered" or "we want a level playing field," most of which are not understood by nonnative English speakers. Interestingly, it takes time and practice for native English speakers to become proficient with the use of International English and to consciously avoid using phrases or terms that are culturally based.[24]

Cultural Perceptions of Organizational Justice

Regarding fairness in the workplace, organizational justice is a central theme within the employee relations domain. A fair workplace helps maintain employee commitment, contributes to job satisfaction and minimizes absenteeism and turnover. There are three broad categories of organizational justice: (1) procedural justice (fairness of methods used); (2) interactional justice (the quality of treatment); and (3) distributive justice (perception of process and fairness of the outcome).

In a culturally diverse workforce, perceptions of justice may vary due to cultural values. A recent study examined cultural factors that influence how employees form overall justice perceptions in the United States, China, Korea and Japan. The study examined employee reactions in industry sectors such as finance, education, service, information technology and manufacturing. According to the study, the effect of perception of fairness on turnover is greater for Americans than for Chinese or Koreans. Americans are more likely to leave their organization as a result of perceived organizational injustice than are Japanese, Chinese or Korean employees.[25] Yet, not all studies point to differences regarding justice based on country culture. The results of one study suggest that cultural dimensions should not be used as a generalization. This study considered whether individualist (low power distance) or collectivist dimensions (high power distance) had the most impact on organizational justice perceptions regarding employee work outcome relationships at a multinational bank with Hong Kong Chinese and American employees. While employees from low power distance cultures were more influenced toward perceived justice, a key finding was that the perceptions of fairness were important to both groups. This study suggests that for managing in different cultures, workplace justice and its corresponding positive effects are important, no matter a country's cultural values.[26]

Turnover is another key aspect related to organizational justice. In an increasingly diverse workforce, turnover due to unfairness in the workplace is very costly. While research on domestic and cross-cultural issues in relation to fairness in the workplace is relatively new, studies demonstrate how insensitivity can damage work relations and result in increased turnover. A recent study of U.S. employees found that more than two million managers and professionals leave their jobs as a result of inappropriate and insensitive comments in their organizations, costing U.S. employers $64 billion annually. The study highlights that illegal discrimination is no longer the greatest threat when it comes to attracting, recruiting and retaining talent. Rather, every-day inappropriate behaviors are the root cause of losing talented employees.[27] By ensuring that HRM policies and practices—including consequences for inappropriate behaviors in the workplace—are fair, consistently applied and culturally appropriate, HR can create a work environment that fosters respect, employee commitment and contribution. However, it should be noted that not all localized policies and practices may be consistent with corporate policies.

Cross-Cultural Decision-Making

Decisions in the workplace are influenced by cultural viewpoints, beliefs, assumptions and values. Cultural values have an impact on why and how decisions are made and implemented. Although cross-cultural decision-making is rarely a topic of discussion, this information provides valuable insight for HR to improve communication in the workplace. Table 8.3 illustrates cultural variations involved in decision-making, based on questions such as (1) do managers of different cultures view problems in similar ways; (2) do they seek out similar kinds of information to investigate problems; (3) do they come up with similar solutions; (4) are different strategies used to determine alternatives; and (5) do they implement their decisions in similar ways.[28]

Culturally influenced decision-making can be seen in various aspects of HRM. Change management is one example where culture influences decision-making. In a culture that is future-oriented, such as the United States, with strongly held beliefs about people's ability to learn and change, HR creates change management programs with the goal to be more productive and efficient in serving internal and external customers (e.g., employee training programs on new technology). In contrast, in a company with a hierarchical management style—common in Japan, for example—where major decisions are made by a senior-level manager, HR would be unlikely to promote a program that emphasizes team decision-making. Whether in a domestic or global workplace, HR needs to be cognizant of cross-cultural decision-making and the corresponding influence on HRM. By being aware of cultural differences in the decision-making process (e.g., the reasons for making decisions, the various ways that decisions are made in different cultures, the party responsible for making those decisions—individuals, groups, various levels within the organization—and the ways decisions are implemented), HR can better gauge culturally appropriate decisions and work with managers of other cultures in the decision-making process. In a culturally diverse workforce, perceptions of justice may vary due to cultural values.

Cross-Cultural Performance Feedback

Lack of cross-cultural sensitivity in the performance appraisal process can result in negative impact on communication, employee morale, teamwork and turnover. It is critical that managers be culturally appropriate when assessing performance and delivering feedback. Additionally, to get better performance results in culturally diverse employee populations, companies may need to reexamine and redefine their perfor-

Table 8.3 Cultural Contingencies in Decision-Making

Five Steps in Decision-Making	Cultural Variations	
1. Problem Recognition	*Problem Solving*	*Situation Acceptance*
	We should change the situation.	Some situations should be accepted as they are
2. Information Search	*Gathering "facts"*	*Gathering ideas and possibilities*
3. Construction of Alternatives	*New, future-oriented alternatives*	*Past-, present- and future-oriented alternatives*
	Adults can learn and change.	Adults cannot change.
4. Choice	*Individual decision-making*	*Team decision-making*
	Decision-making responsibility is delegated.	Senior managers often make decisions.
	Decisions are made quickly.	Decisions are made slowly.
	Decision rule: Is it true or false?	Decision rule: Is it good or bad?
5. Implementation	*Slow*	*Fast*
	Managed from the top.	Involves participation of all levels.
	Responsibility of one person.	Responsibility of team.

Source: From ADLER, *International Dimensions of Organizational Behavior*, 5E, © 2008 South-Western, a part of Cengage Learning, Inc. Reproduced by permission, www.cengage.com/permissions

mance standards to ensure cultural bias does not influence the performance appraisal process.[29] However, as the literature shows, performance management is originally a Western practice. When coming from an international perspective, there are complexities primarily due to cultural and structural constructs that may not directly match the Western use of performance management.[30]

Researchers Philip Harris and Robert Moran point out that at the cross-cultural level, how performance is defined and judged is "culture-bound." In an individualistic society, such as the United States, performance is judged on productivity, timeliness, quality of output, job-specific knowledge and proficiency, with emphasis placed on individual and work outcomes, not on the group and work process.[31] At the same time, culture influences the communication of performance feedback. In a collectivist or high-context culture, such as India and Japan, where in-group harmony and interpersonal relationships are highly valued, it is recommended to give feedback in a manner that is subtle, indirect and non-confrontational. Researchers suggest that for certain feedback processes, such as 360-degree feedback, which involves explicit feedback, employees be trained to understand and utilize such feedback, particularly if it does not match their cultural orientation of communication.[32] Presented by authors Milliman, Taylor and Czaplewski, the following mini-case study illustrates a critical incident in which cultural differences in the performance feedback process contributed to an unexpected response. This situation is an example of one that may commonly occur without cross-cultural training about how feedback is perceived and received in different cultural contexts.[33]

Mini-Case Study #2: Cross-Cultural Performance Feedback[34]

Fred, a team leader in software engineering at a U.S.-based multinational enterprise, leads a virtual work group. His team is working on a new product and is under pressure to meet quality standards and get the product to the marketplace. Some of his team members are located in Malaysia. Since the team was provided with technology for global communications, such as electronic group software and teleconferencing, the company did not provide cross-cultural training. Fred writes an e-mail to his counterpart team leader, Hisham, in Malaysia to inform him that the testing process must end and the next phase of the project must now go forward. Hisham does not respond to Fred's e-mail for many days, and the Malaysian team continues to do testing on the product. For the final stage of the project, Fred flies to Malaysia. Two weeks after the U.S. deadline has passed, the project is successfully completed.

Within the company's goal to operate as a global company, one of the new practices is 360-degree feedback. In his supervisory role, Fred gathers the required feedback and then meets with Hisham. Fred informs Hisham that while he performed well on the project, there were issues upon which he could improve. Fred documents the feedback in an e-mail to Hisham, with a copy to Hisham's supervisor in Malaysia. From Fred's viewpoint, he has completed the performance appraisal in accordance with the company standards, feeling that he has been both fair and transparent. Back in the United States the following week, Fred is quite surprised to learn that Hisham, immediately following the performance appraisal meeting, applied for a transfer to another team. Fred recalls that Hisham was quiet during the performance appraisal. He thinks that the transfer is for the best, particularly if Hisham cannot deal with constructive criticism. After all, Fred knows that the success of the project is what is most important.

In this mini-case study, different cultural dimensions are involved: (1) Malaysia is a high-context culture where communication requires awareness of facial expressions, tone of voice and eye contact, and (2) the United States is a low-context culture where people depend more on words than on external expressions for meaning. Differences in collectivism-individualism also explain the miscommunication between Fred and Hisham. Collectivism emphasizes creating harmony and loyalty between people. Yet, due to Fred's direct and assertive approach in the performance appraisal, Hisham experienced individual criticism and consequently suffered a loss of "face" for his team. On his end, Fred acted within the values of his individualistic culture and emphasized individual responsibility, not group responsibility, in Hisham's performance appraisal. Clearly, Fred is unaware of the cultural context in which he spoke to Hisham.[35] Had Fred received cross-cultural training regarding the Malaysian workplace and appropriately communicated his feedback, Hirsham may not have requested the transfer.

To break the cross-cultural conflict cycle, organizational learning is essential. Examples of learning mechanisms are many: (1) HR puts systems in place to catch cultural issues and then addresses them; (2) supervisors bring cultural dilemmas to the attention of HR; (3) HR learns about cultural conflicts through exit interviews; (4) progress reports sent to managers may flag cross-cultural issues; (5) HR trains managers and team members on communication-style differences between cultures; and (6) prior to sending managers to work abroad, HR provides them with cultural informants, such as mentors and/or managers with multicultural expertise, to offer support and advice.[36] As highlighted in a study on society culture and HRM practices, the methods of communication—downward and upward—are strongly linked to cultural value dimensions. This research points out that in a culture of high power distance, it is unlikely that the manager would use electronic methods in communication. Again, the lesson here is that managers be trained to be culturally appropriate when communicating performance feedback.[37]

Developing Global Mindset

The SHRM's 2008 *Workplace Forecast* cites training and developing global leaders as a global trend to which organizations are now responding.[38] In particular, intercultural competence is emerging as a key focus in global leadership development, with the critical themes of cross-cultural communication skills, developing global mindset and respecting cultural diversity.[39] In fact, global mindset has become an essential competency in global business strategy. As researchers Gupta et al. emphasize, "a deeply embedded global mindset is a prerequisite for global industry dominance."[40]

From a cross-cultural viewpoint, Paul Evans, Vladimir Pucik and Jean-Louis Barsoux, experts in global HR management, point out that it is "global mindset"—a state of mind—that differentiates global managers. Global mindset is the ability to work effectively across organizational, functional and cross-cultural boundaries. The strongest mechanism to develop global mindset is the international assignment. HR can foster development of global mindset by ensuring that talented employees worldwide—no matter their passport country—have equal access to opportunities. Focused learning programs can also promote global mindset. Multinational corporations such as Unilever, Johnson & Johnson and General Electric have effectively used in-house experiential action-learning programs for a broad cross-section of high-potential employees to speed up the development of global mindset.[41]

Global mindset is ongoing, driven by four factors: (1) curiosity about the world and the desire to know more; (2) awareness of one's current mindset; (3) exposure to novelty and diversity; and (4) a specific intention to develop an integrated perspective that weaves together many aspects of knowledge about different markets and cultures. Global mindset is of value for local/domestic organizations as well as companies in the global marketplace. At the local level, for instance, a company might use global mindset to benchmark product and process innovations of competitors outside its domestic borders. For organizations operating in other countries, having global mindset helps people relate to others in different cultural contexts and then develop the foundation essential for "interpersonal glue," such as in cross-border mergers (e.g., Alcatel and Lucent).[42] Ultimately, global mindset greatly fosters global learning, allowing for faster access to other markets or providing quality customer service to diverse groups. As HR supports its organization in training for global competencies, global mindset should head the list of essential cross-cultural factors in HRM.

Career Perspectives Across Cultures

Research about cross-cultural perspectives on careers offers insights on similarities and differences from cultural and national contexts. Career development, a part of human resource planning, is an HRM strategy within talent management. However, Western career attributes and definitions, which dominate the career development literature, are not always representative of how people in other cultures view and formulate careers. Proactive career behavior by individuals to promote their career plans, for example, is uncommon in high power distance cultures, where HR decisions are usually centralized. Where hierarchical status takes priority, decisions for

Table 8.4 Examples of Questions to Assess Global Mindset

Individual	Organization
• In interacting with others, does national origin have an impact on whether you give equal status to them?	• Do you recruit your employees from the global talent pool?
• Does being in a new cultural setting result in fear, anxiety or excitement?	• Do employees of every nationality have equal opportunity to climb to the top of the career ladder?
• When living in or visiting another culture, are you sensitive to cultural differences, without becoming a prisoner of these differences?	• Do you perceive your company as having a universal identity or a strong national identity?

Source: Adapted from Gupta, A. K., Govindarajan, V., & Wang, H. (2008). *The quest for global dominance: Transforming global presence into global competitive advantage, 2nd edition.* San Francisco: John Wiley & Sons, Inc.

promotions may be made by high-level executives. In contrast, HR planning in low-power distance cultures (e.g., United States, United Kingdom) often includes input from managers at many levels.[43] In high power distance and paternalistic cultures (e.g., France), employees often look to their superiors for guidance, whom they assume know what is best for their career development.[44]

Recent studies look at career beliefs, social networking and the influence of political, social and economic changes on career concepts in nations around the world.[45] One study explores career-life success and family social support among successful women in Argentina, Canada and Mexico. In all three countries, women now consider broader measures of career success than have been traditionally viewed, such as learning and contributing to society. In Canada and Mexico, many women now see receiving recognition in the workplace as evidence of career success.[46] A study in Russia notes that new career beliefs and behaviors are emerging, in great part due to multinational corporations entering Russia and introducing Western ideas about career development (e.g., mentoring and coaching, management education and training, professional development).[47] Yet, another study found that social or informal networks are greatly used in the job search process in both the United States and China, with a different focus by workers in each country. Social networks in the United States (an individualistic culture) are used to open doors for opportunities and gain information. In comparison, social networks in China (a collectivist culture) emphasize guanxi (the importance of interdependence of relationships, based on trust and expectations of returning favors).[48] Thus, research illustrates that while cultural viewpoints about career development are gradually changing, differences based on cultural values and past history continue to influence careers in today's global marketplace. This information provides HR with a broader understanding of what is valued in a career through the eyes of other cultures as well as a movement toward global career values.

In Closing

As globalization continues to expand, it is increasingly important for HR to understand the implications of HRM in a changing world. Not all HRM strategies will fit every situation. Communication styles and cultural value dimensions need to be taken into consideration when establishing or changing HRM strategies, policies and practices. Whether in domestic or global business environments, HRM must adapt to cross-cultural factors for the success of the organization and its people.

Chapter 9

The Multigenerational Workforce: Opportunity for Competitive Success

For the first time in history, four generations work side-by-side in many organizations. The working generations span more than 60 years, including so-called Traditionalists, Baby Boomers, Generation X and Millennials/Generation Y. All bring different experiences, perspectives, expectations, work styles and strengths to the workplace. Despite the perceived "generation gap" from differing views and potential conflict, organizations—and especially HR—have the opportunity to capitalize on the assets of each generation for competitive advantage.

Predictions in *Workforce 2020* (published in 1997) focused on demographic change as a major global force shaping the world economy.[1] More than a decade later, SHRM's *2008 Workplace Forecast* upholds these predictions with key demographic trends: (1) the aging population, (2) retirement of large numbers of Baby Boomers, (3) generational issues and (4) a greater demand for work/life balance. At the same time, the loss of talent due to the retirement of older workers will likely drive an increased focus on skills, labor shortages and retention strategies for the current and future workforce.[2]

Thus, in their respective industry sectors, HR leaders have the opportunity to create competitive success by strategically managing generational differences in terms of differing experiences, values and expectations. While not inclusive of all generational workplace issues, this article provides perspectives for HR and organizational leaders on selected key aspects of the multigenerational workforce and offers recommendations, primarily for U.S. organizations.

Today's Four Generations

Generally, the concept of a "generation" is attributed to social scientist Karl Mannheim from his work in the late 1920s.[3] Grounded in shared life experiences and defining historical and cultural events during individuals' formative years, each generation has different collective memories, expectations and values. As such, a generation is defined as an identifiable group that shares birth years and significant life events at critical developmental stages.[4] At the same time, it is very important to avoid stereotyping people from different generations. For example, research shows that people born at the beginning or end of a generation (referred to as "tweeners") can exhibit values and attitudes from two different generations.[5]

Generalities about generations can provide insight on values and expectations in the workplace. The oldest generation, Traditionalists (also known as Veterans, Matures, Depression Babies) grew up following the worldwide economic depression, with World War II as the major event in their childhood. They view work as a privilege and have a strong work ethic grounded in discipline, stability and experience.[6] The Baby Boom generation, born after World War II, is the largest generation in the United States and has had a significant impact on societies worldwide. Defining events of this generation include the space race, rock and roll, and women's liberation. Baby Boomers tend to be idealistic, driven and optimistic.[7]

Different experiences have shaped Generations X and Y. A much smaller generation than the Baby Boomers, Gen Xers were known as "latch-key children" with both parents working. They grew up during the time of high divorce rates and massive job layoffs of the 1980s. They are independent, creative, skeptical and distrustful of authority. In contrast, the younger generation (known as Millennials, Generation Y, Nexters) experienced terrorist attacks in their formative years, including September 11th, and technology has always been a part of their lives. They are confident, team-oriented, patriotic and social minded. Since their parents typically planned their activities, they are accustomed to having structured lives.[8]

An extensive study on generational differences found that leadership style preferences are reflected in selected admired leaders of each generation. Baby Boomers, for example, prefer leaders who are caring, competent and honest, as reflected in their choices of social leaders: Martin Luther King and Gandhi. Generations X and Y want leaders to challenge the system and create change: Ronald Reagan, Tiger Woods, Bill Gates. Each generation ranked honesty, competence and loyalty among the top leadership qualities, with honesty being the most important. For HR and organizational leaders, this means that firms need to recognize and understand the differences and similarities among generations regarding leadership qualities when it comes to the creation of leadership development programs for current and future leaders, for example (see Table 9.1).[9]

Business Case

As highlighted by AARP in Leading a Multigenerational Workforce, intergenerational dynamics offer organizations a highly competitive advantage. That is, management can use different perspectives, strengths and unique values to positively influence the bottom line in key areas: corporate culture, recruitment, employee engagement, retention and customer service.[11]

Yet, while it is commonly held that each generation has highly different values, there are similarities. For example, in a groundbreaking research study, the Center for Creative Leadership surveyed more than 3,000 organizational leaders over a seven-year period to learn how organizations can effectively use similarities and differences among generations. A key finding of this research was that the top three values of all generations were family, love and integrity, although they demonstrated these values in various ways. From a managerial viewpoint, this information is very helpful in better understanding the root cause of differences, misunderstandings and conflict in the workplace.[12] In fact, studies in organizational and human behavior find that people seek similar factors in the workplace, and these commonalities can be leveraged to bond employees in support of a company's mission, vision and goals.[13]

Further, with skills shortages commonplace today, domestic and global organizations must focus on workforce optimization for bottom-line results. Predicted demographic changes highlight the importance of managing talent of all generations (see Table 9.2). In the United States, for example, projections indicate there will be 10 million more jobs than workers by the year 2010. According to the Organization for Economic Cooperation and Development (OECD), working-age populations will decline by 65 million in the industrialized nations of OECD members, such as the European Union. At the same time, worker migration worldwide will likely create a highly competitive global labor market at least until the year 2016, when all Millennials will have entered the workforce, alleviating worker shortage in the developed world.[14] According to the Pew Research Center, by 2050 in the United States, working-age adults will make up 58 percent of the population, down from 63 percent in 2005. Also, depending on economic factors, a greater share of workers ages 50 and older may stay in the workplace longer than in the past.[15] Thus, a renewed focus on training older workers will no doubt become a greater part of talent management. Projections such as these indicate that demographic changes will be substantial, requiring that HR and organizational leaders thoughtfully examine strategic optimization of their human capital.

Workplace Diversity

In recent years, the concept of generational differences as a legitimate workplace diversity issue has gained increasing recognition. SHRM's director of diversity and inclusion initiatives, Shirley A. Davis, Ph.D., points out that in the United States, discussions of workplace diversity tend to focus on topics of race, ethnicity, gender, sexual orientation and disability. "However, in all parts of the world, there is another category of

Table 9.1 Four Generations in Today's Workplace

Generation	Percentage of Workforce	Assets in the Workplace	Leadership Style Preferences
Traditionalists Born 1922-1945 Ages 63-86	8%	Hard working, stable, loyal, thorough, detail-oriented, focused, emotional maturity.	Fair, consistent, clear, direct, respectful.
Baby Boomers Born 1946-1964 Ages 44-62	44%	Team perspective, dedicated, experienced, knowledgeable, service-oriented.	Treat as equals, warm and caring, mission-defined, democratic approach.
Generation X Born 1965-1980 Ages 28-43	34%	Independent, adaptable, creative, techno-literate, willing to challenge the status quo.	Direct, competent, genuine, informal, flexible, results-oriented, supportive of learning opportunities.
Millennials Born 1981-2000 Ages 8-27	14% and increasing rapidly	Optimistic, able to multitask, tenacious, technologically savvy, driven to learn and grow, team-oriented, socially responsible.	Motivational, collaborative, positive, educational, organized, achievement-oriented, able to coach.

Source: Author compilation from several sources.[10]

Table 9.2 Demographic Workforce Predictions

Workforce 2000	Workforce 2020
• The population and workforce will grow more slowly than at any time since the 1930s.	• As retirement ages become increasingly less predictable, workforce planning will become more uncertain.
• The proportion of women and minorities in the workforce will rise dramatically.	• By 2020, according to the U.S. Census Bureau, the proportion of women in the workforce will have gradually increased to about 50 percent.
• The average age of the population and workforce will rise, and the pool of young workers entering the labor market will shrink.	• The continued presence of top-level older employees may cause dissension among their middle-aged subordinates eager for promotion.
• The workforce is aging and thus becoming less willing to relocate, retrain or change occupations, yet the economy is demanding more flexibility.	• Older workers will need different benefits, such as elder care programs.
• Need to recognize the importance of a flexible workforce through company and national policies (e.g., flexible workforce programs, revised pension systems, promotion of retraining and lifelong learning).	• To increase workforce participation, firms and governments will need to accommodate unconventional working arrangements to encourage people to return or remain in the workforce (e.g., parents, older workers).
• Immigrants will represent the largest share of the increase in the population and the workforce since World War I.	• The U.S. population and workforce will gradually become more ethnically diverse.

Sources: Author compilation from several sources.[16]

diversity that cannot be overlooked: multigenerational diversity. Today, there are greater numbers of workers from each age group that bring both new opportunities and challenges. If organizations want to thrive in this competitive environment of global talent management, they need employees and managers who are aware of and skilled in dealing with the four generations that make up the workforce."

The existence of four generations is a major factor in talent management. In its "Competitive Workforce" category, SHRM's Human Capital Leadership Awards Program recognizes organizations with workforce readiness efforts aimed at anticipating and meeting current and future business needs in a changing economic climate. In 2008, Sodexo, Inc. was a finalist in that category for its innovative strategies in multigenerational talent acquisition and engagement. Since recruitment and retention of a multigenerational employee pool are key to Sodexo's business strategy, HR leaders at the company's U.S. headquarters in Gaithersburg, Maryland, launched a multifaceted recruitment initiative. For example, Sodexo established a presence on social networking sites such as YouTube and LinkedIn to attract younger workers and created a new recruitment initiative aimed at veterans that translates military experience and skills into civilian jobs at the company. As a result, in 2007, there was a 24 percent increase in the number of job applicants, including a 38 percent rise in minority candidates and a 32 percent increase in gender diversity.[17]

"At Sodexo, understanding what drives each generation, and what their underlying experiences are, is the key to creating a cohesive work environment where our people feel valued and empowered to work together effectively," said Dr. Rohini Anand, Sodexo senior vice president and global chief diversity officer. "This appreciation of generational diversity, and initiatives customized to meet the needs of each generation, allows each group to fully contribute and be a part of the growth and success of the organization." Clearly, organizations that proactively use the strengths of different generations in the workforce are best positioned for success.

Ethics and Generational Differences

A recent SHRM white paper, Ethics and Generational Differences: Interplay Between Values and Ethical Business Decisions, examined how different generations approach questions of integrity and purpose. The authors point out that "with value systems and motivation at the heart of ethics—and divergent value systems seemingly inherent within the four generational groups—the existence of varied ethical perspectives among co-workers is not a surprise." They emphasize that understanding differing viewpoints on ethics in the workplace will help organizations make sound ethical business decisions.[18]

A common complaint among generations focuses on work ethic. Much of this conflict stems from how the term work ethic is defined and interpreted. Traditionalists and Baby Boomers may criticize the two younger generations about their lack of work ethic, with the oldest generation considering a strong work ethic as demonstrated by being part of the organization (and physically present in the office, in terms of actual hours) for long periods of time. Baby Boomers consider a combination of factors, such as collaboration, teamwork and meetings, as evidence of work ethic. In contrast, Generation X and Millennials see work ethic as working hard—often autonomously—and having a positive impact on the company, while also living a full life outside of their job. Views on the issue of respect also differ. Having "paid their dues," the two older generations expect respect from Generation X and Millennials—yet, the two younger generations consider that respect is earned by making a strong contribution, not by the passage of time.[19]

Despite these differences, research shows that no matter one's age, people value achievement, balance and responsibility and want credible, trustworthy leadership.[20] Such commonalities are important for HR to emphasize in the workplace. As highlighted in Table 9.3, there are various actions that HR can take to help build stronger alliances in the workplace that both nurture and clarify ethical issues for workers of all generations.

Table 9.3 Ten Key Points for Ethical Business Management

1. Develop an internal campaign, with ethics as the #1 value for the 1. organization and employees.
2. Avoid stereotyping employees according to their generation.
3. Clearly identify the priorities of the company and then link them to the priorities and values of employees to support business decisions.
4. When possible, learn the values and motivation of employees and then connect them to individual and organizational goals.
5. Focus on business results, not on methodology (as long as it is ethical). All groups want to contribute and achieve but may do so differently.
6. To make ethical guidelines relevant to everyone, establish ongoing training and support sessions.
7. Look for commonality among employees of different generations.
8. Embrace diversity of opinion and methodology.
9. Err on the side of more communication, such as using more types of media: face-to-face meetings, e-mail blasts, etc.
10. Remember to respect the dimensions of differing generations (age, technological savvy, alternative work experiences, innovation, etc.)

Adapted from: Guss, E., & Miller, M. C. (2008, October). *Ethics and generational differences: Interplay between values and ethical business decision* [SHRM white paper]. Retrieved from www.shrm.org.

Engaging the Millennial Generation

The Millennial generation challenges organizations, HR and managers on many levels. The literature points out that this generation can be "high maintenance," and yet, when companies provide the resources and flexibility to be creative, Millennials also can be highly productive. To attract, engage and retain Millennials, organizations must understand what types of work environment and learning experiences they want. Each generation ranked honesty, competence and loyalty among the top leadership qualities, with honesty being the most important.

If organizations do not adapt their corporate culture to fit the needs of this large generation, this may have detrimental results in terms of hiring, productivity and retention.

These "digital natives" quickly learn and multitask, prefer to work collaboratively with others and thrive on immediate feedback. Although Millennials do not want to be micromanaged, they want clear directions and managerial support and also demand freedom and flexibility to do work at their own pace and in their own way. They want increasing responsibility but need coaching on time management. They are committed to the company "long term"—meaning about a year or two. Such apparent contradictions can boggle the minds of managers from older generations. The key is to build solid relationships by getting to know them, listening and spending time with them. For this "education is cool" generation, managers will want to provide coaching and resources to meet employees' learning goals. From an HR policy and program viewpoint, it is best to avoid the "one-size-fits-all" philosophy. To attract and retain Millennials, organizations need to be willing to customize schedules, work assignments and career paths. Millennials will look to their managers to help them balance work and other commitments. Managers must focus on performance and consistently provide constructive feedback, praise, recognition and rewards.[21]

Companies that are successful in attracting Millennials are creative in their culture, HR policies, programs and work environment. A survey by Human Resource Executive, in partnership with the Great Place to Work Institute, identified "18 Great Companies for Millennials." Facets of corporate cultures sought include:[22]

- Management's actions match its words.
- Employees are appreciated for good work and extra effort.
- Employees are involved in decisions that affect their jobs or work environment.
- Employees are treated as full members of the company, no matter the position.
- Promotions go to those who best deserve them, and the company culture is a team or family environment.

Marriott International Inc., for example, offers workplace flexibility—a benefit highly sought by young employees. In its "Teamwork Innovations" program, employees are encouraged to identify and eliminate redundant work. At one Marriott hotel, teams were able to cut 40 percent off the time that it took to turn over a shift and, with this time savings, were allowed to leave early. At the same time, Millennials like to work for "cool companies." In Portland, Oregon, the Umpqua Bank has internet cafés, coffee bars and couches where customers can relax and watch TV. Some branches even offer yoga and movie nights and have a water dish outside for dogs. The "cool factor" attracts both customers and young employees from high school and college.[23] As portrayed in these examples, organizations that strategically energize their company culture and effectively use the talents and drive of the Millennial generation will have a competitive edge.

HR Policies, Benefits and Programs

Over time, the multigenerational workforce will influence the organizational work ethic, perceptions of organizational hierarchy, work relationships and ways of managing change. The literature suggests that as a result of differing experiences and perspectives, strongly held attitudes and diverse motivators, there will be an impact on two specific areas of human resource policy and employee development: retention and motivation.[24] To successfully retain and leverage talent of all generations, the following studies represent the growing foundation of evidence to make changes in company culture, HR policies, benefits and programs.

No matter which generation, the work environment tends to either attract or repel individuals. An exploratory study examined dimensions of employee fit with work environments and the impact of employee job satisfaction and turnover intention among different generations. The findings suggest that employees in the Baby Boom generation value work relationships as a contributor to employee satisfaction, whereas for Generations X and Y, the work environment fit (potential for career growth, decision-making opportunities, autonomy and job challenge) is a primary retention factor.[25] Companies that are successful in attracting Millennials are creative in their culture, HR policies, programs and work environment.

Work/life balance is a key commonality among the four generations. A recent study that explored generational effects on work-family conflict in the United States suggests that changes reflect family and career stage differences. For example, "family interfering with work" has changed over time for Generation X and Baby Boomers but stayed at the same level for Matures, perhaps due to having fewer family demands (empty-nest family stage). Generation X and Baby Boomers value work/life balance, growth opportunities and positive work relationships. The implication is that managers and HR professionals will want to consider generational differences in work/life program design and monitor patterns of program use by different generational groups.[26]

In a study by the Boston College Center for Work & Family, thought leaders identified top trends that will affect the future of work/life: generational diversity, followed by global challenges, older workers, increasing stress levels and technology blurring. The increasing number of older workers is now a high-profile issue, with the aging workforce a challenge in the United States as well as in Western Europe and certain Asian countries, such as Japan. Companies must find ways to address the needs of various age cohorts based on their different life stages—for example, by keeping in mind different values and life experiences of the workforce when designing strategies that enable all employees to work together productively.[27]

Talent retention can be improved through different approaches to communicating and rewarding employees, using high-tech tools and employing a more high-touch approach where the manager-employee relationship is focused on more personalized rewards. By developing more unified and compassionate workplace cultures, organizations will be more attractive to people of all generations.[28] Such studies provide valuable insight and information to HR professionals to assess HR policies and programs for the multigenerational workplace (see Table 9.4).

Global Generational Trends

Research reveals that comparable generations in countries outside of the United States have both similar and distinct generational workforce issues. As a result of technology, the world is smaller, with greater access to information, products and services, contributing to broadening world views. At a Boston College Global Workforce Roundtable, it was noted that there appears to be a global convergence of attitudes among people under the age of 30. These young people, who do not yet have an agreed-upon identifying label (such as Millennials in the United States), have a global perspective, with a focus on quality of life, engagement in consumerism and a strong drive for personal and professional development.[29] Yet, this may not accurately portray attitudes of young people raised in rural and poor areas with limited exposure to global influences from television and the Internet.[30]

In contrast, the perspectives of older generations are strongly distinguished by local context. That is, these generations are highly influenced by culture, economics and events from their respective experiences, and they bring these viewpoints and values to the workforce. In China, for example, education was limited from 1966 to 1978 as a result of the Cultural Revolution. But for that event, many Chinese workers would likely be in senior leadership roles in organizations today; now, in contrast to their global peers, this group lacks education and experience. Cultural viewpoints also influence the workplace.

Table 9.4 HR Policies and Programs for the Multigenerational Workforce

HR Policies and Programs	Examples
Work/Life Benefits	Flexible hours, telecommuting, family leave, work/life balance policies, allowance for religious holidays, etc.
Rewards and Recognition	Compensation, rewards programs
Health Care	Long-term care, dependent care, elder care, EAPs, wellness programs
Training and Development	Professional development, mentorships, temporary work assignments, job sharing
Succession Planning	Formal leadership development programs, temporary work assignments

Sources: Author compilation from two sources.[31]

In India, the concept of hierarchy has traditionally strongly influenced business decisions, such as strategy, promotions and communications. Yet, in today's Indian workplace, older workers view hierarchy as more important than do people of the younger generation.[32]

Additionally, it should be noted that the concept of the Baby Boom generation exists only in the developed world, with other nations not having the concerns resulting from this large generation. For example, many countries (e.g., Latino Christian, Arab and African nations) did not have a significant reduction in fertility rates, nor did they embrace factors such as access to contraception, the changing role of women in society and more recent focus on work/life balance.[33]

Finally, for the multigenerational workforce in Europe, the literature is rather limited. However, a new study from the Journal of Managerial Psychology explored workplace learning, organizational commitment and talent retention among European managers across generations. The results show that younger generations have stronger learning orientation and lower organizational commitment than older workers. Important practical HR insights include focus on offering leadership development, fostering learning goals and organizational commitment, and managerial emphasis on learning—all key retention factors for the younger generations.[34]

Three Key Management Strategies

1. *Organizational communication:* This key strategy is important to retain talent and avoid potential conflict. A SHRM survey revealed a number of ways to successfully work with a multigenerational workforce, with communicating information in multiple ways, such as oral and written, as the most successful. Different generations have varying levels of comfort with technology, such as e-mail, while others prefer face-to-face communication. Other approaches found to be successful include (1) collaborative discussion, decision-making or problem solving—providing an opportunity to express respect and inclusion of all employees; (2) training managers on dealing with generational differences; (3) teambuilding activities; and (4) creating mentoring programs to encourage workers of different generations to work together and share experiences.[35]
2. *Succession planning:* HR and organizational leaders must be aware of the internal talent pool, encompassing all generations, from which possible successors can be selected and developed. Regarding age-based demographics, HR needs to have a basic understanding of the different values and work attitudes of each generation—important information for cultivating and sustaining a preferred corporate culture.[36]
3. *Mentoring:* The goal of this strategy is to help ensure the transfer of knowledge from one generation to the next. As older workers look toward retirement, mentoring can be an effective vehicle to capture organizational knowledge. Structured mentoring programs are well suited for knowledge transfer. An important step is to survey the younger workers, learn their goals and developmental needs, and then pair them with more experienced employees. Also, using a variety of mentoring models is helpful. Examples include one-on-one mentoring sessions, senior leadership discussion panels, group mentoring programs and even "speed mentoring," where employees sit with organization experts and ask questions. Another model increasingly used is senior staff and leaders coaching younger employees in the onboarding process. This process begins in the hiring period and can last for up to a year, giving younger workers direct attention and professional development early in their career.[37] The following mini-case study presents a successful mentoring program.

Mini-Case Study: Mentoring Between Generations

Launched in 2001, the AARP award program "Best Employers for Workers Over 50" recognizes organizations with best practices and policies that address issues affecting the aging workforce and creating workplace opportunities for all. In 2008, the YMCA of Greater Rochester was ranked 4th out of 50 companies for this award.[38] In the last six years, the YMCA of Greater Rochester has had a formal mentoring program— Mentoring Across Generations—as part of its professional development curriculum. Vice president of human resources, Fernan R. Cepero, PHR, credits its success to the company culture, stating, "Throughout its 155 year history, the organization has focused on leaving a legacy and creating a legacy between generations."

The mentoring program enhances the professional development and personal growth of both the mentor and the mentee. It helps employees understand cultural nuances, gain expertise in a specific discipline and provide ideas and inspiration about career paths. It also exposes employees to different paths of the business and various management levels. As exemplified in the short example from the YMCA of Greater Rochester, mentoring—a critical component of succession planning—builds leadership capacity by increasing the professional strength of the organization's employees.

Dan Friday, a member of Generation Y and buildings and grounds director at the Monroe Family Branch, was new to his position. Tom Ward, buildings and grounds director at the Westside Family Branch and a Baby Boomer, volunteered to mentor Dan, remembering what it was like early in his own career. Over several months, their mentoring relationship developed. As Dan attests, "Tom has coached me on all sorts of issues—from mechanics to staffing. He introduced me to the Association of Facility Engineers, where I've met some very interesting building mechanics and learned about construction projects that I am now considering for improvement to my facility." In fact, Tom has become much more than a mentor. He has helped Dan strip and wax floors, troubleshoot treadmill problems, and even filled in as pool operator when Dan was out for a week. At the same time, Tom has benefited from this relationship. As a subject matter expert, Tom has gained immense personal and professional satisfaction from seeing Dan grow and succeed in his leadership role.

As Mr. Cepero emphasizes, "Mentoring builds strong intergenerational working relationships, strategic use of intellectual capital and increased retention, and, at its core, ensures a continuous flow of knowledge management across generations."

In Closing

As HR professionals work to optimize talent in their respective organizations, research shows that it is critical to leverage the strengths of each generation. Whether in a domestic or global organization, HR has the unique opportunity to create a competitive advantage by guiding policy and program development and management strategies to increase attraction and retention of the four generations in today's workplace.

Chapter 10

Global Talent for Competitive Advantage

In a closely connected world, today's economics have changed how organizations do business. The pivotal point of competitive advantage now focuses on attracting, developing and keeping the right talent. As Dr. Vladimir Pucik, professor of strategy and international HR at IMD Business School, states, "Ask any senior executive in a company that operates across national boundaries, irrespective of national origin, about the major source of tensions in his or her job, and the answer most likely will be the same—the ever-increasing *complexity* of business problems he or she needs to tackle[…] Complexity in the competitive environment drives the need for more complex business strategies, building and sustaining global organizational capability […] and the critical building blocks for this capability are all very closely linked to people, their mind-set, and behaviors—creating an important new domain for the HR function."[1]

This article addresses many aspects of global talent essential for proactive global HR leadership, from global mindset and cultural adaptability, to staffing mobility trends, and safety and security. Beyond the article's are areas such as international employment law, immigration/visas, unions, benefits and compensation practices, tax implications, pensions, and global HRIS systems.

Global Business Practices and Global Talent

Global talent is rising to the top of the talent management agenda for HR professionals and their organizations. A leader in organization culture change, Dr. Donald T. Tosti notes that "global competition is creating an evolutionary process in which a common core of business practices and behaviors will guide the most successful organizations. One key difference between biological evolution and this business evolution is that business leaders can take action now to be sure their organizations will be among those that thrive in the global environment"[2] (see Table 10.1). As highlighted in the Towers Perrin study, *Winning Strategies for a Global Workforce*, "the 'boundaryless' business environment will continue to drive changes in where a company does business, and what it needs from its people to compete efficiently in existing and emerging markets."[3]

Table 10.1 Top Global Expansion Business Practices

- Evaluate policies and programs to ensure organizational objectives are met.
- Align global business objectives and needs.
- Identify a group of qualified potential candidates.
- Plan for long-term career paths.
- Establish criteria to measure assignment success.
- Require completion of a minimum of one assignment as a condition of executive advancement.

Source: Adapted from Brookfield Global Relocation Services. (2010). *Global relocation trends: 2010 survey report.* Woodridge, IL: Author.

Thus, the increasing fast pace of change requires that companies thoughtfully strategize their global workforce planning to remain competitive. According to the 2010 McKinsey Global Survey, executives worldwide believe that the most important global development in the next five years is the shift of the global economic activity from developed to developing economies with growing number of consumers in emerging markets. Corporate challenges center on being able to find the right talent to meet the company's strategic goals, particularly in view of low birth rates and the aging workforce in many developed economies. The survey found that less than 40 percent of executives were confident about having the talent needed in the next five years to meet strategic goals. Many are looking for talent in three areas: emerging markets (44 percent), new talent entering developed labor markets (41 percent) and talent from developing markets moving to emerging markets (35 percent).[4] Ultimately, the strength of an organization is its global human capital and how it is optimized.

Global Mindset

A global mindset is the underlying foundation essential for success in today's marketplace. According to management scholars Evan, Pucik and Barsoux, "global managers are defined by their state of mind." That is, a global mindset is what allows one to work effectively across functional, organizational and cross-cultural boundaries. However, managers are not "born global." It is through experience and learning that one acquires a global mindset and the necessary global skills.[5] Developing global capabilities takes time and is one area where HR can work with management to foster alignment of strategy through the organization (see Table 10.2). Dr. Pucik refers to the term "global brains," that is, the need for managers to be able "to balance competing business, country and functional priorities that emerge in international management process." The advantage of "think globally, act locally"—a phrase that illustrates the concept of a progressive global company—is being able to tap into global capabilities and skills with the goal to satisfy the needs of local customers. Thus, gaining global capability is both about broad concept learning and specific acting/doing.[6]

Table 10.2 Global Mindset Versus Traditional Domestic Mindset

Personal Characteristics	Traditional Domestic Mindset	Global Mindset
Knowledge	Functional expertise	Broad and multiple perspectives
Conceptual ability	Prioritization	Duality-balance between contradictions
Flexibility	Structure	Process
Sensitivity	Individual responsibility	Teamwork and diversity
Judgment	Predictability	Change as opportunity
Learning	Trained against surprises	Open to what is new

Source: Adapted from S. H. Rhinesmith. (1993). *A manager's guide to globalization.* Burr Ridge, IL: Business One Irwin.

For HR professionals to foster global mindset in their organizations, they, too, need global experience and perspective. A recent study by the Society for Human Resource Management explored the most important competencies for senior HR leaders. The results show consensus about competencies for global HR leaders, with global mindset, ranked high among the four regions in the study: (1) effective communication; (2) strategic thinking; (3) global intelligence/global mindset; and (4) cross-cultural intelligence. These findings provide a pathway for aspiring HR leaders to benefit from training and development opportunities that focus on expanding competencies for advanced HR roles. In addition, this information can be used for long-range succession planning to prepare junior HR professionals for future global leadership roles.[7] Competencies also provide a "road map" for global HR. One such resource that helps to clarify the use of global competencies is the Lominger Competencies, which focus on seven specific competencies: global business knowledge, cross-cultural resourcefulness, cross-cultural agility, assignment hardiness, organizational-positioning skills from remote locations, cross-cultural sensitivity, and humility (mostly Asian and Northern European contexts).[8]

Brad Boyson, SPHR, GPHR, a senior-level Canadian HR practitioner and a member of the SHRM Global Special Expertise Panel, currently lives and works in Dubai, UAE. His views on global mindset are of both practical and philosophical importance. Boyson observes, "HR practitioners from developed nations often have a harder time adopting a global mindset because, at least historically, they've seen globalization as a natural extension of what they are already doing. However, as globalization itself introduces different ways of doing business and economies of scale based upon different socio-economic systems, HR practitioners from developing nations have an advantage in terms of adopting and applying a global mindset, as they have always been forced to look 'abroad' for better or more advanced ways of doing things. This habit of looking outward first and then applying a localized solution defines an *applied* global mindset. Unfortunately, all too often, HR practitioners in developed nations tend to problem solve by trying to impose a local best practice beyond national boarders without ever realizing it is a localized practice. To be fair, it's easy to assume something is globally applicable if you haven't personally worked within an alternative system before, especially the dichotomy that exists between developed and developing economies."

To promote the understanding and use of global mindset, a company university can be a strong tool. AGCO Corporation, one of the world's largest manufacturers and distributors of agricultural equipment, is an example of a global company that strategically focuses on training for global mindset. AGCO's vision is to provide high-tech solutions for professional farmers feeding the world, with the mission to achieve profitable growth through superior customer service, innovation, quality and commitment. Officially formed in 1990, much of AGCO's growth has been through acquisitions, leading to a myriad of products, systems, processes, attitudes and approaches to doing business. In 2004, AGCO announced a new global brand portfolio made up of Challenger®, Fendt®, Massey Ferguson® and Valtra®. The key to AGCO's continued success is to maintain the integrity of each of its brands in relation to customers, dealers, vendors and employees under the umbrella of one company. Toward this goal, AGCO developed a strategy, through AGCO University, to share the global message of one company one mindset throughout the organization. The AGCO University offers courses to nurture and develop a global mindset that focuses on meeting the needs of its customers by providing diverse products and services as one company, as well as having a local focus where appropriate (see text box).

AGCO University creates a structural conduit to provide employees with skills, education and continuing development to facilitate the achievement of AGCO's key objectives and strategic initiatives. The following courses, just a small part of the global curriculum, aim directly at ensuring that employees are of one mindset when acting and interacting on behalf of the company.

- *Code of Conduct Training* — Reiterates and demonstrates how employees are expected to behave in the workplace when encountering other employees, customers, dealers, vendors and visitors to the locations.
- *Anti-corruption Training* — Explains what it means to act as an agent or representative for the company. Every country and locale has an accepted culture of conducting business. The information contained in this session demonstrates the impact of conducting business in a fair and equitable manner and how the morale, productivity and profitability of the company are driven by the actions of its representatives.
- *Values Training* — Introduces employees to the Core and Business values of AGCO. Both serve as guiding principles for employees and provide an overall guideline for all activities as members of the AGCO team.

Cultural Awareness

Cultural awareness is essential for business success. An important HR function is to promote linking future career paths and global business success with cultural competence. This is particularly helpful for managers who interact with people globally—whether working with different employee groups, establishing and maintaining business partnerships, and/or developing and expanding the company's global customer base. Cross-cultural intelligence—the ability to switch between ethnic and/or national contexts and quickly learn new patterns of social interaction with behavioral responses—is needed to work effectively in multicultural environments. Ideally, global managers are motivated to acquire new behaviors and skills, and understand the benefits of learning from different cultures.[9]

As discussed in Chapter 8, cultural competence begins with a solid understanding of one's own values and how they shape cultural identity. One is then better positioned to discern and appreciate cultural differences (see Table 10.3). This is important, as decisions in the workplace are influenced by cultural viewpoints, beliefs and assumptions. For example, lack of cross-cultural sensitivity in the performance appraisal process can result in negative impact on communication, employee morale, teamwork and turnover.[10] To be successfully implemented and effective, HR benefits programs, such as pay-for-performance, team-based pay, stock options and/or executive compensation, are highly dependent on cultural context. Therefore, variations in norms and values within and across cultures must be taken into consideration.[11]

Table 10.3 Factors in Cultural Differences

- *Communication:* Verbal and nonverbal
- *Group Dependence:* Degree of importance of the individual or group
- *Hierarchy:* Consideration/perception of rank in relationship to others
- *Receptivity to Diversity:* Country of origin, race, gender, race, religion, ethnicity
- *Relationships:* Important for business relations/interactions
- *Space:* The degree of space and privacy needed for personal comfort
- *Status attainment:* Perceived level of success
- *Time:* Adherence to schedule
- *Tolerance of Change:* Perception of control of one's future/destiny

Source: Adapted from Henson, R. (2002). Culture and the workforce. In K. V., Beaman, Ed. *Boundaryless HR: Human capital management in the global economy.* Austin, TX: IHRIM Press Book.

In his book *Working GlobeSmart: 12 People Skills for Doing Business Across Borders*, author Ernest Gundling, Ph.D., emphasizes the importance of relationship building and global leadership. Dr. Gundling presents a model of 12 key global people skills—for interpersonal, group and the organization—ranging from establishing credibility, building global teamwork and negotiating, to strategic planning, transferring knowledge and managing change. Whether in the headquarters of a multinational corporation or in the global corporation of a foreign office, global people skills are critical for global business.[12] In the multicultural organization, for example, effectively managing global virtual teams requires keen cultural awareness to establish productive working relationships. As noted in Chapter 14, when working with global talent spread across different regions, countries and time zones, communication can either be an enhancer to promote trust or a derailer if a lack of respect for different styles of communication is perceived.[13]

Working globally can require a period of transition, with the inherent new challenges of relationship building and cultural awareness. Peyman Dayyani, SPHR, GPHR, a member of the

SHRM Global Special Expertise Panel, has 17 years of HR management and global roles in the Middle East and Africa. He shares his observations: "The comfort of face-to-face relationships and habit of having uninterrupted meetings in a relaxed office suddenly changed for all of us who had to learn to manage people and operations across different time zones. We were working with less developed regions of the world, where phone lines were interrupted and noisy, Internet connections were slow and video conferencing was, in many locations, a dream to have. Travel bans and security risks were some of the realities we had to face. Our people needed to overcome these challenges with new competencies, such as learning to be more patient, becoming more active listeners (rephrasing sentences a number of times) and being more aware of word usage with people for whom English was their second language. Since we did not have the luxury of body language and emotions to convey the message, effective communication was our most challenging task."

Global Staffing

Global staffing is defined as "the critical issues faced by multinational corporations with regard to the employment of home, host and third culture nationals to fill key positions in headquarter and subsidiary operations."[14] Generally, there are three types of international employees: (1) parent country nationals (PCNS), (2) host-country nationals (HCNs), and (3) third-country nationals (TCNs). When leaving the country, the PCN is typically referred to as an expatriate or assignee, and upon returning home, a repatriate or returnee. Organizations take different approaches to global staffing, from using local hires to relocating talent to other locations. Organizations also draw on a number of global staffing options, such as international commuters, local hires, globalists (those who spend their careers going from one international locale to another), internships (temporary immigrants or trainees), frequent business trips, second-generation expatriates, and returnees (those who return to their home country, already selected or hired by the firm).[15]

International assignments are primarily learning-driven or demand-driven. Learning-driven refers to management development, knowledge transfer and also socializing locals into the company's corporate culture and values. Demand-driven are those that use assignees, often in roles of general manager or director, to assist in specific situations, such as subsidiary startup, technology transfer, rolling out new products and/or organizational control.[16]

Due to the increased focus on global competition for marketplace share and profit, global relocation trends mark key changes in global staffing. The Brookfield 2010 *Global Relocation Trends* survey report (previously conducted and published by GMAC Relocation), a well-known resource for global mobility trends, provides detailed data on employee and family-related relocation issues as well as strategic business concerns. This study has been conducted annually for the past 15 years and thus references trends over time.[17] The top objectives for international assignments, ranked in order of importance, are: (1) filling a managerial skills gap, (2) filling a technical skills gap, (3) building international management expertise/career development, (4) technology transfer, (5) launching new endeavors, (6) transferring corporate culture, and (7) developing local business relationships. In today's business environment, there is now greater central oversight for global mobility, with 96 percent of relocation assignment policy decisions made globally at company headquarters. The study found that a majority of companies (89 percent) gave a high rating—good or very good—on the return on investment of expatriate assignments.[18] In addition, short-term assignments (less than one year) are becoming more widely used than the past two- to five-year expatriate assignments, primarily due to cost, family support and repatriation challenges.

Effective global staffing requires a clear understanding why employees accept international assignments and why they turn them down. The Brookfield study revealed that the value of the international experience on the employee's career is the number one reason for accepting an international assignment: 33 percent of respondents said expatriates were promoted faster; 28 percent believed that they more easily obtained positions in the company; and 28 percent changed employers more frequently. Assignment refusal continues to focus on family concerns (83 percent), spouse/partner career (47 percent) and location/quality of life (25 percent). The two major factors contributing to assignment failure were spouse/partner dissatisfaction (65 percent) and inability to adapt (47 percent). Further, certain locations were found to have the highest rates of assignment failure: #1 China; #2 India; #3 United Kingdom; and #4 United States. The reasons for these failures varied by country: China was due to language, cultural adjustment and the high expense to live in major cities; India, due to accommodation issues, security, cultural differences and living conditions; the United Kingdom, due to difficulties adjusting, family issues and culture; and the United States, due to expat compensation, family reasons, the school system and job performance. In some cases, the assignment ends with an early return—due to family concerns (32 percent), accepting new position in company (21 percent), completing an assignment early (17 percent) and cultural adjustment challenges (8 percent).[19] Since the investment for international assignments is significant, such data are of great value when planning for global staffing and global talent management.

Cultural Adaptability

The value of cultural adaptability for success in international business cannot be overestimated. A key role of the global HR leader is to provide training and dialogue to both educate and support global management and staff to be better prepared for cultural challenges. Whether on international business travel, an expatriate assignment or managing a global team, culture has an impact on relating to others. Clearly, the learning curve can be steep but also worthwhile. Dayyani, of the SHRM Global Special Expertise Panel, points to credibility as a value of expatriate work: "In very short time of almost two years, I had to travel to more than 40 countries and put on half a million miles of air travels, learning many new competencies, from building trust across cultures to becoming a wizard of many electronic gadgets—and ultimately was able to get connected and establish communication in various platforms to home office and remote places. The most worthy take-away was gaining credibility to lead geo-dispersed teams." At the same time, while technology is an important tool to help keep global talent connected to their family and friends, it cannot fully alleviate culture shock. Culture shock is experienced in many ways and in various degrees, no matter one's level of experience working and living in different cultures. Thus, global managers must be knowledgeable about the symptoms and challenges of cultural adaptability. In her book, *Breaking Through Culture Shock: What You Need to Succeed in International Business*, Dr. Elisabeth Marx presents a culture shock triangle for all types of global assignments—from short-term to the business traveler to the long-term assignee. This is a valuable tool for global HR managers involved in preparing and developing managers to work abroad or on global teams. Psychologically, global managers experience the following three levels of culture shock:[20]

- *Emotions*—coping with mood swings and the stress of the transition (goal: to achieve contentment).
- *Thinking*—understanding foreign colleagues (goal: to develop a way of thinking that is culturally effective—change perception/interpretation of behavior and events).
- *Social skills and identity* (goal: to develop a professional and social network, effective social skills and an international identity).

While employees today know that they are responsible for their own careers, the global context brings with it different opportunities, with unexpected and substantial influences on one's life. The impact will be experienced broadly, from personality to career success, with many learning opportunities on the journey. One expatriate study found the 91 percent of managers interviewed perceived a positive impact on personality—becoming more open-minded, confident, tolerant and patient, as well has having a broader outlook. According to 82 percent of managers, there were many positive influences on career, including faster career progression/promotion, gaining more senior roles, and improvement of strategic thinking/negotiation and international skills. Yet, in some cases, managers found that their company did not take full advantage of their experience when they returned. When their international experience was discredited, employees left their organizations to find opportunities where global talent was wanted (see text box).[21]

Changing Employee Attitudes

> *"I grew up, it broadened my horizons and I developed a need for travel and a thirst for knowledge. I felt more flexible and self-sufficient. At the beginning, I was more reserved, but after I adapted, I became more outgoing."*
>
> *"I learned a lot about dealing with headquarters and the experience was a major stepping stone in my career. I also developed a broader expertise in transactions."*
>
> *"My experience has not helped me to progress in my own company but has made me much more marketable outside."*
>
> Source: Adapted from Marx, E. (2001). *Breaking through culture shock: What you need to succeed in international business, 2nd ed.* London: Nicholas Brealey Publishing.

A new study by Towers Watson has important implications for global talent pipelines. The 2010 Global Workforce Study, *The Shape of the Emerging "Deal,"* explored the evolution of the employment relationship worldwide and how people now relate to their companies and work. The findings highlight how the global recession and changing business models require employers and employees alike to reconsider their assumptions about the world of work. The results reflect significant issues that will likely influence decisions to invest in global talent for years. Key findings common throughout the global sample are that employees have:[22]

- Greater desire for security and stability.
- Concern about their ability to ensure their long-term financial and physical health and well-being, as well as career and performance.
- A preference for job security over mobility for career growth.

- Low confidence in the interpersonal aspects of leaders and managers.

To establish a new employment proposition, the ideal is that each organization, with its own unique vision about its people, can bring together traditional and new approaches to workforce management. It is recommended that organizations (1) foster greater self-reliance by the employee, (2) create a greater personalized work experience—to better align with how people add value to the organization, and (3) strengthen the flexibility and agility of the company's management style, structure, processes and delivery of workplace programs.[23] As HR leaders work with their organizations to identify, develop and staff global talent, it is valuable to keep in mind the changing employment relationship for the long-range sustainability of the company.

Spouse and Family Challenges

For global staffing assignments, the burden of adjustment often falls to the spouse and family. Whether for international business travel, unaccompanied short assignments or the traditional assignment of two or more years, the spouse and families of traveling employees experience challenges. The main family issues are cross-cultural adaptation, dual-career marriages and education of the children. In recent years, elder care has emerged as a critical factor influencing decisions to accept global positions. To help ensure the success of the assignment, both for cost and results, global HR functions have gradually increased spouse and family support. Increased support is often the result of input from assignees and their families collected internally as well as from external research studies. According to the Brookfield 2010 *Global Relocation Trends* survey report, among organizations do offer cross-cultural support, 55 percent provided training for the entire family, 38 percent for assignee and spouse, and 4 percent for employee only. Many companies offer programs for the spouse/partner: 85 percent offer language training, 38 percent provide education/training assistance, 34 percent sponsor work permits and 31 percent assist in career planning. In addition, 8 percent have provisions to assist assignees with elderly family members.[24] These types of statistics are valuable benchmarks for global HR in order to develop, change and/or expand policies and programs for global workforce planning.

In addition, work/life balance is growing in importance in today's society. A key driver of employee satisfaction in developed countries, work/life balance is now becoming a topic in emerging markets and developing economies. It encompasses quality of life due to greater demands in the workplace, changing roles of men and women, different family structures, increased focus on health in families and changing demographics.[25] Two recent studies about families and global assignments highlight the challenges around work/life balance and the interlinking importance of work, family and communication. Conducted by The Interchange Institute, *Voices From the Road* and *Voices From Home* consider the impact of unaccompanied international assignments on the lives of employees and their families. The studies found that the partnership of the employee, family and organization are very important, both from work and personal perspectives. The Institute's founder and executive director, Anne P. Copeland, Ph.D., notes that "companies should not assume that, just because the spouse is staying at home, there are no family or personal problems. Although unaccompanied assignments work for some, many families are still disrupted and distressed by the uncertainties and unpredictability of the assignments, the financial strain, and the absence of one partner."

Voices From the Road examined factors related to positive outcomes of international assignments among nearly 1,500 employees working in one of 57 countries on five continents. Personal factors (mental health, substance abuse, marital issues) and work outcomes (attitudes about work, ability to get work done, willingness to take another assignment) were considered. Among the top contributors to the success of an assignment were the degree of involved decision-making of the employee and spouse about the assignment, choice about assignments, HR policies (such as family-friendly policies), family support services and financial support from the company.[26]

Voices From Home considered the views of the spouse. The study participants were 88 percent female, with citizenship from 21 countries and spouses working in 17 countries. The study found that financial costs were an issue—only about one-third said they had adequate financial support during the assignment, and many cited new financial costs. Higher levels of satisfaction and better adjustment were reported when assignees and their spouses had input about the timing of home visits and when there was less ambiguity about the length of the assignment. It was also discovered that when couples felt pressured into accepting the assignment, there were more negative outcomes, such as depression for the spouse and behavioral issues for the children. The study recommends that organizations support and facilitate professional counseling for couples and/or connections with support networks of those in similar situations. Managing challenges may be alleviated by advice and tips from experts and peers with these experiences.[27] Both studies, available at www.interchangeinstitute.org, are valuable resources for global HR professionals seeking to improve international assignee success.

Miguel R. Olivas-Luján, Ph.D., a professor at Clarion University of Pennsylvania (USA) and Tecnológico de Monterrey (Mexico) and a member of the SHRM Global Expertise Panel, points out, "While the literature attributes a large percentage of expatriate failure to lack of spousal adjustment, children's needs should not be overlooked. Children in the toddler and younger ranges might be the ones that end up adjusting more smoothly, as their language skills are still in formation and they are not embedded in social circles that will be missed in the new location. On the other end of the spectrum, those in their teenage years often show the opposite characteristics (fully developed language skills and a high degree of social embeddedness), which correlate with higher difficulty in adjusting to their new environment." Dr. Olivas-Luján, a published scholar on cross-cultural business issues, notes, "The newest forms of telecommunication technologies—in particular, social networking sites and the diffusion of teleconferencing gear—can have both positive and negative effects on their users. On one hand, using these technologies to stay in touch more frequently with extended family and friends may lead to missing them less and to continued social support to adjust to the new environment. On the other hand, the combined facts that the ability to communicate with family and friends more frequently exists, yet distance precludes other types of interpersonal interaction, might exacerbate the negative effects of the culture shock. Research is needed to illuminate this emerging issue." He emphasizes the importance of coping mechanisms: "Effective coping mechanisms such as ensuring early buy-in or conceptualizing the experience as an exciting possibility that will bring about benefits to the family as well as to each individual might make all the difference in the way the family members adjust during the expatriate assignment. This is important to minimize the detrimental effect of a family-to-work conflict spillover for the assignee. Besides, shouldn't the family be a major beneficiary of all career moves for the assignee?"

Safety and Security

Duty of care is a term that implies the (legal) obligation of an employer to safeguard its workforce. In the discussion of global talent, both the employer and the employee have responsibilities for safety and security. The breadth of duty of care widens in the global context to include risk management threats such as natural disasters, terrorism, crime, disease, political unrest, to name a few. Proactive strategic planning for the safety and security of a global workforce, including international business travelers and assignees, requires a partnership between global HR and other parts of the organization (such as risk management, global mobility vendors, the legal department). However, many companies may not be prepared to deal with unexpected situations and emergencies. Global HR can demonstrate leadership in this area by helping to ensure coordinated collaboration within the company for proactive and thoughtful policy and program management for safety and security.

Two recent publications highlight the importance of the respective responsibilities of the employer and employee in terms of safety and security in cross-border work. Published by International SOS, *Duty of Care of Employers for Protecting International Employees, Their Dependents and International Business Travelers* recommends an integrated strategic approach for safety and security, focusing on three key perspectives: (1) legal, (2) corporate social responsibility and (3) cost/benefit analysis. Best practices are considered, as well as the responsibilities of different stakeholders—government, senior management, HR and employees—for the health, safety and security of expatriates and their dependents, as well as international business travelers.[28]

When HR professionals are preparing employees to travel for global staffing assignments, a practical tool to provide them with is a copy of Travel Wise: How to be Safe, Savvy and Secure Abroad. The author, Ray S. Leki, who has more than 20 years of experience working with company leaders and diplomats around safety, focuses on personal responsibility and internal competencies of the international traveler for a safe and successful journey. Using a comprehensive and holistic approach, this book provides a process to help one gain a solid understanding of one's abilities and knowledge in four areas: (1) motivation to travel, (2) personal and interpersonal skills, (3) cross-cultural skills, and (4) security awareness.[29]

Repatriation and Retaining Global Talent

With keen competition for global expertise, repatriates are an excellent source of global talent. Yet, repatriation, the final phase of the international assignment and a time of transition, is often challenging and rewarding on both the personal and professional fronts. As intercultural management consultant Craig Storti notes in his classic, *The Art of Coming Home*, "The ultimate context for understanding and appreciating reentry are the experiences that precede it. [...] Reentry, for all its minor and a few major annoyances, can't begin to diminish the luster of an expatriate experience. Indeed, it is in some ways precisely because the overseas experience is so rich and stimulating that reentry becomes a problem."[30]

Once back home, many repatriates are eager to use their global experience. However, they can easily be discouraged by the positions available in their organizations, leading to low job satisfaction. As a result, some seek employment elsewhere, and then the company loses its investment to a competitor. The most recent data show average annual turnover/attrition of repatriates as 13 percent, the same as the historical average.[31]

Assignees often gain valuable global expertise, make important business contacts and develop strategic management skills. Repatriates who had a positive experience may consider other global roles, from coaching to consulting to another assignment. One way to avoid losing repatriate talent is through strategic global talent management. Therefore, it is recommended to hold repatriation discussions well in advance of assignee return. The 2010 *Global Relocation Trends* report found that 92 percent of companies had repatriation/re-entry discussions with assignees (as compared with the historical average of 73 percent). One quarter of respondents had these conversations before departure, 29 percent—six months or more before return, 38 percent—less than six months before return, and 8 percent did not discuss repatriation at all.[32]

By working with repatriates before they return, global HR leaders can find the right place to use their much needed skills and expertise for the benefit of the organization.

In Closing

For both the new and the seasoned global HR professional, global staffing holds many challenges and opportunities. With continuous changes in the marketplace, resources such as global mobility trends, expatriate studies, management research and economic indicators all serve to provide valuable information that can be factored into strategic planning for global talent management.

PART III

Employee Relations and Organizational Development

Chapter 11

Leadership Development: Optimizing Human Capital for Business Success

"Many organizations continue to jump from one quick fix to the next, never stopping to truly understand the issues of leadership and the changing dynamics that are at work in the marketplace." [1]

In today's changing times, effective leadership is a key component of organizational success. With the impending retirement of the baby boom generation, changing demographics and limited resources, leadership development is rising to the top as an organizational priority. Corporate investment in leadership development in 2000, for example, was estimated at $50 billion. At the same time, a new paradigm is emerging, shifting from authoritative leadership and position power to collaborative leadership and knowledge power.[2] And organizations are increasingly under pressure to show return on investment for training and development. Reflecting business needs, the *SHRM 2006 HR Strategic Management Survey Report* points out that 74 percent of HR professionals perceive leadership development as one of the core areas where HR can make a strategic contribution.[3] From a strategic standpoint, therefore, HR is ideally placed to lead the way to foster talent for future leaders.

Linking Leadership Development with Business Success

Leadership development is defined as formal and informal training and professional development programs designed for all management and executive-level employees to assist in developing the required leadership skills and styles to deal with a variety of situations.[4] Increasingly, organizations are linking leadership development with business value and organizational success. A recent study found that the more organizations do toward developing leaders, the greater the financial success.[5] When linked with organizational strategy, leadership development programs and leadership competencies effectively support profound long-lasting change.[6] However, according to a recent survey of globally recognized leaders responsible for leadership development, leadership development must first be aligned with the business of the organization before its value can be determined. At Colgate-Palmolive Company, for example, leadership is governed by three core values—caring, continuous improvement and global teamwork—and the company carefully monitors how development fits with its business model and objectives.[7]

Leadership development is fraught with challenges and opportunities (see Table 11.1). Today's fiercely competitive marketplace requires staunch devotion to excellence and the ability to see the big picture that affects the changing face of leadership. For example, successful organizations have moved from security to pay for performance in knowledge-intensive work environments that demand adaptability, innovation and flexibility. Therefore, firms that produce effective leaders who engage people's passion for a better tomorrow will truly foster business success.[8]

Table 11.1 Five Dilemmas of Leadership Development

1. The extent to which and the way in which leadership can really be taught.
2. The changing nature of leadership.
3. The comparative nature of leadership.
4. The measurement and evaluation of leadership development interventions.
5. The integration of leadership programs with other organizational systems–such as career development or reward systems–and the degree of linkage with business strategy.

Source: Adapted from Storey, J. (2004). Leadership development through corporate universities. *Training & Management Development Methods,* 18, 4, 441+.

Critical Leadership Skills

In the discussion and context of leadership development, there are some important points to keep in mind. First, the terms "leader" and "manager" are often used interchangeably, although the literature points to differences between leadership and management. The primary difference, simply put, is that managers control and solve problem whereas leaders motivate and inspire. Similarities include creating relationships to accomplish an agenda and working to ensure that people get their jobs done.[9] Second, there is debate regarding whether leadership can be taught. The overarching agreement, however, is that the learner must have a personal commitment to learning the necessary leadership skills, behaviors and competencies and then exhibiting these behaviors.[10] Third, there is also debate about whether leaders are made or born.[11]

According to the Center for Creative Leadership, resourcefulness, composure, straightforwardness, decisiveness and building and mending relationships are essential leadership skills for business success.[12] In contrast to other skills, such as technical skills that change over time, intangible skills are of enduring value. Additional key "soft skills" include initiative, communication, collaboration/teamwork, people development/coaching, personal effectiveness/personal mastery, planning and organizing, and presentation skills.[13] The Gallup Leadership Institute Summit on Authentic Leadership points to the importance of leading with authenticity. Authentic leaders, highly aware of how they behave and think, positively affect sustained performance and are optimistic, confident and resilient with high principles, values and ethics.[14] Talent management skills, including diversity management across cultures, genders and age groups, in conjunction with strategic thinking for global competition and technology application, are also essential.[15] Consequently, when seeking future senior-executive material, organizations often value personal leadership traits more highly than business-oriented capabilities. Thus, being open to change and growth, having the courage to make decisions that "feel right," building strong relationships both internally and externally, and motivating and inspiring others are necessary skills for success.[16]

One of the most critical skills in today's competitive marketplace is building and maintaining trust. Building trust—through transparency, honesty, communication and actions—does not happen overnight. Being viewed as credible and trustworthy requires that one deliver on agreements or explain why it is not possible, be clear about expectations and take responsibility for one's mistakes. An ongoing dialogue is essential. For example, it is important to spend time getting to know the desires and hopes of each person on the team. If trust is violated through actions or in the eyes of the employee, the leader must work it out directly and quickly. Along with actions, saying "I am sorry" and "I'll fix it" goes a long way toward reestablishing trust. Trust leads to sustainability, portable both domestically as well as globally.[17]

Poor leadership skills, however, along with unethical behavior and incompetence, contribute to leadership failure and can be costly (e.g., poor company reputation, loss of customers, increased turnover). Leaders fail because of how they act and who they are, particularly when under stress. Common causes of derailment are arrogance, bullying, self-centered ambition and betrayal of trust. Certain "flawed" behaviors—such as arrogance, emotional instability and abrasiveness—are more damaging at upper-level positions, which have high stakes and thus potentially higher costs of failure. Solutions include getting feedback, using a coach, analyzing potential factors of derailment (e.g., business failures, stress from events, problems, environments) and using small failures to prompt awareness through learning and change.[18]

Finally, since today's leadership roles are increasingly complex and diverse, the role itself determines certain key skills. Operational roles—the more traditional management positions—require self-confidence and flexibility. Advisory roles that provide support in a specific area (e.g., HR or IT) require excellent people skills, influence and organizational knowledge. Collaborative roles that accomplish work through others are highly proactive, requiring tenacity at gathering information. Overall, the more strategic and sophisticated the role, the wider the essential repertoire of leadership skills.[19]

An Integrated-Solution Approach to Leadership Development

Many organizations struggle to find the right strategy to bridge the leadership gap. Some focus on a single-method approach (e.g., classroom learning) while others use the multi-solution approach with a hodgepodge of programs and no strategic process in place. In today's complex business environment, the integrated-solution approach, with its holistic and strategic focus, works best to (1) transfer vital skills and ideas to leaders; (2) enhance performance; (3) reinforce corporate culture and values; (4) drive business results; and (5) adapt to changing business realities. One of the advantages, for example, is the focus on critical moments in the leadership lifestyle, such as the first time being a people manager or moving into an executive position. During transitions, leaders need to learn new ways of thinking about their roles or risk derailing or failing. The integrated approach offers a synergistic, strategic and sustainable pathway for organizations to build leadership capacity. Alignment to organizational strategy with long-term planning for best use of resources requires serious commitment on the part of the organization, senior leaders and HR (see Table 11.2). With its comprehensive strategy, the value of the integrated-solution approach is that it focuses on the selection of appropriate development options and, most importantly, aligns them with business goals and objectives, ensuring that organizations can be proactive and responsive because they are aware of what is happening in the business.[20]

Table 11.2 Eight Steps to Implementing an Integrated-Solution Approach to Leadership Development

1. Develop a comprehensive strategy for integrated leadership development.
2. Connect leadership development to the organization's environmental challenges.
3. Use the leadership story to set the context for development.
4. Balance global enterprise-wide needs with local individual needs.
5. Employ emergent design and implementation.
6. Ensure that development options fit the culture.
7. Focus on critical moments of the leadership lifecycle.
8. Apply a blended methodology.

Source: Weiss, D., & Molinaro, V. (2006). Integrated leadership development. *Industrial and Commercial Training*, 38, 1, 3-12.

Mini Case Study: Integrated Leadership Development

This mini case study illustrates a successful leadership development initiative designed to match the organizational culture and firm readiness.[21]

The vice president of HR of a large engineering firm wanted to implement an assessment center process to launch a leadership development initiative. However, in discussions with the executive team, there was resistance. Also, considering all the organizational priorities, the CEO was concerned about the level of financial commitment required and the firm's ability to effectively accomplish this goal. After much reflection, the HR executive realized that the organization was not ready for this type of solution because it did not yet have a culture in which leaders were open to receiving feedback that an assessment center would generate. Rather than risk failure, the VP of HR introduced a staged approach. In the first year of the initiative, an online self-assessment tool was implemented, giving leaders the opportunity to assess themselves based on the firm's leadership competencies. In the second year, a multi-rater assessment was implemented, in which leaders were assessed on leadership competencies by direct reports, managers and peers. In the third year, an assessment center process that focused first on high-potential candidates was introduced. The initiative was successful, as both the culture and the readiness of the firm were respected.

Succession Planning

Across the organization, effective succession planning integrates talent management with strategic planning.[22] The goal is to anticipate future leadership requirements by finding, assessing and developing the human capital necessary to accomplish the organization's strategy.[23] Succession management requires visible and consistent support from the CEO and senior management (see Table 11.3). As companies become more complex and global, evolving toward a knowledge-era mindset, the focus expands from emphasis on individual leaders to leadership teams with complementary skills and a shared vision.[24] However, demographic trends indicate a significant decline in the workforce of 35- to 45-year-olds over the next 15 years, with fewer people available for management positions. Consequently, executive talent will be in high demand, and at the same time, younger managers will not yet be ready to take on leadership responsibilities.[25] Since competition for leadership expertise will be intense, organizations must develop succession plans now to ensure their future. Yet surprisingly, many firms are not strongly focusing on succession planning, as confirmed by the SHRM 2006 Succession Planning Survey Report, in which only 29 percent of companies reported having a formal succession plan in place.[26]

Table 11.3 Seven Common Elements of Successful Succession Plans

1. Visible support from the CEO and all members of top management.
2. Clearly defined leadership criteria.
3. A defined plan to find, retain and motivate future leaders.
4. A simple, easy-to-follow, measurable process.
5. The use of succession planning to reinforce the corporate culture.
6. A process that focuses primarily on leadership development.
7. A process that is a real organizational priority.

Source: Berchelman, D. K. (2005, Fall). Succession planning. *The Journal for Quality and Participation*, 28, 3, 11-13.

To help offset the looming leadership crisis, HR can both spearhead and manage succession planning. For organizations new to succession planning, a good starting place is to assess key positions in the current organizational chart, the staff holding these positions and their anticipated retirement dates, and develop a projected organizational chart. From there, the process depends on company goals and the current stage of succession planning. Some firms may decide to redesign and/or rethink their approaches to find, develop, retain and motivate future leadership by focusing first on needed leadership skills, while others may take a more comprehensive approach, looking at talent throughout the entire organization and then developing programs to utilize current leadership strength as well as build new competencies. Some firms may already be at an advanced stage of succession planning, closely looking at individuals as leaders, team leadership and/or individuals who can lead the entire organization.[27]

Developing the Leadership Pipeline

Talent development is the most critical aspect of managing human capital. Research shows that "best companies for leaders," working hand-in-hand with succession planning, create a leadership pipeline through (1) encouraging leaders at all levels to create work climates that motivate all employees to perform at their best; (2) making leadership development a priority for everyone, not just an HR issue; (3) providing job shadowing opportunities for mid-career managers; (4) helping leadership teams as well as individual leaders work better together; (5) ensuring high-potential individuals have 360-degree feedback; (6) providing mid-level managers with leadership development early in their careers; and (7) providing external coaches to senior managers.[28] By using a number of leadership development options, companies can foster a more inclusive and extensive group of potential leaders (see Table 11.4).

As highlighted in the *SHRM/Catalyst Employee Development Survey Report*, 80 percent of organizations use a number of initiatives to develop future leaders (e.g., formal coaching, job rotation, high-visibility assignments, formal career mentoring, leadership forums, identification of high potentials, succession planning). In general, large organizations use leadership training (88 percent) and development planning (79 percent) more than medium-sized organizations (81 percent and 76 percent, respectively) and small organizations (50 percent and 57 percent). And 49 percent of organizations effectively identify high-potential employees, while 25 percent do not.[29] Casting a wide web to expand the leadership pipeline translates into more potential talent. For example, at Sonoco Products, a large manufacturer of packaging products, the succession process considers lower-level employees with leadership potential as well as senior management. By identifying linchpin positions (those essential to the long-term health of the firm) and including middle management, a company can develop a broader talent pool. A transparent succession planning process also helps to identify additional talent. For example, at Eli Lilly, a top company in succession management, the HR managers and the succession management team can access the company intranet-based succession management tool to consider an employee's current level, potential level, experience and development plans.[30]

Ensuring a diverse mix of people in the leadership pipeline—such as women and racial/ethnic minority groups—further adds to available skills. However, research shows that organizations are not optimizing leadership development opportunities for diverse groups. Common barriers to minority advancement, for example, are the scarcity of mentors and personal networks, the lack of visible assignments and significant line experience, and, for women in particular, family responsibilities. Solutions include holding managers accountable for training on diversity and associated attitudes and behaviors as well as progress on diversity metrics. Organizations can also provide work/life support to their workforce. However, research shows that only 38 percent of companies have formal diversity and inclusion initiatives, and of these, 25 percent offer leadership development programs to women and racial/ethnic minority groups. In general, formal career mentoring for women (14 percent) and racial/ethnic minority groups (13 percent) is underutilized. Large organizations with diversity initiatives and more staff devoted to diversity are twice as likely to use formal coaching and high-visibility assignments for women and racial/ethnic minority groups than are small and medium organizations.[31]

Yet developing more and better leaders is not the sole focus of the leadership pipeline. Broadly, certain themes highlight the state of leadership development today: (1) leadership development increasingly occurs within the context of work; (2) there is critical reflection about the role of competencies in leadership development; and (3) companies are revisiting the issue

Table 11.4 Types of Leadership Development Options

Assessment	Coaching	Learning	Experience
Psychometric assessment	Internal	Individualized development planning	Stretch assignments
Multi-rater feedback	External	High-profile learning events	Outside positions and projects
Competency assessment	Mentoring	Leaders developing leaders	Action learning
Assessment centers		Partnering with thought leaders	
		Technology-based learning	
		Business school affiliations	
		Development of intact teams	

Source: Weiss, D., & Molinaro, V. (2006). Integrated leadership development. *Industrial and Commercial Training*, 38, 1, 3-12.

of work/life balance. Rather than focusing on what may be lacking, it is very important to develop and leverage strengths, along with minimizing weaknesses and looking at the whole person. Topics for leadership development increasingly include managing stress and personal renewal to avoid burnout, with health and well-being at work gaining attention.[32]

Corporate Universities

In recent years, the corporate university (CU) has gained popularity as a vehicle for leadership development. The concept of the CU emerged in the mid-19th century, when companies such as DuPont set up technical schools for prospective employees when they encountered problems recruiting talent with the requisite skills. Generally, a small core staff works closely with prestigious partners to deliver programs. The CU creates deliberate formative experiences, with comprehensive and sustained leadership development programs that serve a number of strategic priorities—integration, culture building and knowledge management—and are key change management initiatives that can, for example, restore intellectual capital lost through delayering.[33] The CU also forwards strategic drivers. BAE Systems, for example, has used its CU for post-merger integration, developing a learning organization, focusing on knowledge management across business units and developing senior leaders. Overall, the concept of the CU continues to evolve, reflecting the organization's priorities.[34]

Leadership Styles, Worldviews and Organizational Behavior

Composed of values and orientations toward people, a worldview portrays a philosophy of life. How leaders view the world is illustrated by their leadership styles and, correspondingly, by their behavior. The interrelations of worldviews and leadership styles promote specific workplace cultures that, in turn, influence organizational behavior. Worldviews also influence what key traits are emphasized for leadership development. For example, will a leadership program focus on creating partnerships? Perhaps not, if senior leaders have a bureaucratic leadership style. Enhancing relationships, for example, is a skill supported by enabling and charismatic leaders. Training that reshapes mindsets around power and influencing skills is promoted by enabling, charismatic and visionary leaders, as are action-learning and self-worth/assertiveness skills. By comparing the worldviews of its organization's leaders to organizational behavior, HR can better identify and promote appropriate training for competitive advantage in its specific industry.[35]

Assessing the Value of Leadership Development

From competition, globalization and increased expectations of shareholders, pressure to perform puts organizations in the "hot seat" to measure human capital initiatives. When considerable resources are devoted to leadership development, organizations need to know if and how these programs make a difference. Interestingly, intangible assets—as a percentage of market value—have risen from 38 percent in 1982 to 85 percent in 2000.[36] However, determining the impact of intangibles—as training is often considered—can be a challenge. In fact, according to the *SHRM/Catalyst 2005 Employee Development Survey Report*, 78 percent of organizations do not analyze the return on investment (ROI) of leadership training. For those organizations that do measure the ROI of development methods, the highest ROI comes from apprenticeships/internships (20 percent), leadership development (18 percent) and formal coaching (18 percent).[37]

Designed to provide business leaders with an interlinked view of strategy, one possible place to house the assessment of leadership value is in the four-quadrant balanced scorecard. Leadership development falls in the quadrant for innovation, learning and growth, with subtopics of human and organizational capital.[38] To measure leadership development value against strategic goals, many organizations create their own metrics. Wachovia Corporation, for example, uses business indicators to illustrate enhanced performance following training and the reduction in the number and amount of legal claims. Often, it is potential, performance and growth that offer good measures. Unilever, for example, assesses the value of leadership development by answering specific questions, such as "are leaders clear about what the business wants to do" and "did the business grow its bottom line?" Thus, it is hard business results, influenced by effective leadership development, that illustrate an impact on the bottom line.[39]

Global Leadership Development

A recent global leadership survey that explored how organizations identify and develop future leaders illustrates the leadership gap that companies are struggling with today. A negative correlation was found between a firm's need to hire outside leaders and its confidence to meet future growth needs. In the next five to seven years, for example, 75 percent of companies expect to hire 25 percent or more of their leaders from the outside. However, only 57 percent of organizations have been formally identifying and developing high-potential talent for less than three years.[40] This information has important implications for the pipeline of global leaders, suggesting that the global leadership gap may be even wider than originally known.

A survey of CEOs and 1,000 senior executives of more than 75 companies in 28 countries highlights that "global literacy is the new leadership competence required for business success. To be globally literate means seeing, thinking, acting and mobilizing in culturally minded ways." Two key predictors of success in the global marketplace are leadership development across all levels of the company and valuing multicultural experiences/competencies. As the world becomes more economically integrated, the ability to value and leverage cultural differences is one of the top global literacies.[41]

Evans, Pucik and Barsoux, experts in global HR management, point out that it is the global mindset—a state of mind—that differentiates global managers due to their ability to work effectively across organizational, functional and cross-cultural boundaries. HR can foster development of the global mindset by ensuring that talented employees worldwide—no matter their passport country—have equal access to opportunities (see Table 11.5). The strongest mechanism to develop a global mindset is the international assignment. In addition, multinational corporations, such as General Electric, Unilever and Johnson & Johnson, have effectively used in-house experiential action-learning programs for a broad cross-section of high-potential employees to speed up the development of the global mindset.[42]

Table 11.5 Most Effective Practices to Develop Global Business Leaders

1. Longer-term international assignments.
2. International cross-function team participation.
3. Internal management/executive development programs.
4. Development of global management teams.
5. Mentoring and/or coaching.
6. International leader development centers.
7. 360-degree feedback.

Source: Kramer, R. J. (2005). Developing global leaders: *Enhancing competencies and accelerating the expatriate experience.* New York: The Conference Board.

Thus, in today's global marketplace, effective cross-cultural leaders are those who are able to behave differently in different cultures and respect different values, work ethics, business protocols and the cultural diversity of their workforce. Successfully leading organizations in the 21st century requires emotional and cultural intelligence to understand regional and ethnical cultural diversity of global working environments and cross-cultural communities worldwide. The concept of emotional intelligence has been around for some time. Yet cultural intelligence is a relatively new concept, described as the ability to switch national and/or ethnic contexts and quickly learn new patterns of social interaction with appropriate behavioral responses. Linking global business success and future career paths with cultural competence is an important area for corporate trainers to emphasize, so that managers are motivated to learn new behaviors and skills and understand the benefits of learning from different cultures. Yet while role plays, case studies and simulations are helpful to develop cultural intelligence, it is immersion in the culture itself that truly makes the difference.[43]

For multinational corporations, moving talent across organizational silos via succession management helps develop leaders in different businesses and geographies. Procter & Gamble is particularly rigorous about global talent management, requiring a prior overseas assignment for candidates for president of a business line. Some companies are exploring actions to help speed up global leadership development. A relatively new approach is sending high-potential employees on foreign assignments early in their careers for a period of six months to a year. However, 86 percent of companies that use this development method have rated it as not very effective or only moderately effective. Another innovative approach is to move experience to people, rather than people to experiences, by reengineering development opportunities (e.g., company action-learning projects for international collaboration experiences). Yet while it may seem like a good idea to accelerate development, complex leadership and cultural lessons are often best learned in stages. It takes time to truly develop a global leader, from working with different cultures and understanding complex relationships to developing cultural skills and attitudes to behave effectively in a multinational context.[44] Today, with the dramatic economic growth in Asia-Pacific in recent years and a forecast that by 2015 this region will account for 45 percent of the world's gross domestic product, much of the attention of the business world has been focused on Asia-Pacific. Local and international companies are working hard toward effective leadership development. A major challenge is the current limited supply of leadership capability in contrast to the anticipated need and the resulting severe competition for talent. For example, in some sectors, Bangalore and Shanghai have annual turnover rates greater than 40 percent. International organizations are seeking to reduce the number of expatriates and localize leadership. Key benefits of local leadership are speaking the local language and understanding the nuances of Asian cultures. Other drivers to develop leaders in Asia-Pacific include substantial growth prospects for business, availability of raw talent, expansion of learning infrastructure in commercial and government facets, diversity and inclusion programs, corporate social responsibility programs, and international expansion along with the success of local/regional firms. However, the challenges are many: incumbent expatriates, low mobility, high turnover and escalating salaries from competition for talent, capability of HR professionals in some locations, and preservation of established company cultures, networks and behaviors.[45]

Studies on Leadership Development

Recent studies highlight today's best practices and challenges regarding leadership development.

A New Paradigm for Leadership Development[46]

Due to the changing role of business (e.g., demographic shifts, globalization and degradation of natural resources) and the corresponding critical challenges that demand immediate responses from organizations, a new paradigm for leadership development is evolving. The Center for Creative Leadership is examining leadership at the organizational level, focusing on building connections across boundaries, establishing leadership practices for interdependent work and developing interdependent cultures. The underlying belief is that being highly flexible in a changing environment increasingly requires organizations to use collaboration, action-learning and shared mental models to not only drive leadership capability but also become more proactive in addressing critical challenges. Critical challenges necessitate new learning, creativity and rapid decisive action, yet they also require individuals and organizations to slow down and carefully reflect on situations.

What Makes Great Leaders: Rethinking the Route to Effective Leadership[47]

The most-admired organizations on the Fortune 500 list have strong leadership development practices: (1) emphasis on ongoing development efforts closely linked to strategic business goals and supported by formal reward programs; (2) frequent use of competency models as well as a wide variety of developmental programs to select and advance leaders; (3) low tolerance of inappropriate behavior in order to "meet the numbers;" and (4) emotional intelligence of leaders. Successful leaders create workplace environments that foster performance, pride and purpose, always remember whom they are leading and do not support performance at any cost. They can build relationships with diverse groups of people, create a believable vision, motivate others and negotiate a wide range of business and social situations.

Leadership Succession Planning Affects Commercial Success[48]

This global leadership survey of 19 industries explored how organizations identify and develop future leaders. The study findings note a significant negative correlation between a firm's need to hire outside leaders and its confidence to meet future growth needs. To successfully develop future leaders, specific resources are important for high-potential individuals: (1) a chief executive who is actively involved in the development of future leaders; (2) significant roles that truly tax the abilities of high potentials; (3) coaching relationships within the organization; (4) senior executives who are involved in the mentoring relationships; and (5) external executive education programs.

How Top Companies Grow Great Leaders[49]

In a survey of 375 U.S. public and private companies, 20 companies were found to be the most effective at leadership development. A key enabler was active involvement by the board of directors and the CEO. In top companies, 83 percent with active CEO involvement in leadership development performed at the 75th percentile or higher in total shareholder return, compared with 56 percent that performed below the 25th percentile. Additionally, at 65 percent of top companies, board members were directly involved in leadership development. A wide range of developmental opportunities was provided: 95 percent offered mentoring, compared with 45 percent of other companies, and 90 percent had a defined process for assimilating leadership into new positions, compared with 44 percent. Effective companies emphasized developing talent across the organization, with 85 percent of top companies holding leaders accountable for developing others, compared with 46 percent of other companies. Further, 20 percent or more of a leader's annual incentive was dedicated to accountability of people development, compared with 10 percent at most companies.

Trends for Leadership Development

In closing, many forces—information technology, global competition, retiring baby boomers, the need for rapid and flexible organizations and teams and differing employee needs—are shaping future leadership requirements. "Nontraditional business" factors, such as international markets, world economic trends and focus on regions (e.g., the Asia-Pacific), are influencing leadership needs. Keeping up with international trends will be essential for business success. In the future, HR will see new perspectives regarding leadership that will significantly change the thinking about, approaches to and practices of leadership development (see Table 11.6).[50]

Table 11.6 Six Trends for Leadership Development

1. Importance of leadership competencies.
2. Globalization/internationalization of leadership concepts, constructs and development methods.
3. The role of technology for communication with a geographically diverse workforce.
4. Increasing interest in the integrity and character of leaders.
5. Pressure to demonstrate return on investment.
6. New ways of thinking about the nature of leadership and leadership development.

Source: Adapted from Hernez-Broome, G., & Hughes, R. L. (2004). Leadership development: Past, present and future. *HR. Human Resource Planning, 27*, 1, 24-33.

Chapter 12

Motivation in Today's Workplace: The Link to Performance

In today's marketplace, where companies seek a competitive edge, motivation is key for talent retention and performance. No matter the economic environment, the goal is to create a workplace that is engaging and motivating, where employees want to stay, grow and contribute their knowledge, experience and expertise.

> *Motivation* is generally defined as the psychological forces that determine the direction of a person's level of effort, as well as a person's persistence in the face of obstacles. The *direction of a person's behavior* refers to the many possible actions that a person could engage in, while *persistence* refers to whether, when faced with roadblocks and obstacles, an individual keeps trying or gives up.[1]

The responsibility for motivation is three-fold: it falls on the senior leadership, the direct manager and the employee. Numerous factors are involved, from trust, engagement and values (individual and organizational) to job satisfaction, achievement, acknowledgement and rewards. Motivation is essential for working autonomously, as well as for collaboration and effective teamwork. The ultimate focus of the organization is to successfully retain talent, meet goals and go beyond expectations. It is the role of HR and organizational leaders to foster an environment for excellence. Through a foundation of research, theory, studies and practical examples, this article addresses the questions of what motivates employees, what managers need to do, and what supports motivation and, thus, performance.

What Influences Motivation?

Motivating employees for better performance encompasses these critical factors: employee engagement, organizational vision and values, management acknowledgment and appreciation of work well done, and overall authenticity of leadership. Chana Anderson, CCP, SPHR-CA, director of HR and a member of the SHRM Employee Relations Special Expertise Panel, says that motivation is influenced equally by the employee and the company: "Motivation and engagement is truly a 50-50 relationship between the employee and employer. Employees are expected to come to the workplace with the intrinsic motivation and desire to be successful, be value-added and contribute to the obtainment of an employer's vision. Conversely, it is incumbent upon the employer to provide resources, opportunities, recognition and a cohesive work environment for employees to be successful."

Employee Engagement

Engagement influences motivation. It is reflected in the extent to which employees commit, how hard they work and how long they stay. People join organizations for different reasons, motivated by intrinsic and extrinsic rewards. Intrinsic rewards are reflected in actions believed to be important. Examples include an employee who wants to help people by providing excellent customer service or a senior manager who gains a sense of accomplishment from overseeing a large corporation. Intrinsic outcomes include responsibility, autonomy, feelings of accomplishment and the pleasure of doing interesting work. Extrinsic-motivated behavior includes actions performed with the goal to have material or social rewards, with outcomes such as job security, benefits, vacation time and public recognition. It is the responsibility of managers to motivate employees, with the goal for employees to contribute to the organization. Managers can best motivate employees by offering rewards that are meaningful to them.[2]

Vision and Values

Employees are often motivated differently. To develop a work environment that promotes motivation, organizations need to know what is important to their employees and then to emphasize these factors. In fact, some companies and researchers are beginning to look at "work spirituality"—not in a religious sense, but in a sense that what an employee does aligns with his or her greater sense of life and purpose. Aside from monetary gain, work provides people with fulfillment on various levels, from earning a living and "doing good work" to aspiring to a vision and ultimately having an impact on the quality of life. These reasons can change over time in response to changes in people's home life and responsibilities.

Further, in response to drastic economic changes and natural disasters, companies can change over time as well.[3]

Management Acknowledgment and Appreciation

How employees are treated is a strong determinant of employee motivation and performance. Edward E. Lawler III, author and consultant for human resource management, emphasizes that "treating people right is fundamental to creating organizational effectiveness and success. It is also easier said than done." According to Lawler, this includes "a highly complex set of actions on the part of both organizations and employees. Organizations must develop ways to treat their employees so that they are motivated and satisfied; employees must behave in ways to help their organizations become effective and high-performing." This winning combination for performance requires a partnership between the organization and the employees. Lawler states: "One can't succeed without the other. To provide people with meaningful work and rewards, organizations need to be successful. And to be successful, organizations need high-performing individuals. The challenge is to design organizations that perform at high levels and treat people in ways that are rewarding and satisfying." To describe this mutually beneficial relationship, Lawler uses the term *virtuous spiral*, a relationship that occurs when the organization values its employees, and in return, workers are committed to high performance.[4]

Leadership and Making a Difference

In today's pressure-cooker environment, performance is carefully noted at all levels of the organization. No matter an individual's title, everyone has the opportunity to lead in some capacity and have a positive impact on performance. Understanding the value that can be achieved through different roles is one way of providing motivation, performance and thus leadership skills. A recent article published on Knowledge@Wharton, titled "Putting a Face to a Name: The Art of Motivating Employees," emphasizes that workers have better results when they can identify with those they serve. Specifically, face-to-face interactions and task significance ("*what I do makes a difference*") are key drivers for motivation and performance. Research by Adam Grant, Ph.D., a Wharton management professor, indicates that making human connections is critical for motivation, leadership and high job performance. He found that face-to-face interactions—no matter how superficial—can lead to significant improvements in performance, and that motivation and performance increase simply by an employee's awareness of the impact of his or her job on others. Dr. Grant has observed this result through studies of all types of jobs and roles in the workplace, from customer service representatives, managers, nurses, doctors and medical technicians to security guards, engineers, salespeople, police officers and fire fighters—based on when people can directly see the impact of their efforts.[5]

Mini Case Study

In a study published in the *Journal of Applied Psychology*, Dr. Grant found that lifeguards at a community recreation center who read about how their ability to avoid fatalities made a difference were stronger leaders/performers. Their work improved by 40 percent in contrast to lifeguards who merely learned that lifeguarding can be personally enriching. Grant points out that in today's economy, where work is often virtual without the end user physically present, "it is important for employers to build in systems that reinforce employees' awareness of whom they are helping."[6] As HR leaders work on processes and systems designed to improve motivation and performance, it is important to be cognizant of the issue of technology and how it can create distance between employees and the end users of their work. Dr. Grant suggests that focus on the mission of the organization is one way to overcome the challenge of a virtual workplace and lack of direct interaction and is a successful strategy for creating the energy for motivation necessary to achieve high performance and quality of service.

Leadership for Motivation

To reach the hearts and minds of employees, leaders need to be authentic with an impelling vision. "It is exceedingly important for a leader of any organization to communicate his or her vision constantly to ensure that there is no doubt about the direction a team is heading," says Ken Blanchard, world-renowned management coach. He emphasizes: "One of the most destructive traits a leader can have today is arrogance—acting like you've got it together all the time. On the other hand, one of the most endearing qualities a leader can have is to be in touch with his or her vulnerability. It's that side of a leader that keeps the vision from crumbling under the pressure of circumstance."[7] In addition, leaders need to connect the organization's vision and values to the employees' day-to-day work and help them see how the work they do every day connects to the bigger picture. The 2009 study *Best Companies for Leadership* conducted by Bloomberg BusinessWeek.com and the Hay Group reveals that leading companies were focused on leadership even during the recent economic downtown. This annual study ranks the best companies for leadership and examines how they develop leaders.

The 2009 study found a shift in what the top 20 leading organizations value regarding leadership. Specifically, the most valued qualities in leaders are strategic thinking and inspiring leadership. In a press release, John Larrere, national director of Hay Group's Leadership and Talent Practice, and co-leader of the Best Companies for Leadership Study, stated: "For organizations to succeed, they will need to understand what key leadership elements are paramount in driving their organizations toward growth. It's more than just getting people to produce the right outcomes. It's about getting them to be passionate about their work and grooming them to handle the challenges ahead. The Best Companies for Leadership have tabled this out."[8] According to this study, companies are now focusing their efforts on positioning for the future. To do so, 94 percent of the best companies have leadership development programs to enable employees to deliver on goals/strategies, 90 percent provide all employees with the opportunity to develop and practice the capabilities needed to lead others, and 87 percent have a sufficient number of internal candidates ready to assume open leadership positions. In fact, 94 percent of the best companies actively manage a pool of successors for mission-critical roles, 83 percent invest a great deal in their people, and 80 percent promote growth opportunities. In addition, 95 percent use corporate social responsibility to recruit employees, 66 percent have a high proportion of women in senior leadership, 91 percent make it easy for people to work from home, and 91 percent have an appreciation of global issues as a key job requirement. Finally, the best companies for leadership focus on employee engagement through commitment and discretionary effort and on employee enablement, with optimized roles and a supportive environment, leading to financial success, customer satisfaction and employee performance—*all* to drive organizational performance.[9]

In today's economy, leaders need to be mindful of economic pressures when looking for ways to motivate employees. Some organizations find cost-effective ways to provide opportunities through "developmental assignments," where people can grow their skills in other areas to be ready for promotions when they may occur. A good manager will take the time to consider ways to motivate employees, whether performance levels are good or need improvement. For the leader, it is beneficial to take a step back and consider, on a personal level, what is motivating oneself. Important questions to ask are: (1) what are your own values; (2) what keeps you motivated; (3) how are your own engagement levels; (4) are you committed to the values of your company; and (5) do you take pride in your work and in your organization? By taking the time to examine these questions and thoughtfully answer them, a leader can gain a refreshed and even enlightened viewpoint to perform better—both for him/herself and for his or her staff—and be able to better optimize for improvement. By identifying three areas that need most attention, for example, a leader can develop a plan and put it into action.[10] "It is exceedingly important for a leader of any organization to communicate his or her vision constantly to ensure that there is no doubt about the direction a team is heading."

Employees need to have acknowledgment and respect and know that their contributions are valued. It cannot be stressed enough how demotivating it can be when managers do not recognize, acknowledge or appreciate employees and their hard work. Two strategies that can help motivate employees are (1) to provide training (including current job, new technologies and the ability to keep up with changes in the employees' areas of expertise) and (2) promotional opportunities (promote from within).[11]

Positive and supportive leadership clearly makes the difference for an engaged and motivated workforce. In an interview with *Hospitals and Health Networks*, Jo Manion, R.N., Ph.D., points to the bottom line for hospital and patient care, as outlined in her book, *The Engaged Workforce: Proven Strategies to Build a Positive Health Care Workforce*.[12] Since excellent health care is critical for everyone at different points in life, employee motivation that results in excellent

Inspired Staff Make the Difference in Difficult Times[13]

In the health care field, engaged and motivated employees make the difference in patient care. From her years as a nurse and executive working in hospitals, Dr. Manion emphasizes that it is hospital leaders who hold the key to promoting passion in employees for their work, thus retaining essential talent and saving the organization money. By establishing a workplace that promotes well-being, leadership can inspire staff, resulting in loyalty to the organization and to the patients and their families. "If you have engaged workers who are happy to be there, who feel happy about what they do, who feel respected, who feel honored, then they treat people the same way: It ripples. Patients can pick up unhappiness in employees in a nanosecond." She urges leaders to know and understand their employees. Also, through workforce mapping, HR leaders can better understand the demographics of the workforce, learn who plans to retire in five years and then be able to look to the future for retention and hiring. The quality of patient service depends on an inspired and motivated staff.

Source: *The Engaged Workforce: Proven Strategies to Build a Positive Health Care Workforce* (American Hospital Association, 2009)

patient care is one example of motivation that all can relate to on personal and professional levels (see text box).

Motivational Theories

As HR professionals seek to support their organizations in attracting and retaining the best and brightest talent, motivational theories can offer insight into how to motivate employees, what is important and what the rewards may be—with the ultimate goal of improved and/or sustained performance by individual employees and the organization as a whole. Motivation is at the heart of performance, essential for success for both the organization and its workforce, as a group and as individuals. Dr. Teresa A. Daniel and Dr. Gary S. Metcalf, authors of a SHRM white paper "The Science of Motivation," emphasize that "people join organizations for specific reasons and usually with some purpose in mind." The white paper highlights the following theories that have shaped the concept of motivation in the workplace:[14]

Expectancy Theory

Victor H. Vroom's theory suggests that motivation is high when employees believe that high levels of effort lead to high performance and high performance leads to attainment of desired outcomes.

Maslow's Hierarchy of Needs

People seek to satisfy five basic needs: physiological, safety, belongingness, self-esteem and self-actualization needs. Abraham Maslow placed these needs in a pyramid, with the most basic on the bottom and self-actualization at the top. When the lower-level needs are met, the next higher level begins to motivate behavior.

Herzberg's Motivator-Hygiene Theory

This theory from Frederick Herzberg focuses on two factors applicable to the workplace: (1) meeting basic expectations (hygiene factors) and (2) leading to increased performance (motivation factors). Examples of basic needs are a comfortable working environment, adequate pay, good relationships with coworkers and effective supervision. Motivation factors for high job satisfaction include opportunities for recognition, advancement and professional growth.

McClelland's Needs for Achievement, Affiliation and Power

In this theory from David McClelland, each person has three needs: (1) achievement—strong desire to perform well; (2) affiliation—being liked, having positive interpersonal relationships; and (3) power—the extent to which an individual desires control or influence on others. People have these needs to varying degrees.

Equity Theory

Formulated by J. Stacy Adams, this theory is about people's perceptions of fairness of their work outcomes in relation to their work inputs. It suggests that motivation is influenced by comparing one's own outcome/input ratio with others'. If an individual feels that the ratio is unfair (e.g., underappreciated, paid less), that individual's performance may decrease. In contrast, where equity is perceived, employees are more motivated to continue contributing their current levels of input for their current levels of outcomes. Motivation is usually the highest when employees perceive that they are treated with equity.

Goal-Setting Theory

Ed Locke and Gary Latham are the leading researchers of this theory. The focus is on motivating workers to contribute by meeting goals set to improve the overall performance of the organization. They suggest that goals that employees work to meet are prime determinants of their motivation and therefore performance. Goals need to be both specific (quantitative and measurable) and difficult (hard, yet not impossible).

Maslow's work on the hierarchy of needs showed that when individuals strive to fulfill their potential, they are happier. An article in the *Journal of Applied Management and Entrepreneurship* examined the influence of Maslow's humanistic views on business training and the challenges of motivating employees to learn.[15] Learning and new skills remain an essential part of organizational strategy to achieve competitive advantage. A benchmark survey conducted at the height of the recent credit crisis found that 50 percent of companies were looking at technology to improve their customer satisfaction and business success, including retaining staff and providing training to upgrade skills and attract the best caliber of talent. The following example of the pharmaceutical company Pfizer illustrates the criticality of professional development. To develop key talent and engage the company's global workforce to improve its competitiveness, Pfizer focuses on developing "Next Generation Learning Tools."[16]

Mini Case Study

In a survey of its workforce, Pfizer learned that 78percent of respondents were reluctant to improve their education due to travel time to class and work commitments. To address the need to retain talent and improve skills, Pfizer partnered with Hibernia College for a Master of Science in Pharmaceutical Medicine program for physicians and nonmedical professionals seeking to move into leadership positions. Providing flexibility, this program allowed for an interactive self-paced study, online recorded lectures and live online tutorials for direct contact with faculty. Pfizer gained business benefits: selection for the program was seen as a reward by employees, and 76 percent of students said they felt valued by the company. As a result of the company investing in them, employees were more likely to say that they will stay with Pfizer. The online master's program is seen as a strong vehicle to help the company "build the knowledge, technical skills and leadership capabilities of Pfizer's employees," noted Soeren Rasmussen, senior director at the Department of the Chief Medical Officer at Pfizer.

Another resource on motivational theories is the book *Work Motivation: History, Theory, Research, and Practice.* It offers in-depth information about behavioral science frameworks for motivation in the workplace, with a chronological review of research and theories from the end of the 19th century to the present. As pointed out by author Gary P. Latham, Ph.D., a leader in the field of motivation, the practice of science is essential for "predicting, understanding, and influencing the motivation of people in organizational settings."[17]

New Approaches

In addition to classic motivational theories, a number of recent writings contribute new ideas to the literature on workplace motivation:

1. *Primal Leadership: Realizing the Power of Emotional Intelligence.* In their 2002 book, authors Daniel Goleman, Richard Boyatzis and Annie McKee bring together decades of research on leadership. They argue: "The fundamental task of leaders is to prime good feeling in those they lead, and that occurs when a leader creates resonance—a reservoir of positivity that frees the best in people. At its root, the primal job of leadership is emotional." This theory has significance for bringing forth motivation and commitment in leadership and employees for attainment of organizational goals. In addition, Goleman's writing on emotional intelligence includes a critical facet applicable to motivation: *relationship management/inspiration.* "Leaders who inspire both create resonance and move people with a compelling vision or shared mission. Such leaders embody what they ask of others and are able to articulate a shared mission in a way that inspires others to follow. They offer a sense of common purpose beyond day-to-day tasks, making work exciting."[18]
2. *Psychological Capital: Developing the Human Competitive Edge.* In their 2007 book, researchers Fred Luthans, Carolyn M. Youssef and Bruce J. Avolio present their PsyCap theory with a compelling view of factors critical to motivation and performance. Resilience is a key component of PsyCap, defined as "the capacity to rebound or bounce back from adversity, conflict, failure, or even positive events, progress and increased responsibility." The PsyCap resiliency process is not a linear experience; rather, the assets and risk factors—as a group—are both cumulative and interactive in nature, with implications for performance and the development of resiliency of leaders, employees and organizations. For example, confidence, hope and optimism are assets in the resiliency process. The resilient leader has the ability to grow in times of turmoil, managing and integrating assets, risk factors and values. Such leaders use resiliency as a tool to assist employees to see difficult times as opportunities for advancement (career resiliency), thus owning more of the responsibility for success for themselves and for the organization.[19] As Luthans notes, "The current reality is not if employees will need to draw from their psychological capital resilience in order to recover and reinvent themselves, but *when.*"
3. *Drive: The Surprising Truth About What Motivates Us.* In his 2009 book, author Daniel H. Pink states, "The secret to high performance and satisfaction—at work, at school, and at home—is the deeply human need to direct our own lives, to learn and create new things, and to do better by ourselves and our world." Pink challenges the organizational "carrots and sticks" approach to motivation, noting that traditional rewards ("if-then") do not give people what they want and, in fact, tend to diminish intrinsic motivation and performance and can encourage unethical behaviors and foster short-term thinking. The three elements of true motivation—autonomy, mastery and purpose—will lead to greater performance, particularly when the objective is in the service of a higher cause.[20]

A Study on Employee Engagement and Motivation

The Ashridge Business School, one of the world's leading business schools, conducted a study about motivation from the employee viewpoint. While financial rewards were often mentioned, the most common were intrinsic motivators. The top most important motivator was the work itself, followed by the need for work to be challenging and interesting as well as valued and recognized by the organization. The key motivators were praise and recognition from the manager and the organization, and celebration of success. The study also found that a very important theme is the employee desire for autonomy and freedom to do his or her job, the ability to make decisions and the authority to deliver the work in a way the employee considers the best. Another important employee motivator is being trusted to get the job done—without being micro-managed. Other key themes are communication, objectives and goals, and a shared vision. Ultimately, the quality of leadership is paramount to good employee morale. Poor leadership will result in poor employee engagement and thus in poor performance. In addition to the critical function of the manager as a role model, the following key relationships are identified as essential for motivational success—all interrelated and contributing toward feelings of motivation:[21]

1. Organizational structure and processes—performance management, reward systems, training, interesting work—must be supported by a clear vision, strong communication processes, quality decision-making and an organizational culture of mutual respect.
2. Organizations need to pay attention to the working environment. For example, too many meetings and poor meeting management will have a negative impact on employees' level of motivation.
3. The individual employee needs to know what motivates him or her and be aware of how work satisfies these needs. The manager and/or organization can support this process by facilitating opportunities for employees to meet, talk and share their views with colleagues and managers.
4. Colleagues: Working with people who respect and support each other is positively motivating.

A New Model for Employee Motivation

In their 2002 book, *Driven: How Human Nature Shapes Our Choices*, researchers Paul R. Lawrence and Nitin Nohria identify four basic emotional needs/drives. These drives, based on research in cross-disciplinary fields such as biology, evolutionary psychology and neuroscience, are: (1) *acquire* (obtain scarce goods, including intangibles such as social status); (2) *bond* (form connections with individuals and groups); (3) *comprehend* (master the world around us); and (4) *defend* (protect against external threats and promote justice). Using these four drives, Nitin Norhia, Boris Groysberg and Linda-Eling Lee developed a new employee model for motivation, published in *Harvard Business Review*. They conducted two major studies to find out what actions managers can take to satisfy these drives and increase employee motivation. The study surveyed about 5,000 employees in two global companies (a financial company and an IT services firm), as well as employees from *Fortune* 500 companies, about commonly measured work indicators: engagement, commitment, satisfaction and intention to quit.[22]

These studies revealed that organizational levers of motivation can influence certain drivers and motivational indicators. For example, a reward system can satisfy the drive to acquire by discriminating between poor and good performers, tying rewards to performance and providing opportunities for advancement. A good example is that of Sonoco, a manufacturer of packaging for industrial and consumer goods, which took this approach with a pay-for-performance system. The company established very clear links between performance and rewards based on individual and group metrics. As a result, employee satisfaction and engagement improved, and the company was named by Hewitt Associates in 2005 as one of the top 20 talent management organizations in the United States.[23]

The studies also found that company culture is the most effective way for an organization to forward the drive to bond. Specifically, organizational culture can create a strong sense of camaraderie by promoting openness, collaboration, friendship and teamwork. The drive to comprehend is promoted by designing jobs that are meaningful and foster a sense of contribution to the organization. Performance management and resource allocation are tools that can increase the transparency of all processes, thereby emphasizing fairness and building trust.[24] Ultimately, culture, performance, engagement, job design and reward systems need be aligned to maximize motivation.

Table 12.1 Twelve Important Ways to Motivate Employees

1. Provide employees with the information and resources they need to do a good job.
2. Ask employees for their input by involving them in decisions that affect their jobs.
3. Find out directly from employees what motivates them.
4. Personally congratulate employees for their excellent work.
5. Recognize the needs of employees.
6. Establish good channels of communication–be (physically) accessible and available.
7. Use performance as the basis for promotion.
8. Have a promote-from-within policy.
9. Publicly recognize employees for good work (if culturally appropriate to do so publicly).
10. Include recognition as part of morale-building activities to celebrate group success.
11. Have clear goals.
12. Foster a sense of community.

Source: Adapted from Top 20 ways to motivate employees. (September 2008). *SuperVision*, 69/9, 26.

Recognition and Rewards Programs

As emphasized earlier, for employees to remain motivated, recognition is essential. Direct line managers have one of the most important roles regarding recognition. Their communication style—or lack of communication—stands out as critical for successful recognition. Recognizing good performance is also a key factor in talent retention. Different types of reward and incentive programs are effective at motivating employees. Motivation may be promoted through monetary and nonmonetary rewards.

A recent SHRM survey report found that 58 percent of HR professionals overall indicated that their organizations offered some form of incentive bonus plans: 50 percent offered a bonus plan to executive employees and 45 percent to nonexecutive employees. Incentive bonus plans can promote high performance because the bonus is usually tied directly to company and/or individual performance. In addition, some benefits programs include employee recognition. Seventy percent of HR professionals indicated that their organizations recognized milestones such as birthdays and service anniversaries. More than half of HR professionals said their organizations offered some type of noncash, companywide performance awards such as gift certificates or an extra day off.[25]

Motivating the Millennial Generation

As highlighted in Chapter 9, the Millennial generation brings forth new challenges for motivation and engagement. This group of young workers has a distinctly different set of expectations than other generations.[26] Cam Marson, author of *Motivating the "What's in it for me" Workforce*, notes that while Millennials expect to be accommodated by their employer, it is strongly recommended that young workers learn everything they can from the older generations. He points out that the Millennial workers have a responsibility in the work relationship, too, and that it is not all about them.[27]

Further, in a unique position in time, Millennials are the first generation to be part of a truly global economy. Most have had access to technology all of their lives. A 2010 study by Accenture explored how students and young workers in 13 countries use technology in their personal and professional lives. The findings are important for HR and organizational leaders because there is a direct line to talent management. The study points out that companies that "fail to embrace Millennial behavior are at risk of failing to attract and retain new hires, while also seeing their competitive edge erode from lack of innovation in information technology." Regardless of country, Millennials are jumping ahead of the boundaries of corporate IT. They expect to use their own technology/devices in the workplace, and 45 percent of Millennials globally use social networking sites at work, even if there is a corporate policy prohibiting it. Additionally, 72 percent of Millennials in India, 52 percent in the United States and 45 percent in China say that an important factor in their choice of employer is the organization's use of state-of-the-art equipment.[28] Thus, to be competitive today, HR and organizational leaders must understand what motivates the Millennial generation and learn to use these factors to the advantage of both the employee and the employer.

Global HRM and Motivation

In an interview about motivation, SHRM talked with Kenneth Somers, a member of the SHRM Global Special Expertise Panel. Somers has more than 30 years of experience in senior HR leadership roles, working both domestically and internationally in global organizations. This exchange offers a close-up view of key aspects about motivation and performance in today's global marketplace.

SHRM: In the global HRM context, when you think of motivation—regarding the individual employee and as a key factor for organizational performance—what are some of the top issues that come to mind and why are they important in today's global workplace?

Somers: This is a place where the research and my own anecdotal experience coalesce. Employees everywhere are recession and RIF weary. Those whose positions have not been affected by reductions are looking for signs that "it" is over. Neither businesses nor governments have defined the "new normal." Most people are hunkered down and only marginally engaged. The corollary is that businesses will be impeded in their attempts to tap into employees' discretionary capacity.

SHRM: In your experience in the global marketplace, what are some of the primary motivators for employees and why are they important for HR leaders and organizational leaders to know?

Somers: I believe there are more motivators we hold in common than those that differentiate us. In my experience, employees everywhere want to feel respected and treated fairly, to work for an employer in which they have pride and to have an opportunity to grow. What is critical is for HR and business leaders to understand how these universals manifest in varying cultures. Understanding and applying those learnings with sincerity and consistency is the table stakes for successfully motivating performance across borders.

SHRM: What are some of the ways that HR leaders can create a workplace that is motivating in a global company, and why would this make a difference for overall performance—of employees and, thus, the organization?

Somers: There are many things that employers can do to stimulate greater engagement. If you agree that the bigger challenge is to create sustainable engagement, it then follows that sustainable engagement flows from consistent, high-quality people leadership. Employers need to take these steps:

- **Communicate with staff on a regular basis:** Everyone understands the world has changed. Explain what is going on, how it affects the business and the resulting impact on people. Tell the truth without drama. But even more importantly, tell a story about where you are going. Engagement also flows from people buying into a future and wanting to be part of it.
- **Follow communications with actions that are consistent with the messaging.** If part of the future story is to capture market share from a previously untapped segment, create and implement measures that show staff you meant what you said and are acting on the message.
- **Share status reports.** This is part of ongoing communications but is particularly focused on letting people know "how we're doing." Celebrate successes and be candid about needed course corrections.
- **Recognize achievements.** You may not be able to award big bonuses or significant merit adjustments, but a lot can be gained by saying thank you and encouraging further development and success.
- **Give feedback.** Many leaders would prefer to crawl under their desks in times like these. We need to be visible to be able to accomplish the prior points. And when it comes to managing performance, remember that your teams know who is pulling their weight and who is not. Engagement also depends on people perceiving a leader's ability to step up and do the right thing—especially when it is hard.

While the particular "how's" of these ideas will vary from country to country and from culture to culture, I think the principles are fairly universal.

SHRM: Finally, in a global workplace, what are three of the most important ways a manager can portray behaviors and attitudes that relate to employee motivation?

Somers: This is simple to say and, of course, harder to actually do. But it boils down to these:

- **Model the corporate values—all the time.** If business leaders behave consistent with the espoused corporate values, those in the population who don't subscribe will self-select out.
- **Listen with genuine intent.** People want to be heard. They will not always agree with your decisions, but they will be more accepting if they feel they have had a chance to express views and/or concerns.
- **Deliver on the commitments you make.** In many geographies, you get only one chance to demonstrate your reliability.

Conclusion

Organizational success cannot be achieved without strong leadership and a focused, thoughtful work environment that promotes motivation. No matter the industry, HR leaders need to be in touch with what is important to employees and to work with senior management to foster a motivated workplace based on trust, recognition and acknowledgment, for optimal engagement and performance.

Chapter 13

Performance Management: Getting It Right from the Start

Most would agree that establishing a company performance management system is a significant undertaking. But how can you ensure that you get it right from the start? HR practice leaders have grappled with this issue for decades. Academic and professional journals abound with ideas and approaches too numerous to count. Yet making recommendations and choices about program components from among a perplexing number of growing choices and their associated variables remain a dilemma.

What we do know for certain is that a steady shift has occurred over time in the workplace in relation to human resources. Work now requires more knowledge and skills than ever before, i.e., organizations are more dependent on human capital as an intangible asset (Figure 13.1).[1, 2] As a result, organizations are, or it would appear they should be, interested in optimizing the way this asset is managed. Establishing an effective performance management system is an organization's way of doing just that. After all,

> *"...a great deal of theory concerned with human motivation and human development argues that an effective performance management system should be a key building block of every organization's human capital management system. To tie performance to rewards (the key to motivating performance), organizations need to have accurate measures of individual performance. To develop, individuals need feedback about their strengths and weaknesses. Organizations, meanwhile, need performance information to direct their training and development resources to those individuals who can gain the most by them. Finally, organizations need performance information to correct performance problems and assess the effectiveness of their improvement efforts."*[3]

Figure 13.1 | Why Is It So Difficult to Execute Strategy?

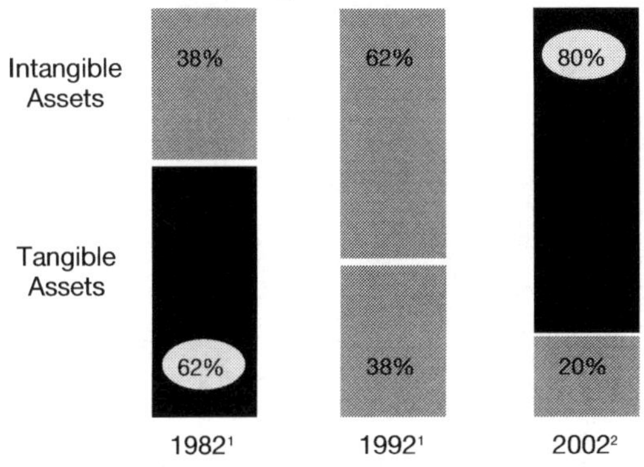

1. Brookings Institution analysis of S&P500 companies
2. Kaplan & Norton

Background

However, many of us have heard the adage, "the road is paved with good intentions." Based on a review of pertinent research studies, it would seem then that a parallel could be drawn between performance management systems and corporate business plans. According to Robert Kaplan and David Norton, the authors and developers of the Balanced Scorecard, less than 10 percent of all strategic business plans are effectively executed. Companies worldwide are facing unprecedented competitive pressures. Whether we are ready or not, competitive pressures will force the transformation of the performance management function in most organizations. In fact, the compensation function in organizations with high-performance work systems (HPWS) is already showing signs of change. These organizations understand that pay and performance management can play a strategic role in attracting and retaining key employees, and they are beginning to engage in innovative approaches to performance management to improve business performance. As a result, HR practice leaders specializing in total rewards management are now required to have a thorough understanding of the business in order to align performance reward programs properly.

Finally, while companies worldwide want their employees to perform well across the board, there is an increasing focus on key talent—those critical few employees who, by virtue of their skills, will and do play an important role in creating shareholder value. How will organizations go about identifying, rewarding and retaining this talent? These are the individuals who form and maintain pivotal relationships with customers, fulfill the vision for the organization, lead and motivate others, establish goals, remove obstacles, identify resources and tools, and know when it's time to move new leaders forward who can make a difference.

Making the Business Case

HR practice leaders have long held the belief that a company's performance management system can lay the foundation required to support the strategic planning efforts of the organization. Although the empirical research to support these hypotheses and demonstrate the economic impact of performance management activities is limited, there are credible research studies available to amply demonstrate what can be accomplished when a qualified plan is placed in motion. Four of these studies are highlighted here.

Corporate Culture and Performance Study

This groundbreaking 11-year study included more than 200 companies from 22 industries and compared financial and operational performance measures of companies with performance-enhancing cultures to those companies whose cultures did not exhibit performance-enhancing characteristics. It demonstrates how unwritten rules and/or shared values can either lead to the success or to a failure to adapt to changing markets and the environment (Table 13.1).[4] As the authors point out, fundamental to the process of establishing a "performance-enhancing" culture is effective leadership.

Table 13.1 Impact of Performance-Enhancing Culture on Corporate Performance

	Organizations With Performance-Enhancing Cultures	Organizations Without Performance-Enhancing Cultures
Revenue growth	682%	166%
Employment growth	282%	36%
Stock price growth	901%	74%
Net income growth	756%	1%

From "Corporate Culture and Performance," John P. Kotter and James L. Heskett, p. 78

High-Performance Work System Index

The second study, which was based on 429 firms in 1998, is actually the fourth biennial survey (i.e., prior survey years: 1992, 1994, 1996) representing a combined total of 2,800 firms. As with the previous study, this survey compared specific HR management policies and practices determined to influence the quality of high-performing employees over an extended period of time. Survey results for the bottom 10 percent of firms (42) versus the top 10 percent of firms (43) were compared. At the conclusion of the study, the results totaled $158,101 versus $617,576, respectively, in sales per employee, versus $3.64 to $11.06 market value to book value per share of stock, and a turnover rate of 34.09 percent to 20.87 percent, respectively. This distinction represents a 391 percent return on investment for the top 10 percent of firms. How was this accomplished? According to the authors,

> *"the most striking attribute of these comparisons is not any one HR management practice—it is not recruiting or training or compensation. Rather, the differences are much more comprehensive—and systemic ... the very best firms in our sample are much more likely to have developed a clear strategic intent and communicated it effectively to employees."*[5]

Current Performance Management Practices: Center for Effective Organizations/University of Southern California

This 2003 survey of 55 HR managers from medium and large companies, mostly members of the Fortune 500, was conducted by the Center for Effective Organizations at the University of Southern California (USC). As noted by the authors, there is little research data to establish the impact of many practices recommended in the writings on performance management, nor is there much information available to HR practice leaders about what companies are actually doing at this time. This study attempts to bridge the gap between these two voids. A representative sampling of the data collected and resulted is provided in Table 13.2.[6] This particular dataset suggests that senior management plays an important role in the establishment of the performance management system in most companies. However, the findings also indicate that, as a general rule, there is little accountability in relation to how well managers may or may not do appraisals, nor are there "calibration meetings" in use for comparison purposes to ensure the validity of the system companywide. Interestingly, there is a strong direct relationship between leadership by senior management and ownership of performance by line management, and in favor of the use of calibration meetings as part of the performance management system. That is, the stronger the leadership by senior management, the more likely line management took ownership of their performance. As such, the authors concluded that senior and line management ownership in the performance management system should be fostered, to include

Table 13.2 Managerial Behavior

	Percent Frequency						Correlation Coefficient	
	Little or No Extent	Some Extent	Moderate Extent	Great Extent	Very Great Extent	Mean	Perf. Management System Effectiveness	Differentiation Effectiveness
Leadership by senior management	5	13	16	35	31	3.7	.63***	.47***
Appraisal of how well managers do appraisals	54	15	22	6	4	1.9	.51***	.31***
Calibration meetings that compare ratings of the effectiveness of the system	24	18	18	20	20	3.0	.33*	.37**
Measures of the effectiveness of the system	20	36	15	18	11	2.6	.60***	.33*
Line management participation in system design and development	16	20	22	27	15	30	.39**	.25
	6	19	28	31	17	3.4	.72***	.43***
Ownership of performance management by HR	9	16	22	31	22	3,4	.22	.08

Note: For Correlation Coefficients * = Significant at the .05 level. ** = Significant at the .01 level. *** = Significant at the .001 level.

accountability for the completion of the performance appraisals in keeping with company requirements, as well as their calibration corporatewide to check for rater bias.

Working Today: Understanding What Drives Employee Engagement–The 2003 Towers Perrin Talent Report

The fourth study, completed in April 2003, represents the views of more than 35,000 employees in U.S. companies, and updates and expands a prior study completed just two years ago. As noted in the study, engagement remains the ultimate prize for employers, and the "endgame" is the same for everyone: discretionary effort. Competitive advantage has become a difficult goal to achieve and an even more difficult advantage to retain. Building momentum through an engaged workforce takes more than an expression of management commitment—what leading employers are learning is that consistent management practices in a positive and challenging work environment, day in and day out, make the difference. Highlights from this report in relation to how employees view their pay and bonus programs are summarized in Figure 13.2.[7]

Figure 13.2 | Employee Views of Pay

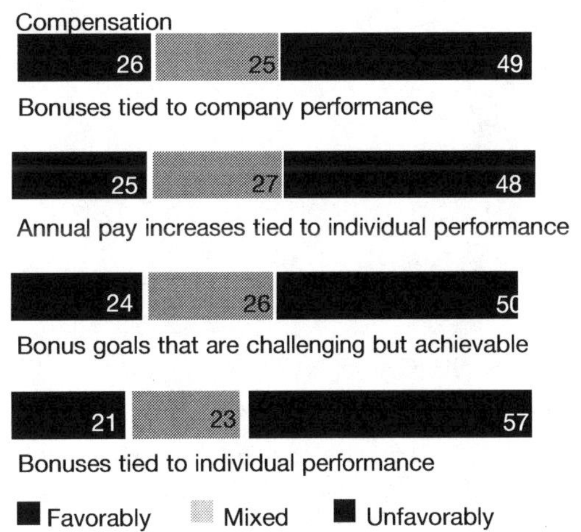

Source: The 2003 Towers Perrin Talent Report.

Performance Management–Critical Success Factors

Periodically, a question will be raised about why people are so fascinated with monitoring the popular press on which companies have topped the list of *America's Most Admired Companies* (AMAC)? By way of background, to be eligible for consideration, a company must be listed on the *Fortune* 500. From there, a questionnaire is sent to more than 12,000 executives within the companies, to include their respective board members, and the financial analysts who represent that particular industry. Ballot recipients then vote within their respective industry. The Most Admired Companies in America study ranks participants based on eight key attributes; a ninth is added for the Global Most Admired Companies Study (see Table 13.3).[8] A company's final score is the average of all the scores that the company receives on the various attributes. If the financial indicators are separated, four out of the eight or nine remaining attributes speak to what the human resources or the human capital assets contribute to the organization: innovativeness, the overall quality of the management, the ability to attract and retain talented people, and the quality of the products or services. The success of each of these factors is ultimately dependent on the people that are engaged, the opportunities for growth and development offered to them, and the degree of focus the organization is able to maintain over time. But, getting back to the original question—over the last five years, shareholder returns for AMAC have been 26 percent versus 11 percent for their peer companies, or two and a half times the return.

Table 13.3 *Fortune* Survey of Most Admired Companies

Eight key attributes:
1. Innovation
2. Quality of management
3. Long-term investment value
4. Social responsibility
5. Employee talent
6. Quality of products or services
7. Financial soundness
8. Use of corporate assets
Global organizations only:
9. Effective global business performance

Getting It Right from the Start

A number of parallels can be drawn between the findings of the AMAC study, in particular, and the research studies provided earlier in this article. There is no question that there are many paths that can be taken and serious commitments made to the design, development and implementation of a formal performance management system within one's organization. There are no *one-size-fits-all solutions* for any organization. Each organization is unique and must find its own niche in the marketplace. However, most would agree that whether our organizations are large or small in revenue or in human capital, there are certain fundamental criteria that could apply to all equally. The following *"critical success factors"* are recommended as ground zero for all organizations serious about establishing an effective performance management system and *getting it right from the start.*

Critical Success Factors:

- ***Mirror your corporate culture and values***—Ensure that the core values and beliefs important to your organization are fully integrated into your performance management system.
- ***Design development and planning phase***—Make provisions for executive involvement by having *visible CEO and senior management support* from the outset. This will facilitate buy-in and companywide acceptance for the process. Include management and employees in the design phase to ensure that they understand the process from the ground floor up and are active contributors.
- ***Focus on the right company performance measures***—Agree as a team on those *"vital few"* measures (the core 10 to 20) that will give your organization a clear *line of sight* and the highest degree of confidence it needs to determine how well it is doing in relation to major goal achievement. These are the measures that should be shared with line management and synchronized with other reporting processes to keep the entire organization informed of its progress in relation to all other supporting goals and objectives.
- ***Link job descriptions to the performance management system***—Ensure that your employees can see the *direct relationship between the job competencies* they are required to bring to the job, their job descriptions, and the goals and objectives targeted in their performance plan; if the link is unclear, this document should be brought into alignment and re-visited at least annually thereafter at each performance review.
- ***Differentiate performance fairly and objectively***—The ability to differentiate performance is critical. Performance differentiation requires the appraiser to acknowledge that there will, in all likelihood, be gradations of employee performance. For example, the vast majority of employees may perform their jobs according to expectations based on their level of experience and time in service. However, some may far exceed expectations and others may fall far short of required expectations. Companies are more likely to achieve the results that they desire when they are conscientious about assessing the talent of their employees fairly and objectively in accordance with clearly delineated standards of performance and/or in terms of relative contribution (i.e. essentially compared to the contribution of others) that can be defended by the organization.
- ***Train managers in performance management***—Make an *upfront investment* in training to ensure that managers have the skill sets required to participate fully in the

performance management system planning process. This should include all members of line management to ensure that everyone is on the same page, is speaking the same language, and are using the same tools and techniques.

- ***Link compensation to the performance management system***—According to the USC study previously referenced, the relationship between rewards system practices and performance appraisal effectiveness is strong for all performance management items. The study found, however, that the strongest relationship item is appraisal results and salary increases. "Apparently, tying the results of performance appraisals to financial rewards does lead to the performance appraisal system being effective. The finding that effectiveness is higher when rewards are tied to appraisal results is important, because it contradicts the frequently made argument that appraisals are more effective when they are not tied to financial rewards."[9]
- ***Differentiate linkage to total rewards system***—If there is a secondary or tertiary *total rewards* component to your performance management system, it is imperative that this aspect of the plan be communicated and linked effectively *right from the start.* A 2002 study by the Hay Group uncovered the following findings: 90 percent of organizations have a written compensation policy, even though many employees do not understand it; 73 percent of organizations did not reveal information about their pay system to employees; only slightly more than half of the managerial and professional and less than 25 percent of the other employees know their own salary range; and 61 percent said they were not effective or even marginally effective at motivating employees by promoting their pay program. To be effective, reward programs must be aligned with performance, must be communicated and must be understood to have a motivational effect.
- ***Hold managers accountable for the communication process***—Although communication is everyone's job, ultimately someone must be responsible. Require managers to *actively search out, offer and acquire performance feedback on a regular basis.* By taking the lead in the ongoing communication process and demonstrating the behavior required to make the system work effectively, line management will also be functioning as a coach and mentor to the employees under their supervision.
- ***Set clear expectations for employee development***—Employee development will be crucial to the success of the performance management system. With flatter organizations and narrower spans of control, it will be essential for today's organizations to seek alternative ways to develop employee talent through ongoing skills mastery, special projects and assignments, team leadership opportunities, and formal education and training. As such, it is not unusual for organizations to establish a required minimum number of employee development hours per annum per employee to facilitate this process.
- Track effectiveness of performance management system—To determine the effectiveness of the performance management system, an evaluation of the system is required. The system should be structured to ensure that company and employee performance goal alignment can be confirmed at any point in the performance management cycle, and the probability of meeting targeted performance objectives can be calculated. This will permit confirmation of cost management and ROI goals and objectives, which should be preset throughout the reporting cycle.
- ***Adjust performance management system as required***—Based on the results of the periodic analysis of the company performance management system, the system measures ("vital few") should be adjusted for each requisite reporting period. This information must be communicated back, in turn, to line management in a timely manner. This step is a critical link in the effective communication and implementation of the program and brings the performance management process full circle by reinforcing the employee behaviors required to achieve the goals and priorities of the organization on a continuing basis.

Performance Appraisal–Some Choices

According to Edward Lawler, "Performance appraisals should be driven by a *hierarchical process* in which supervisors evaluate their direct reports at all levels in the organization. All too often, however, senior executives in an organization are not appraised and do not appraise their subordinates. The result is that performance appraisals become something the people at the top tell middle management to do to lower-level employees."[10] To the extent possible, HR practice leaders should strive to reverse this trend and encourage the active inclusion of senior management in the performance appraisal process.

Bearing in mind that the performance management system is intended to serve multiple purposes, the importance of the performance appraisal process to the success of your performance management system should not be underestimated. Performance appraisals will and can impact a host of critical human resource delivery systems and must be viewed within the context of the total performance management process. Based on their design, performance appraisals have the potential to influence career progression, succession planning, organizational training and development, retention, total compensation and other key human capital asset investment programs. As such, the implementation of such programs will require careful planning and integration, to include a provision for ensuring that they are meeting the needs of the organization philosophically, strategically, and in full compliance with all internal and external company requirements. Examples of performance appraisal systems include:

Graphic Rating Scales (GRS)

GRS lists a number of factors, including general behaviors and characteristics (such as attendance, dependability, quality of work, quantity of work, and relationships with people) on which an employee is rated by the supervisor. Supervisors rate individuals on each factor, using a scale that typically has three to five gradations (e.g., unsatisfactory, marginal, satisfactory, highly satisfactory, outstanding). Thus, the system allows the rater to mark the performance of an employee on a continuum. Because of its simplicity, graphic rating scales tend to be one of the most frequently used forms of performance appraisal.

Ranking

Ranking consists of listing all employees from highest to lowest in order of performance. The primary drawback of the ranking method is that the extent of the differences in performance among the individuals is generally not well defined. Points may be assigned to indicate the size of the gap to overcome this drawback.

Forced Distribution

In forced distribution, the ratings of the employees in a particular group are disbursed along a normal bell-shaped curve. The supervisor would apply a certain percentage of the ratings within his or her group to each performance level on the scale, based on the number of employees within his or her group. In order for this method to be fair and equitable, it must assume that the widely known bell-shaped curve exists in a given group in relation to job performance. As a general rule, the spread of performance appraisal ratings does not typically resemble the normal distribution of the bell-shaped curve. Instead, 60 percent to 70 percent of the workforce of an organization rates in the top two performance levels. While this pattern could reflect above average to exceptional performance on the part of many employees, it could also reflect leniency bias, i.e., a tendency by the supervisor to rate at the high end of the rating scale.

Behaviorally Anchored Rating Scales (BARS)

BARS attempts to assess an employee's behaviors instead of characteristics. Descriptions of possible behaviors are matched against those that the employee most commonly exhibits. The assessment tool contains sets of specific behaviors that represent gradations of performance used as common reference points or *anchors* for rating employees on various *job dimensions*. Developing a BARS assessment tool is expensive and time-consuming. It is based on extensive job analysis and the collection of critical incidents (examples of very good and bad performance information) for a particular job.

360-Degree Feedback

360-degree feedback is the process of collecting perceptions about a person's behavior and the impact of that behavior in the workplace from that person's work associates. These individuals typically include an employee's supervisor and other members of line management, direct reports, fellow co-workers, internal and external customers, and vendors and suppliers. Other names for 360-degree feedback are multirater feedback, multisource feedback and group performance review. This form of assessment is favored, in particular, for employee development purposes.

Management by Objectives (MBO)

MBO is a process through which goals are set collaboratively for the organization as a whole, various departments and/or subfunctions, and each individual member. With MBO, individuals are evaluated, usually annually (although interim meetings to certify progress are recommended), on the basis of how well they have achieved the results specified by the goals. MBO, or goal setting, is particularly applicable to nonroutine jobs, such as those of managers, project leaders and individual contributors.

Certifying Your Performance Management System

Any organization making a concerted commitment to *performance management* has made a significant investment in time, effort and resources. As such, it will be crucial that this system be assessed on a periodic basis, just like any other resource of value in the organization.

The following self-diagnostic is offered as a resource in this effort. This tool can be tailored to meet the particular needs of your organization.

Periodic System Assessments

Is your existing performance management system (PMS) meeting the criteria set by your organization? An annual audit of your performance management system should be performed to ensure that it is aligned with its culture and business strategy. Using a graphical rating scale of 1 (strongly disagree) to 5 (strongly agree), rate your performance management system in relation to the following statements:

- Our PMS reflects our company's mission and values; it reflects our desired company culture.
- Our PMS has the full commitment and active participation of our CEO and senior management team.
- Our business strategy is clear, including our key business drivers and the metrics used to track them (e.g., financial, operational, employee engagement, customer and client).
- Our managers understand how to cascade our company goals down through the organization to ensure that they are effectively linked to individual employee goals.
- Individual goals are truly linked to our business drivers, and effective two-way communication links are clearly established.
- Our performance appraisal process distinguishes between observable behavioral dimensions and the frequency of those behaviors (examples: appraisals based on core competencies or the mastery of certain behaviors).
- Our PMS incorporates feedback from multiple sources (e.g., 360-degree feedback and/or another form of multirater feedback).
- Our PMS outlines clear standards of performance and rewards eligibility for high performers, solid performers and marginal performers in the following scenarios:
  - Merit increases.
  - Annual incentives.
  - Long-term incentives.
  - Discretionary incentives.
- Our PMS provides an ongoing comprehensive training program for:
  - Managers conducting performance appraisals.
  - Individuals being appraised.
- Our PMS provides additional support services for professional and career development to managers and employees.
- We are able to accurately determine the ROI of the PMS.
- Our existing technology supports our PMS objectives as designed (i.e., in accordance with system requirements) to include:
  - The various raters and reviewers we wish to involve in the process.
  - The capture of information throughout the performance cycle (including planning, forecasting, progress review, end-of-year evaluation).
  - Sharing data across HR and other business applications (including pay, learning and development, workforce, and succession planning).
  - Providing the necessary level of data security and archiving.
- Our PMS is capable of real-time analysis of performance data to identify trends in relation to:
  - Performance differentiation.
  - Pay differentiation.
  - Performance gaps/developmental needs.
- Our internal business partners are able to access and use the PMS.

Upon completion of the self-assessment, you should have a good starting point to begin to weigh the strengths and weaknesses of your performance management system.

In Closing

As noted in the introduction, if an organization's performance management system is effective, it will be a "key building block" to its human capital management system. It should serve as the basis for accurate measures of individual performance and thus individual rewards. It should be designed to provide feedback to employees about their strengths and weaknesses and, therefore, recommendations on developmental opportunities that will impact career progression for the employee and succession planning for the organization. It should also serve as a viable feedback mechanism regarding training and development requirements for all competency and skill levels throughout the organization. Finally, it should be the central means by which performance challenges and opportunities are identified, solutions are implemented and the effectiveness of these efforts assessed.

These options are limited only by the imaginations and creativity of the individuals who are assigned, or who volunteer, to work on them. It will be up to the management of the organization to ensure that it does not stand in the way of progress, ensuring that the possibilities are effectively communicated to its employees, that recognition and rewards are forthcoming to them, and ongoing investments continue to be made in developing its most important asset, the people it employs.

Chapter 14

Successfully Transitioning to a Virtual Organization: Challenges, Impact and Technology

In today's world, organizations increasingly conduct business in a virtual workspace, whether their employees are located in different countries, cities or venues in the same city. The virtual workspace can be defined as an environment where employees work away from company premises and communicate with their respective workplaces via telephone or computer devices. The virtual organization has different and/or greater challenges than the traditional face-to-face workplace environment, with lines of work crossing over geographies, markets, countries and cultures, alliances, partnerships, and supplier networks. "The virtual office is the office of the future," says John R. Wilson, J.D., Esq., president and CEO of GoffWilson, P.A., and a member of the SHRM Global Special Expertise Panel. "As technology advances and 'live' video becomes high definition, the need and expense of brick and mortar offices diminishes. However, we lose some of the human factor, which is unsettling and difficult to replace, no matter the technology or organizational skills of those involved. A major challenge for the human resource professional will be to instill within the virtual office the nuances felt only with real human interaction."

The very nature of virtual work requires planning and thoughtful design. The development and evaluation of virtual teams present a unique opportunity for HR to partner with many different elements of the business. The benefits to the business stakeholders of a successful virtual work program can be significant, yet difficult to achieve without a strong strategic HR function. Further, with increasing dependence on technology for communication in the workplace, the role of leadership is changing. The glue to the virtual organization is leadership, the right competencies and attributes, trust and rapport, and management of virtual workers and teams.

Organizations can learn from experiences of others in the virtual workspace. To learn what companies are doing to effectively transition to virtual work, the Society for Human Resource Management (SHRM) interviewed HR professionals and researchers in U.S.-based and global organizations. With an emphasis on a solutions-based approach, this article explores key factors to successfully transition to a virtual organization and includes real-life scenarios to illustrate both effective and ineffective approaches, with a focus on leadership styles, the effectiveness of virtual working teams, communication, technology, virtual meetings and management, and global virtual teams. HR and organizational leaders will find this article of value to better understand the challenges of the virtual workplace, discover ways to address these challenges and implement solutions that will promote business success.

Leadership Styles

Effective leadership is the number one factor that influences success in a virtual organization. Maintaining cultural identity, employment brand and employee/manager satisfaction requires consistent and regular communication. Leadership skills are even more essential for virtual work. They include a strong focus on relationships, emotional intelligence, a track record of results and innovation, a focus on process and outcome, and the ability to give positive and constructive feedback. Also important is the ability to teach and coach others and provide recognition both formally and informally in ways that show appreciation and motivate continued success. HR should be part of any pilot program to help leadership understand, anticipate and mitigate management problems. When HR has experience in participating in a virtual team, it lends credibility for HR to fully participate and respond to problems as they arise.

For a virtual team leader, flexibility is paramount. "Leaders need to be more flexible in how and when they communicate. Some people connect on instant messenger while others prefer text messages.

Protocols of communication get more and more sophisticated. The more flexibility I have, the more I can connect with my diverse team," points out Elaine Orler, president of Talent Function Group LLC and a member of the SHRM HR Technology and Management Special Expertise Panel. "To me, digital connection, including voice, can provide enough connection to co-workers. It is important to establish a digital rhythm with each member of the virtual team. I text, versus e-mail, if something is urgent, use instant messenger when we are in meetings, etc. It is still possible to be very connected to members of your team." At the same time, it is equally important to position leaders for success. For example, HR professionals should consider these factors in structured interview processes, provide examples to learn how candidates would think and act in different virtual situations (e.g., with workers spread across geographies, cultures and time zones), and have top candidates meet with senior leaders who can speak about the challenges and expectations of collaborative virtual work. Ultimately, leaders need to be able to engage everyone to work toward a common vision, purpose and destiny.

"In the virtual organization, the role of a leader tends to shift from one of controller to one of coordinator or coach. The leader manages by principle, develops a bias for a cross-functional organization, promotes open sharing of information and empowers the virtual worker," says John G. Schieman, vice president of Global Programs and Marketing at Global Dynamics, Inc., a leading provider of customized solutions to meet the challenges of globalization, virtual environments, and diversity and inclusion in more than 60 countries for over 25 years. The Global Dynamics' model to enhance leadership skills in a multicultural virtual organization, based on the company's experience in the field, is outlined in Table 14.1. "It's essential for organizations to promote trust and effective working relationships, with one of the first steps being the establishment of virtual guiding principles and organization charters," Schieman points out. Consider the following two scenarios: the first focuses on building trust, and the second shows how assumptions and lack of cultural awareness can lead to unexpected and unwanted surprises.

Table 14.1 A Model to Enhance Leadership Skills for Success in a Multicultural Virtual Organization

Enhancers	Derailers
Promote trust and maintain effective working relationships with virtual workers.	Inability to establish the additional levels of trust required with remote workers.
Establish virtual guiding principles and organization charters to ensure the organization is in alignment.	Inadequate communication skills required for virtual network effectiveness.
Identify and define virtual worker roles, responsibilities and accountability.	Lack of comfort and expertise with technologies required for success in the virtual organization.
Establish a reward and recognition process commensurate with the virtual organization characteristics while maintaining consistency with traditional organization structure.	Inability to address conflict resolution within the work group.
Demonstrate cultural competency when interacting globally.	Lack of sensitivity toward different styles of communication.

Source: SHRM interview with Global Dynamics, Inc. (www.global-dynamics.com)

Best Practice

A senior vice president of a global pharmaceutical company was given responsibility for the Americas. The individual, who resided in the United States, was unfamiliar with the cultures of Latin America. Initially, he attended a course to enhance his cultural awareness. Next, as he prepared to communicate critical electronic messages to his new organization, he decided to translate his message into local languages and confirmed that each message was culturally correct. As he planned to visit each cultural region, he scheduled a cultural coaching session to assist him in building trust and securing relationships.

Critical Incident

A senior executive of a global financial services company was given responsibility for Japanese operations. The executive, who resided in the United States, was told that there had been relationship and communication difficulties between the U.S. and Japanese organizations. His plan was to communicate his U.S. model and request that the Japanese operation conform. Initially, he sent an e-mail to all Japanese associates indicating he was planning a visit to Japan for one day to introduce his operational plan and obtain their commitments. He failed to recognize the importance of hierarchy in his communication by sending the message to everyone. He scheduled a one-day visit, not allowing enough time to understand the culture and build relationships. During his trip, he misunderstood verbal and nonverbal communication, concluded that he had Japanese commitments, only to discover upon his return that there were no commitments given.

Team Work: Effectiveness and Communication

Working with and managing a virtual team is very different from managing an on-premise group. "Collaboration tools, goal definition and coaching are areas where HR can help a manager enable a virtual team. Managers need help to understand how embracing technology—such as instant messaging, screen sharing and web conferencing—may make them more flexible and effective. In fact, developing this set of competencies is necessary even for managers of on-premise teams, since these technologies are as familiar as the telephone to many new entrants in the workforce," points out Kristin Lundin, SPHR, product manager at Salary.com and a member of the SHRM Technology and HR Management Special Expertise Panel. She emphasizes that "when adopting or even evaluating virtual teams, HR needs to lay out the strategy for aligning activities done remotely with those done at physical company locations and how they can creatively integrate remote employees."

Research shows that to connect human beings, it is essential to thoughtfully select the most appropriate technology. For exam-

Promoting Inclusion

"Today's virtual meetings often involve participants from multiple cultures, and this requires global leadership skills and culturally appropriate communication to foster engaged participation that leads to improved collaboration," points out Lorelei Carobolante, SCRP, GMS, GPHR, SCRP, CEO/president of G2nd Systems and a member of the SHRM Global Special Expertise Panel. She describes a situation that illustrates an easy but important way to promote trust and inclusion:

A senior manager, who resides in the United States, was leading an engineering team that relied on multi-site expertise to develop a new product for a global semiconductor manufacturing company. In his experience, managing meetings with a combination of virtual and in-person venues was much more difficult than either one or the other, because participants in the conference room would unintentionally dominate the discussions without including the rest of the team. Remote participants felt irrelevant and unable to significantly contribute. To leverage the expertise of all, the manager sent Starbucks cards to all remote participants (coffee and tea were available for the in-person group) in advance of the meeting to establish a feeling of inclusion from the beginning. Throughout the meeting, the manager made a conscientious effort to ask the remote participants to provide their perspective first, helping the group achieve its objectives.

ple, e-mail is not the best medium to communicate an inspirational message. Particularly in the early stages of establishing a virtual team, it is important to consider technology that allows individuals to see and hear expressions, since nonverbal cues are key to trust and rapport. Virtual team members may also have conflicting commitments, such as being involved in multiple projects and multiple teams. To balance time and work commitments, the leader needs to carefully consider other responsibilities of team members when setting goals. Since in many instances virtual team members may never meet each other, the virtual team leader's role is essential to help develop confidence among team members to create a team identity.

When team members identify with their team, they are more likely to be engaged and energized to fulfill the team's goals. Miguel R. Olivas-Luján, Ph.D., a professor of management at Clarion University of Pennsylvania and Tec de Monterrey, Mexico, and a SHRM Global Special Expertise Panel member, points out that where possible, it is still important to meet face to face, especially at the start of the project: "This is more relevant to tasks that are not central to the teams' main job, such as temporary task forces, virtual teams formed with a particular purpose where participants are not discharged of their main duties to accomplish the goal. Through the years, I have noticed that virtual work groups have a flurry of activity and interaction just before and a few weeks after every face-to-face meeting. Often, much more is achieved during those weeks than during the rest of the year."

In companies where a significant amount of the work is either knowledge-based or involves producing technology that is easily transferred, virtual teams present a unique opportunity to build a win-win situation between employers and employees by offering an attractive work/life balance for employees while also reducing facilities and infrastructure costs for employers. "Technology has developed to a level where many knowledge workers have broadband access either off-premise or at home," points out Lundin. "Even in retail or manufacturing, some roles are not dependent on the physical plant to be productive. In some locations in the United States and other developed nations, even wireless broadband has become ubiquitous. This provides the ability for an employee to have a work experience that is productive and very similar, regardless of the employee's physical location."

Yet, productivity in the virtual workplace can be challenging. Olivas-Luján notes, "I recall a couple of research projects in which the cultural diversity of the team participants made it almost impossible to get things done on time. In contrast, another effort that gathered responses from employees in about 22 countries turned out results much faster because the leader set up a structure that could be considered autocratic, yet was highly efficient. She provided standard instructions, offered advice and made sure each country co-author knew exactly what to expect. This experience is also consistent with the research that suggests that diverse teams often take longer to reach the 'performing' phase and become more productive than homogeneous teams. The outcomes are more creative and effective than those of homogeneous teams if the leader is able to manage the diversity."

A recent SHRM poll on HR's involvement in the virtual workforce reveals a variety of key transition factors (see Figure 14.1). This research found that within the next 12 months,

Figure 14.1 | In what ways does your HR department currently support your organization's virtual workforce?

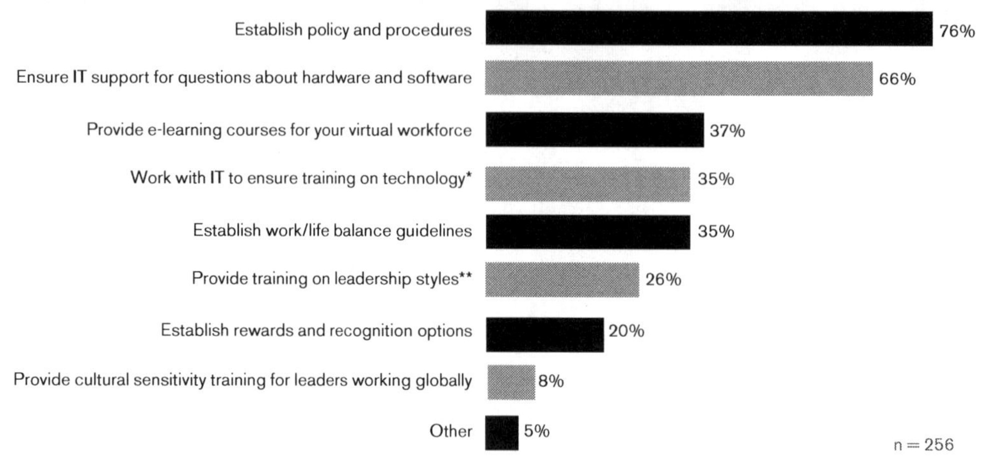

* e.g., web conferencing software, webinars for working virtually, social networking tools, e-learning programs.

** styles that promote trust and maintain effective working relationships with virtual workers.

Note: Asked only of respondents who said their organizations offered virtual work options. Percentages do not total 100% as respondents were allowed multiple choices.
Source: SHRM Poll: Transitioning to a Virtual Organization (2010)

22 percent of organizations expect the percentage of their employees who work virtually to increase, 76 percent expect it to remain the same, and 3 percent will decrease the percentage of virtual employees. The poll shows the various ways in which HR is working to support the organization's virtual workforce. In addition, according to a SHRM survey report *Workplace Flexibility in the 21st Century: Meeting the Needs of the Changing Workplace*, 43 percent of HR professionals say that in the next five years, a larger proportion of their workforce will be telecommuting.

Virtual Teaming Technology

Virtual teams are highly dependent on collaboration technology and infrastructure. For employees who never see and/or meet each other, it can be a daunting effort to establish trust and rapport, effectively communicate and share information on an ongoing basis. Obviously, technology is a large component of managing and enabling a virtual team. HR professionals should be closely aware of what technologies are being offered and used by remote workers so that they can help managers transition to managing virtual teams. "HR leaders need to guide their teams to evaluate and become familiar with all of the various technology that the virtual team will be using," says Lundin, of Salary.com. "Understanding and using these technologies will enable HR professionals to coach managers and leaders on the needs of the virtual employee and to understand how to best support those managers and employees."

The expansion of virtual teaming technology provides a variety of communication tools for virtual teams. "Technology should be a strong conduit for virtual team success. That technology is not solely based on corporate infrastructure, but rather is an extension of that infrastructure to create and bond the team as a community of peers," emphasizes Orler, of Talent Function Group LLC. "Virtual communication and information sharing can be accomplished using a number of vehicles, such as e-mail, intranets and the Internet, video conferencing, teleconferencing, webcasts, shared electronic whiteboards and groupware (e.g., Lotus Notes). Every organization, as it expands to work at a virtual pace, will encounter challenges when working virtually."

Yet, as Olivas-Luján points out, "Familiarity trumps sophistication. As my colleagues and I have moved from e-mail to synchronic discussion groups (chat rooms) and now to social networking-based communications, I used to try to get my colleagues to employ the newest technology (instant messenger, Skype, etc.). However, some were too busy to learn, others needed more hand-holding, and it was just not productive. I now try to use the lowest common denominator (e-mail with attachments or shared documents in some cases) and don't push the 'newest and the latest.' Ultimately, the expectations and needs of companies to use technology appropriately will drive change in the workplace."

The following examples show how organizations are being proactive to connect with their workforce by using technology as a strategic tool to ensure seamless work and stronger communication despite a lack of face-to-face interaction with key stakeholders in the company.

Performance Management

A medical testing organization is creatively using virtual teaming technology to connect managers and their direct reports in the performance management process. A group of sales managers has direct reports whose job duties keep them in the field. This group's efforts are vital to the organization's success, and weekly field reports are an inherent part of the performance review process. Managers use an online system to record their field reports on a daily basis. This Internet-based system is available via their wireless PCs and accessible anytime. Consolidated online reports are also available to senior management and allow real-time monitoring of the organization's sales efforts to support immediate oversight of their revenue growth strategic goal.

A Change Initiative

An office services firm was implementing major benefits changes for its U.S. employees. Part of the benefits strategy change was a shift away from a paternalistic approach to more employee responsibility. The company knew this represented a major change management opportunity. It wanted to have its best change management team lead efforts to announce, engage and manage change efforts but without letting advance word leak out. The change management team was scattered across the United States, but had to work closely together for several months to effect the desired change results. To work as a virtual team, a secure blog was created for the change management team members. Only team members had access to ongoing discussions and draft change documents. The blog was a convenient way to provide real-time collaboration as well as a record of discussions and decisions for team members who could not make the live conversations. Team members learned to use the blog as the central repository for all planning and implementation tools. It was the most accessed site on a daily basis, even if no synchronous communication was required between members. The change team's success using the blog for virtual team collaboration was noted as a key element of the change process. The blog tool has since been used by other virtual teams throughout the organization.

Virtual Meetings and Management

1. **Shared project/program management tools** ensure that documentation is consistent and relevant across the team and enable real-time updates and changes (e.g., SharePoint by Microsoft, Connect Pro by Adobe, and eRoom by EMC2, off-the-shelf products (some free) such as Jive, Basecamp and Google Docs).

2. **Instant messaging, text messaging.** Mobile devices are the number one most common tool used around the world (see www.mocom2020.com/2009/03/41-billion-mobile-phone-subscribers-worldwide). With company plans, text messaging globally for simple status checks is less expensive than phone calls, and in many countries, it is a more effective way to reach someone. Text messaging is not limited to just a mobile device; it can be integrated into e-mail notifications and various other standard desktop tools.

3. **Voice over IP and video chat** can create a sense of community among a virtual team and are a low-cost alternative to international calling plans, from high-tech innovative virtual conference rooms offered by Cisco Systems to mainstream readily available products such as Skype or GoogleTalk.

4. **World clock.** The greatest obstacle to a global virtual workforce is finding the time to meet without forcing anyone to work unrealistic hours to participate. Several free programs offer the ability to review time zones and check availability, and this simple consideration can foster unity in the team and a sense of equal sacrifice and commitment.

5. **Dynamic project planning tools.** Microsoft Project continues to be the traditional tool for project management, but the market is moving to real-time dynamic project support tools. The new web 2.0 features word clouds, mind maps and context-based search, with options to share information by timeline, dependency, owner or goal. Applications such as MindJet and solutions by Matchware are easy to use and intuitive, leading to increased productivity.

Seamless Service

A major outsourcing firm leverages teams in Europe, North America and Asia to successfully deliver client projects. While some work efforts can be completed around the clock and take advantage of time zone differences to speed up processes, team members must also work together in real time. A variety of virtual teaming technologies are used to facilitate their interaction and collaboration. Web conferencing technology is used for synchronous and asynchronous communications. Team members who cannot make a conference call can listen to and view a recording of an earlier session when they are available. Team members can also track problems online and address issues while working in their respective time zones. This technology helps span time zones and allows seamless work efforts.

Virtual Meetings, Management and Team Building

Motivation and engagement are among the top challenges for virtual teams. Building the sense of team makes all the difference to establish rapport and trust, encourage creativity and innovation, and accomplish the mission and goals of the team. Managers need to find ways to provide public forums for recognition, avenues to share ideas, take advantage of training and development opportunities to strengthen the team, and celebrate the achievements of both individuals and the team. The following three real-life stories portray examples of solutions to motivation and engagement challenges.

Recognition[2]

A senior manager at a high-tech company was discouraged to provide recognition for his distance sales group, which had recently moved into a virtual organization environment. The manager was finding it difficult to offer praise and recognition in a public forum, where salespeople tend to thrive. Prior to the company transitioning these employees to home offices, the manager had brought the sales team together on a regular basis, where they could stand up and be recognized for their accomplishments. While the sales goals were monitored on a monthly basis, the manager was finding it more difficult to maintain momentum without the face-to-face monthly meetings, despite energy-producing events such as the team signing a company for a significant contract or a new product being launched in the marketplace. The manager went to the HR director to ask for recommendations. As a result, the company chose to invest in web-conferencing and videoconferencing as tools to better motivate company teams (sales included) and create better real-time opportunities for recognition.

Virtual Training Can Be Effective and Fun

The Inspection Division of Manheim, the world's leading provider of vehicle remarketing services, recently won the bronze award from Brandon Hall Research Excellence in Learning for its use of simulation/gaming in a learning program. The division launched a state-of-the-art online training program for its 1,300 highly technical vehicle inspectors, who were accus-

Eight Ideas to Celebrate from a Distance

1. Celebrate both individual and team accomplishments.
2. Celebrate the mileposts, not just getting to the goal.
3. Hold an annual or semiannual achievement review event.
4. Respect team member preferences on how to celebrate.
5. Acknowledge personal milestones, such as birthdays, weddings, birth of children, anniversaries of tenure in the company, educational accomplishments, community service, etc.
6. Present e-gift certificates to the team. Leaders can bring these to on-site visits.
7. Invest in "portable parties"—send party kits (such as party hats, horns, party favors, confetti) to each member and celebrate via tele- or video-conferencing.
8. Create a location on the company intranet to post best practices and learnings.

Source: Adapted from Fisher, K., & Fisher, D. (2001). *The distance manager: A hands-on guide to managing off-site employees and virtual teams.* New York: McGraw-Hill.

tomed to in-person/hands-on training. Due to its significant growth, the company had to shift to virtual learning, and the change was initially met with apprehension. As it turned out, the combination of interactive games, video and commentary were very well received. The company's national trainers reached out to the inspectors for their feedback, answered their questions and made it as easy as possible. Personal follow-up took the fear out of the new approach, and now inspectors throughout the organization routinely use this award-winning program.

The Virtual Office and Employee Engagement[3]

At the company headquarters, there was a growing need to consolidate office space to save costs. As a pilot, one of the regional teams began to work from home offices. Although the real estate savings from eliminating office space were significant, the team's manager found that team engagement levels decreased, as did productivity, due to the lack of informal interaction, essential for sharing and generating ideas. The company ended up putting back some of the office space, using a "hotelling" concept, with networked office space available on a first come, first served basis. This change allowed for monthly face-to-face meetings, promoted an increased sense of team and was cost-effective for other teams as well, as additional employee groups began to work virtually.

Table 14.2 Tips for Effective Virtual Meetings and Management

- Prepare and distribute agendas in advance; ensure agendas reflect input requested from participants.
- Initiate meetings with "roll call" of all participants; review agenda, meeting objectives and timeframe.
- Identify the key roles of facilitator and scribe.
- Position participants in locations "free" of distractions or background noise.
- Promote climate of collaboration and inclusion; encourage every attendee to participate and express his or her view.
- Encourage participants to effectively use available technology.
- Conduct meeting evaluation at the close of the session.
- Establish expectation for distribution of the meeting minutes.
- Establish "next steps" and make follow-up assignments.

Source: SHRM interview with Global Dynamics, Inc. (www.global-dynamics.com)

Global Virtual Teams

A commonly quoted advantage of global virtual teams is the ability of an organization to leverage competencies and skills from all parts of the world. These teams are seen as having the capability to solve very complex problems and open up possibilities for substantial process creativity and innovative solutions. Global virtual teams are typically assigned to projects aligned with an organization's strategic goals and may be short term (less than 12 months) or long term. They offer additional advantages to remain competitive, such using synergies, providing costs savings (e.g., travel), enhancing knowledge transfer and enabling access to low-wage resources through globalization.[4]

Leaders of global virtual teams deal with different dynamics than those of a traditional team, including different styles/work etiquette and different cultural viewpoints. Time can be a challenge (working either synchronously/"real time" or asynchronously/accessed any time, such as e-mail), as can culture and language (English may be the second or third language for some members, with cultural context communication in meaning or translation of documents), and humor (best to avoid online humor, as it does not translate well in e-mail).[5]

Working with clients in the transition to a virtual organization, Schieman, of Global Dynamics, Inc., has found that a model for effective multicultural virtual team should demonstrate the following characteristics: (1) successful team performance exceeds the sum of the individual performance and contribution; (2) team style is established by all team members and leverages the cultural diversity of the group; (3) accountability exists at both the individual and entire team level; and (4) reward and recognition are based on the success of the entire team, consistent with cultural norms. The following examples illustrate some of these points.

Understanding Cultural Differences

Two high-level information technology virtual teams were formed, each with members from the United States, India, Japan, Brazil and Germany. Both team leaders were American. Each team was tasked with the design and development of a web-based business application, which had to be available for use within six months. The first team leader created a team charter without any understanding of cultural values and without involving team members in the creation of the charter. The leader decided that iterative, prototype development would be the best approach and that he would empower all team members. He assigned that function to team members from Japan and India. Establishing milestones and maintaining schedules was critical on the project since the development life cycle was only six months. This project experienced numerous false starts and delays and failed to deliver on time.

The second team leader, recognizing that she did not fully understand cultural differences as they related to the strength of her team, participated in a cross-cultural awareness training program. She decided, similar to the first team leader, that prototyping was a good approach. She met with her team members, discussed her thoughts and asked for feedback and suggestions. The Japanese and Indian team members stated they would be more comfortable with final specifications. The U.S. team members volunteered to do the prototyping. The Japanese and Indian members agreed to develop the final product based on the completed prototype. The Brazilian member volunteered to evaluate the "ease of use" capabilities of the design. The team leader asked each person to provide his or her milestones, time schedules and interdependencies with one another. She and the German team member agreed that he would create and manage the final project plan. This team leader developed an understanding of the strengths each individual and culture contributed to the team and leveraged those characteristics while creating an inclusive working environment. The project was delivered on time, within budget and was well received.

Finally, solid experience in conflict resolution is recommended to successfully manage and address the complex dynamics of a global virtual team. (For further reading, see Chapter 8.)

In Closing

Whether in a domestic or global virtual work environment, today's virtual workplace is rapidly changing as new technologies are introduced. HR should take a leadership role to support its organization to remain competitive in an increasingly virtual marketplace. No doubt, within months of the publication of this report, there will be new technologies to support the virtual worker and offer better opportunities for collaboration and productivity. HR and team leaders need to ensure that all staff understand the various technologies that will make the most effective use of time and resources but will also support people, communication and achievement of the business goals.

Chapter 15

Business Ethics: The Role of Culture and Values for an Ethical Workplace

In the business world today, issues of trust, respect, fairness, equity and transparency are gaining more attention. Business ethics includes organizational values, guidelines and codes, legal compliance, risk management, and individual and group behavior within the workplace. Effective leadership, with open dialogue and thoughtful deliberation, develops the foundation of an ethical workplace, is woven into the fabric of the organizational culture and is mirrored in ethical decision-making. Toward this end, all organizational leaders have a key role in establishing corporate values and modeling ethical behavior for their workforce, organization and community.

The importance of ethical leadership has grown exponentially. A 2009 special report from the Business Roundtable Institute of Corporate Ethics and the Arthur W. Page Society focuses on the issue of leadership and trust. *The Dynamics of Public Trust in Business—Emerging Opportunities for Leaders* emphasizes that trust is a critical factor in business. The report points out that "even in the best of times, the dynamism of trust requires continual monitoring and rebalancing as economic and social situations change." Companies can create positive business ethics by generating goodwill, communicating openly and taking advantage of opportunities for leaders to create value based on a foundation of accountability, responsibility and integrity. Ultimately, trust—through good business ethics—"positively impacts business success in a number of critical areas, such as employee performance, customer retention and innovation."[1]

While not inclusive of all aspects of business ethics, this research article focuses on organizational culture and values as integral in the foundation of an ethical workplace. The primary audiences—human resource professionals, people managers and senior management—will find this article useful to thoughtfully consider the state of business ethics in their respective companies, identify related challenges and opportunities, and rethink how better to communicate, restructure and/or reframe policies and practices that influence the organization's ethical stance.

Business Imperative

Organizational culture and ethical leadership are at the core of business ethics. Each shapes and reinforces corporate values, and influences employee attitudes and behaviors. Broadly defined, business ethics includes ethical conduct, legal compliance and, in some cases, corporate social responsibility. Ethics-related outcomes can be seen in nearly every aspect of a company, from employee perceptions of fairness, to employee engagement and retention, and ultimately, as U.S. and global executives note, to reputation and sustainability (see SHRM's 2008 Executive Roundtable Symposium on Sustainability and Human Resource Management).[2]

The establishment of business ethics as policy is not new. A number of business codes were established and in use in the 1920s. In fact, the retailer J. C. Penney Company introduced a company code of conduct in 1913.[3] The focus on business ethics, particularly ethics policies and programs, rapidly grew in the United States in the 1980s and 1990s in response to government and legal pressures. The Defense Industry Initiative (DII), created in the 1980s in response to government regulations, was developed for defense contractors to comply with a high standard of conduct. DII was the first organized attempt at creating standard ethics and compliance programs. In 1999, a survey of a sample of *Fortune* 1000 companies by researchers Weaver, Treviño and Cochran found that only 20 percent had adopted ethics polices prior to 1976 and 60 percent since the mid-1980s.[4] A series of high-visibility corporate scandals (such as Enron, Arthur Andersen, WorldCom) resulted in the Sarbanes-Oxley Act (SOX) of 2002, the goal of which is to foster truthful communication between company officers and shareholders in publicly traded companies.

In today's global marketplace, HR, ethics and compliance officers, and organizational leadership must also be cognizant of cultural differences that influence business ethics. In different countries, there are cultural variations around business ethics, such as cultural norms, legislation, communication styles, etc. In Europe, for example, there is a history of socially mandated employee involvement in businesses, where the U.S. style of codes of conduct may not be applicable. Other cultural differences, such as indirect communication styles and the need to save face, require sensitivity for ethics-related communications. U.S. corporate ethics programs tend to reflect American cultural norms, such as individualism. In contrast, collectivist societies use different communication styles to address interpersonal and ethical problems. Whether in domestic or global companies, ultimately, the commitment to business ethics and the foundation is built through organizational culture, with ethical values reflected in the workplace.

Leadership and Organizational Culture

Corporate integrity is reflected in leadership. "Because sound ethical behavior continues to erode within society, it is vital that an organization's leaders model the ethical behavior they require from staff members," notes Norman Howard, Director of Human Resources, W. K. Kellogg Foundation. "Thus, the culture of an organization plays a critical and essential role in defining the importance of ethics both in how it respects employees and how it conducts business."

An ethical culture is developed through communication, rules, leadership, rewards, rituals and stories. The realm of business ethics and organizational culture includes the views of employees and management, individual and organizational values, and constant compliance and principle-driven ethics. Attitudes and behaviors are reinforced over time through codes of conduct, behavioral modeling by senior staff, ethical decision processes and ethics training. Three key questions to ask within an organization are: (1) how does the company culture portray organizational values; (2) do company policies reflect corporate values that form the platform for ethical leadership and corporate governance; and (3) are employees treated fairly and consistently?[5] Leadership determines how effectively this is accomplished. As pointed out in an article titled "The Ethical Commitment: Building Value-Based Cultures," employees want to trust management and know that their needs and well-being are considered. Managers demonstrate trustworthiness when they listen to employees, account for their actions and explain reasons for decisions.[6] Data from the 2009 National Business Ethics Survey, conducted by the Ethics Resource Center, reveal employees' views about whether leadership sets a good example of ethical behavior, with 80 percent approval for top management and 86 percent for direct supervisors.[7]

Finally, regular assessments of company ethics by HR and senior management are critical (see Table 15.1). This may include policies and programs, the code of conduct, ethics communications, ethics training and employees opinion surveys. Key questions to consider are: (1) is the company sending the message that it promotes ethical behavior; (2) is it concerned with the welfare of employees or is the goal to protect the company; and (3) is the formal ethics program outsourced for cost savings (on the Internet), thoughtfully focused on the nuances of the organizational culture, and to what degree is senior management involved?[8]

Table 15.1 Ten Questions to Assess Your Company and Its Procedures About Decision-Making

1. Do you give your employees an opportunity to express their views before decisions are made?
2. Are all employees treated with respect and dignity?
3. Does the company promote consistent application of the rules across situations?Does the company discourage the influence of personal biases on decisions?
4. Are the needs of employees considered?
5. Are decisions made based on accurate information?
6. Is honest feedback provided about why decisions are made?
7. Are the rights of employees respected?
8. Are managers consistent in their views about appropriate ethical standards?
9. Are opportunities provided to appeal decisions that employees disagree with?

Source: Adapted from Tyler, T., Dienhard, J., & Thomas, T. (2008, Winter). The ethical commitment to compliance: Building value-based cultures. *California Management Review, 50*(1), 31-51.

Organizational Ethics Standards and Practices

In some organizations, HR may be responsible for ethics in terms of programs, discipline and communication. In a company without a formal ethics and compliance function, the chief HR professional often serves as the ethics officer, and the HR department promotes ethical conduct and training. The SHRM/Ethics Resource Center 2008 survey report *The Ethics Landscape in American Business: Sustaining a Strong Ethical Work Environment* documents that the majority (83 percent) of HR professionals believe that the HR department is a primary resource for ethics-related issues. Many feel that they are not part of the ethics infrastructure, yet are often requested to assist or remedy situations caused by ethical violations. However, the key findings show that HR professionals, in general, are in agreement that nonmanagement employees, supervisors and top management: (1) support them in following their organization's ethics standards; (2) talk about the importance of workplace ethics and doing the right thing in their work; (3) set a good example of ethical behavior; and (4) are held accountable if they are found to be in violation of the organization's ethics standards.[9]

The platform for an ethical workplace is the code of conduct. It describes a value system and ethical principles and outlines specific ethical rules embodied by the organization. Written standards of ethical conduct cover a number of areas, such as compliance and laws, confidential or proprietary information, conflicts of interest, use of company assets, and acceptance of or providing gifts, gratuities and entertainment. The purpose of a code of conduct is to raise ethical expectations; focus on dialogue about ethical issues; encourage ethical decision-making; and prevent misconduct and establish a platform for enforcement.[10] Through the code of conduct, with clear language and specific illustrations of how ethical principles apply to the workplace setting, organizations put employees—including management—on notice that there are consequences of not complying and expectations for certain behavior.[11]

Two broad incentive categories encourage ethical behavior: reward and recognition systems, and performance evaluation systems. Companies may use public acknowledgment of individuals or teams who go "above and beyond the call of duty" as a vehicle to reinforce ethical behavior. For example, an annual ceremony to present the "President's Award for Integrity and Business Ethics" is one way to thank employees for their exemplary work and set examples for others. Performance reviews may include a section on corporate values, such as how the employee demonstrates respect, inspires others, engenders trust and confidence, keeps commitments, etc. Such recognition helps maintain focus on the company's philosophy about business ethics, the real impact on the workplace culture by the employees and the company's standing in the marketplace.

Ethics and Generational Differences

Understanding generational differences—and finding common ground—helps improve communication in the workplace (see Table 15.2). The SHRM white paper *Ethics and Generational Differences: Interplay Between Values and Ethical Business Decisions* examined how different generations approach questions of integrity and purpose. The authors point out that "with value systems and motivation at the heart of ethics—and divergent value systems seemingly inherent within the four generational groups—the existence of varied ethical perspectives among co-workers is not a surprise."[12]

Table 15.2 Key Points for Ethical Business Management of Different Generations

- Develop an internal campaign, with ethics as the #1 value for the organization and employees.
- Avoid stereotyping employees according to their generation.
- Clearly identify the priorities of the company and then link them to the priorities and values of employees to support business decisions.
- When possible, learn the values and motivation of employees and then connect them to individual and organizational goals.
- Focus on business results, not on methodology (as long as it is ethical). All groups want to contribute and achieve but may do so differently.
- To make ethical guidelines relevant to everyone, establish ongoing training and support sessions.
- Look for commonality among employees of different generations.
- Embrace diversity of opinion and methodology.
- Err on the side of more communication, such as using different types of media: face-to-face meetings, e-mail blasts, etc.
- Remember to respect the dimensions of differing generations (age, technological savvy, alternative work experiences, innovation, etc.)

Adapted from: Guss, E., & Miller, M. C. (2008 October). *Ethics and generational differences: Interplay between values and ethical business decisions* [SHRM white paper]. Retrieved from www.shrm.org.

A common area of tension among generations focuses on work ethic, and conflict often stems from how it is defined. Traditionalists and Baby Boomers may criticize the two younger generations about their lack of work ethic, since older generations often equate strong work ethic to being part of the organization (and being physically present in the office) for long periods of time. Baby Boomers consider a combination of factors—collaboration, teamwork and meetings—as evidence of work ethic. Generation X and Millennials see work ethic as working hard—often autonomously—with a positive impact on the company while also living a full life outside of their job. Yet, research shows that no matter one's age, people value achievement, balance and responsibility, and want credible, trustworthy leadership (see Chapter 9).[13]

The commitment of the Millennial generation (Gen Y) to volunteerism points to idealism and the confidence that one individual can positively affect society. Volunteerism is an opportunity for organizations to showcase ethical and moral behavior through community service (see *Volunteerism—Moving Up on the Strategic Agenda*).[14] A recent study from Deloitte found that nearly two-thirds of respondents aged 18 to 26 prefer to work at firms that offer opportunities to their employees to volunteer their professional skills at nonprofit organizations.[15] "It is the idealism that this generation of young employees brings to the workplace that can also portend the potential vulnerability of their moral compass," says human resource consultant Joy Gaetano, SPHR, president of Gaetano Group and a SHRM Ethics Special Expertise Panel member. "An organization that can establish clear ethical guidelines, set policy standards and provide a culture that nurtures ethical decision-making and values gains respect as an 'employer of choice' where a young employee can focus on optimizing his or her workplace talent rather than feel compromised by workplace conduct."

Ethical Decision-Making

Values drive decision-making. In the sometimes confusing maze of decisions, employees and managers may at times feel conflicted by their personal values and the corporate message. In today's busy workplace, managers have to make decisions quickly, are influenced by short-term pressures and therefore may fail to adequately focus on social norms and ethical principles. When confronted with ethical decisions, guidelines about ethical-decision making are valuable tools and can be presented in a corporate ethics program, during a staff meeting or as part of an employee-manager mentorship. These guidelines provide a framework for learning (e.g., where do workers learn what is acceptable in the workplace) as well as opportunities to reinforce corporate values. Such discussions are important in management training—for new managers, managers new to the company and longer-term managers alike—to highlight how value-based decision-making fits within the organization's mission and vision (see Table 15.3).

Table 15.3 Questions and Lessons for Ethical Decision-Making

- What is the biggest ethical dilemma you have experienced in your career?
- How did you respond?
- What was the outcome?
- What did you learn?
- How did you transfer this learning or experience into teachable moments for others?

Source: Tichy, N. M. (2003). Students meet ethical dilemma in their workplace challenges. In N. M. Tichey & A. R. McGill (Eds.), *The ethical challenge: How to lead with unyielding integrity* (pp. 211–230). San Francisco: Jossey-Bass.

The concept of moral motivation—*why should I do the right thing?*—is the focus of a recent article in the *Journal of Business Ethics*. The authors explored moral motivation through the lens of applicability to corporate ethics programs. The value of this study lies in offering a basis for discussion of how and why decisions are made (i.e., what is the ethical foundation/reasoning). The ethical theories of moral philosophers (Aristotle's ethics of virtue, Kant's categorical imperative and Mill's utilitarianism/greatest happiness principle) identify key ethical leadership skills that are important for today's workplace: (1) practical wisdom—personal integrity and good character, (2) moral reasoning—compliance with corporate ethics, and (3) moral feelings—cost/benefit analysis (for all stakeholders).[16]

Mini-Case Study: John's Decision

John Hart was a division manager at Atlantic Soda, a large bottling conglomerate with more than 30 companies. He was asked to meet with Bill Goodwin (his boss) and Bob Martin (regional division manager for a competitor, Mid-Major Pop). John had joined the firm six months earlier and was known for his track record of hard work and excellent sales results. In Atlantic's culture of rewarding performance and talent, John had already been promoted twice. At the meeting, Goodwin discussed the intense price competition between Atlantic Soda and Major Pop. He suggested that they establish a mutual set of prices. The two principals agreed. However, John would have the responsibility to implement this arrangement in his region.

This true story illustrates an opportunity for an ethical decision. Pressures were exerted by John's manager to sway the decision. John had options to consider: personal/company achievement or his personal and the company's integrity. He made the wrong choice and went to jail for his part in the price fixing, a violation of the Sherman Antitrust Act.[17]

Corporate Ethics Programs

Ethics training is a key part of business ethics. It assists employees and management in clarifying their own ethical paradigms and doing the right thing when confronted with ethical dilemmas. In conjunction with a code of ethics, ethics training serves as an organization's guiding framework. Training can be delivered in many ways, such as web-based training, webcasts and in-person training programs, thus accommodating schedules and different learning preferences and taking advantage of cost-savings opportunities. Legislation makes compliance critical (see *U.S. Sentencing Guidelines for Organizations*, adopted in 1991 and updated in 2004, www.ussc.gov/orgguide.htm). Publicly traded companies subject to the Sarbanes-Oxley Act of 2002 (SOX) must have a code of ethics designed to deter wrongdoing, including a statement promoting financial integrity that clearly applies to senior financial officers (see SHRM article about the Sarbanes-Oxley Act). Additional U.S. federal laws that cover unethical business practices include the Foreign Corrupt Practices Act of 1977 (FCPA), which prohibits corrupt payments to foreign officials for the purpose of obtaining or keeping business; mail and wire fraud statutes, 18 U.S.C. § 1341, 1343; The Travel Act, 18 U.S.C. § 1952, which provides for federal prosecution of violations of state commercial brib-

Figure 15.1 | The Increase and Decrease of Misconduct Over Time

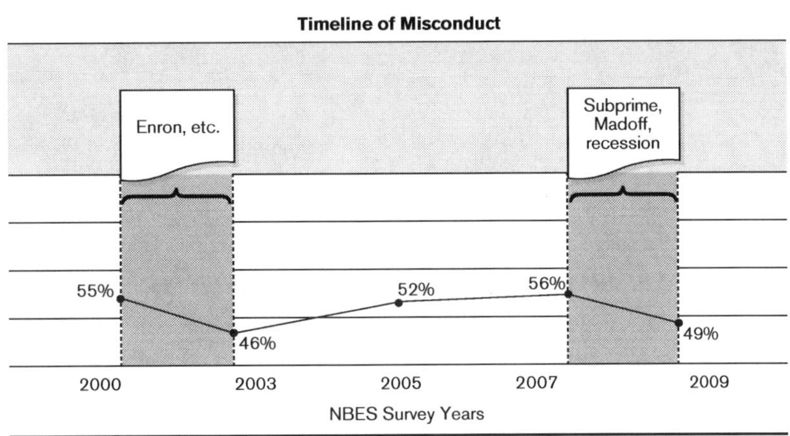

Source: Ethics Resource Center. (2009, October). 2009 *National Business Ethics Survey*, www.ethics.org

ery statutes; and Federal Sentencing Guidelines, particularly §8.B2.1, regarding the components of an effective compliance and ethics program.

Based on the Federal Sentencing Guidelines, the Ethics Resource Center (ERC) outlines six elements necessary for a comprehensive ethics and compliance program: (1) written standards for ethical conduct; (2) training on ethics; (3) a mechanism to seek ethics-related advice or information; (4) a process to report misconduct anonymously; (5) disciplinary action of employees who violate the organization's ethics standards or the law; and (6) inclusion of ethical behavior within each employee's regular performance appraisal. The SHRM/ERC 2008 survey report on ethics found that most organizations do not have a comprehensive ethics and compliance program. Only 23 percent of HR professionals reported that their companies had all six elements, yet other factors were in place: 88 percent of HR professionals said that their organizations disciplined employees who violated the company standards, 75 percent had written standards for ethical conduct, 74 percent had a mechanism to report violations confidentially or anonymously, and 66 percent had orientation or training on ethics. In contrast, more than 50 percent of organizations did not have a specific mechanism for employees to seek advice on ethics-related matters, and 57 percent did not evaluate employees on ethical conduct in their performance reviews. The most common types of misconduct seen by HR professionals were abusive or intimidating behavior toward employees (excluding sexual harassment); e-mail and/or Internet abuse; inaccurate reporting of actual hours worked; employee behavior putting the employee's interests above those of the organization's; and employees taking sick days when they are not sick.[18]

The *2009 National Business Ethics Survey* from ERC found that during the recession, 81 percent of employees have confidence in their company's executives, only 23 percent believe that the recession has negatively affected the ethical culture within the company, and 10 percent believe that in order to stay in business during the recession, their company has lowered its ethical standards. Employees see their leadership—even during these difficult economic times—as trustworthy, with 81 percent of respondents trusting that company executives are telling the truth about the well-being of the organization. The study also found that with more focus on business ethics, misconduct decreases: specifically, misconduct declined after 2002, when SOX was passed, then increased over the next four years, and then declined again during the recession (see Figure 15.1).[19]

Ethics and Perceptions of Fairness

Perceptions of fairness are closely tied to business ethics, at the root of which are questions of justice. Also known as "organizational justice," it encompasses fairness of outcomes and allocation of resources, fairness of decision-making processes and fairness of interpersonal treatment from the supervisor. In today's litigious environment, organizations must be transparent, equitable, consistent and fair in their policy development and administration. The following example illustrates how policy applied inconsistently can negatively affect employee morale. Individual values and moral positions of an employee may end up in juxtaposition with the policies and behavior of the employer, through confusion, inconsistency, and poor management communication and practices, bringing forth questions of fairness.

Mini-Case Study: A Lack of Transparency

An employee had worked for nearly 30 years at a well-established, fiscally sound bank in the commercial market. Unexpectedly, she found herself needing to take time off for the care of her sick husband. Saturday morning, her husband was rushed to the hospital to undergo emergency surgery, and on Monday he was placed in intensive care. On that Monday, the employee made a request to her manager to use some of her 10 months of accrued sick leave to care for her husband. FMLA was approved, but she was told that according to the HR department, she must use vacation time rather than sick leave.

After being out for a couple weeks, with more than two-thirds of her FMLA entitlement remaining, the employee returned to work. Her manager and a senior HR officer ushered her into a meeting to discuss the terms of her return to work. "We're concerned about your ability to come back. We can't have you taking long lunches or leaving early to visit your husband." The employee assured them that this had not been her plan but asked why it would be a problem if an occasional need were to arise. "If we let you do it, we'd have to let everyone do it." Although she had planned to retire in less than six months, at this point, the employee was very upset and her view of the company was negatively affected by this exchange and lack of support. She later learned that sick leave use for family members was discretionary at the determination of the manager. An HR officer also informally counseled her, saying "if your own doctor were to say you are too stressed to work, your sick hours would more than carry you through your planned retirement date, plus you'll get another annual profit-sharing check." This sentiment was echoed to her by several other bank officers.

The poorly communicated and inappropriately administered policies—such as the FMLA leave—coupled with lack of sensitivity by management and subsequently perceived unfairness—largely contributed to the distress of the employee. This example illustrates how lack of transparency of company policies can create confusion and lead to an unethical subculture. In this case, vague policies allowed line and human resource managers to permit or deny leave on a case-by-case basis. While denying sick leave may save the company money in the short term, the cost is also reflected in decreased employee morale, with the likely loss of valuable human capital.

Transparent procedures are important. They allow managers to emphasize the importance of decision-making for all employees to minimize the belief that some receive favorable treatment or differences based on other biases. When focus is placed on respecting employees and their rights, the quality of interpersonal relationships in the workplace improves. When people are treated with dignity and courtesy, commitment to the organization increases along with productivity.20 Ultimately, the question that HR and organizational leaders should ask is, are our own policies inadvertently shaping our corporate cultures in ways that will undermine the reputation of the company and ultimately cost the company the loss of talent, production, customer service and profits?

Global Perspective

One popular topic for HR professionals in the last few years has been the need to develop a global mindset, but this need has been viewed mostly through the context of individual development. SHRM interviewed Lorelei Carobolante, SCRP, GMS, GPHR, SHRM Global Special Expertise Panel member and CEO/president of G2nd Systems, who has extensive expertise in the area of intercultural communications.

"We often fail to recognize that the establishment of such cultural norms within an organization has many more business ramifications than the often-cited cases of employees assigned to foreign locations and their struggle to become effective contributors," says Carobolante. "As our workforce, anywhere in the world, is becoming more culturally diverse, developing a global mindset is just as important at the local level as it is globally. It applies as equally to a manager in Singapore as to a manager in Toledo, Ohio. For example, we often associate ***communication style*** with culturally different norms and therefore typically consider it merely an issue of 'etiquette.' Sometimes, we also appreciate its effect on productivity, but we rarely recognize its ethical implications."

"When a manager provides employees with the same desk, the same computer, the same tools, but fails to provide instructions that are equally understood and interpreted by native and non-native English-speaking employees, not only does the manager foster a lack of productivity from employees who cannot understand the subtle implications derived from culturally based expressions, but the manager then does not actively support (and can potentially damage) an employee's ability to excel, be successful and develop his or her professional career," Carobolante continues.

"When a manager is able to communicate in a culturally neutral fashion, employees are not put at a disadvantage in their ability to succeed as a result of poor communication skills by the manager. Even if an employee is uncertain about the meaning of what he or she is told, the employee most likely will not ask for clarification—for fear of been perceived as less intelligent [or having an English proficiency or cultural-difference problem]."

This example clearly illustrates the relationship between business ethics and productivity, and the ethical responsibility for clear communication on the part of the manager, as Carobolante explains. A lack of understanding of these dynamics often leads to:

1. Poor team performance, as some employees can establish relationships, while others find it difficult.
2. Inconsistent productivity across the organization, as some employees are well attuned with the goals, while others, though equally talented, tend to isolate themselves.
3. Employee dissatisfaction, as isolation tends to facilitate a sense of inequality and unfair treatment and leads to decline in employee engagement—a direct connection to productivity.
4. Ultimately, employee retention problems, as talented individuals who do not feel appreciated and lose faith in their ability to grow within the organization will leave the company.

As Carobolante concludes, "What is most difficult to recognize is the ethical responsibility associated with today's new globally diverse workplace, which requires managers to communicate effectively across multiple cultures at the same time so that all employees will have equal levels of participation, thus being able to contribute their expertise, creativity and commitment to reach the organization's goals."

In Closing

The message sent by leadership through organization culture determines the tone of business ethics in the workplace—how it is defined, perceived, promoted, demonstrated and "lived." Based on a foundation of solid and clear corporate values for ethical behavior, the right decisions can be made, thus fostering trust, fairness, transparency and compliance. With organizations becoming more global and more virtual, leaders must understand people of different backgrounds, cultures, values and perspectives. Ultimately, the ethical workplace is the common link between culture, values and leadership and productivity, organizational reputation and sustainability.

PART IV

The HR Professional

Chapter 16

Creativity and Innovation in Human Resource Management: A Sign of the Times

In a changing global economy, creativity and innovation are essential for success. Creativity in organizations offers opportunity for efficiencies, new ways of working, improved performance and increased growth. While the types of breakthroughs associated with science and technology are not typically those found in the HR space, creativity and innovation are the hallmarks of human resource management (HRM).

The 2008 study by The Boston Consulting Group and the World Federation of Personnel Management Associations, *Creating People Advantage: How to Address HR Challenges Worldwide Through 2015*, identifies three primary areas for action by HR and organizational leaders: (1) enabling the organization, (2) anticipating change, and (3) developing and retaining the best employees.[1] From a holistic and macro perspective, this *Research Quarterly* explores the critical roles of creativity and innovation in HRM, points to potential areas for creative and innovative approaches, and provides suggestions, solutions and examples from senior HR and business management professionals.

The Business Case

The growing number of books, studies and articles about creativity and innovation reflect their importance for all types of organizations—large and small, public and private, domestic and global. In people management, creativity is not just about ideas. It is also a pathway toward creating value, manifested in various ways and in different stages. Creativity and innovation begin with the process of generating and developing ideas and then move to collaboration and implementation, with the end result a positive influence on profitability.[2]

At the macro level, creativity and innovation in human resource management begin with alignment with the company mission and strategy. As a first step, focus on organizational culture is essential, as culture determines openness to new ideas and sets the tone for creativity. HRM philosophy, practices and policies and related HR services and products must be creative and innovative in both the short and long term, resulting in heightened value for a stronger, healthier and more viable organization.

The Meaning of Value Creation

Within the discussion of creativity and innovation, value creation is an important concept to understand because it is the foundation for success. At the organizational level, maximizing value means that stakeholders see goals achieved, contributing toward fulfilling the organization's mission. The ultimate goal of value creation is ***sustained value creation.*** Within value creation, there are two levels: personal and organizational. Both the individual and the organization must have a clear understanding of what is meant by strategy and success, including related activities and measures (see Table 16.1). Note that the value driver is the determinant of the outcome, not the outcome itself. In the best-case scenario, value drivers have a positive long-term impact.[3]

Table 16.1 Five Factors of Value Creation

- A definition of what value means to the organization and to you as an employee.
- A solid understanding of the multiple value creation perspectives and activities at the individual and organizational levels.
- A clear understanding of the organizational strategy and a clearly defined personal success strategy.
- A personal measure of success that exceeds organizational expectations.
- Mastery of speed without sacrificing quality.

Source: Adapted from Thakok, A. V. (2000). *Becoming a better value creator: How to improve the company's bottom line—and your own.* San Francisco: Jossey-Bass, Inc.

To truly be a value creator, HR must have an in-depth knowledge of the business strategy. Thus, it is important to understand the following key factors of value-context in one's organization and their influence on value creation: (1) how does one create value, (2) how people behave in organizations, and (3) what organizational dynamics enhance or diminish value creation. As the role of HRM for value creation continues to expand and grow, the types of key questions for HR to ask include:[4]

1. *How does HR create value?* Examples: attracting and retaining the best talent, reducing overall departmental cost structure.

2. *How does HR destroy value?* Examples: hiring the wrong people, excessive spending, inefficient use of resources.

3. *How do the financial goals of the company impede HR value creation?* Examples: too many initiatives, cutting back on the quality of the employee benefits package.

4. *How could HR redefine these goals?* Examples: take a long-term perspective toward developing HR, give HR more profit and loss focus and responsibility.

5. *What performance metrics does HR typically use?* Examples: increasing retention, process management (HR transactions), development of leadership and functional competencies.

Thinking Strategies for Creativity

Max Planck, the creator of quantum physics, said that new ideas are generated by creative imagination and making unusual associations. Fostering different thinking strategies opens more opportunities for creative application in the workplace. Below are three examples of successful thinking strategies for idea generation.5 While some approaches may not be typical in the HRM context, they can be used to leverage imagination, idea generation and implementation. Creative thinking strategies can translate into solutions of innovative changes or shifts in people management philosophy, organizational strategy and corporate values, as well as HRM policies, programs and initiatives.

Idea Bank

The concept of the idea bank is to use items to generate thoughts and ideas. Fill a container (such as a file, shoe box, drawer, coffee can) with items that might trigger ideas by association, including interesting quotes, pictures, cartoons, poems, doodles, articles, designs and advertisements. When working on a challenge, take out a few of these items and try to make associations and connections. Ask yourself questions that may pull out thoughts or ideas related to other connections. If the goal is to improve the business organization, for example, try drawing pictures, such as a circle. The circle could be seen as a cell within DNA. What could the connection be between the cell that carries genetic information and the organization? The result might be a list of values that could become the starting point of corporate values and codes of conduct, such as being respectful of each other in the workplace and being cooperative and collaborative in order to increase productivity.

Visual

Solutions can be created from working with visuals, using them to stimulate conversation and ideas, as demonstrated in this story. Dealing with poor economic times, the CEO of a Japanese perfume company asked his senior management team for ideas to survive the recession. He used a visual to prompt their thinking. He gave them a picture of a king crab, with instructions to study it and find ideas that they could apply to their organization. Examples of the connections that the senior team made include: (1) a crab sees 360 degrees: we must improve our market intelligence; (2) a crab has distinctive features: we need to develop a distinctive package that more clearly differentiates our products from our competitors'; (3) a crab is a scavenger: we need to allocate resources to table out other uses and markets for our products.

Thought Walk

A change in environment can lead to new thoughts and ideas. Jean-Jacques Rousseau, the famous French philosopher, did some of his most creative thinking when traveling alone. Taking a walk can provide refreshment and stimulus. Use objects seen or collected on a walk around the office to help focus on idea-building and solutions. Walking around the workplace and coming back with a list of things that were interesting, and then brainstorming with colleagues, can lead to listing related or unrelated characteristics, building ideas around them, and then finding more ideas. HRM processes that could be improved through team collaboration is an example of how this thinking strategy can be used.

Enabling the Organization

Chapter 3 states that "organizational leaders shape the workplace environment for learning—for idea generation, innovation and ultimately for sustainability."[6] The key organizational practice for successful innovation is visible commitment from senior management to establish and promote an innovative culture. Barriers to innovation include acquiring and developing the right talent and increasing the number of employees involved in the innovation process.[7] The two key phenomena directly tied to innovation in organizations are harnessing creativity and the renewal of the company. In some companies, innovation is strongly embedded in the corporate culture—the IT industry, for example, with Google, Microsoft and Apple. To thoughtfully create the culture needed for strategic innovation, HR and senior management can use a number of organizational levers. Three critical levers include the ability to judge risks and when to take them, managing ambiguity, and embracing unexpected events as learning events. At the same time, it is important to keep in mind that managing innovation is a paradoxical process: there must be both stability and openness to change.[8] HR is uniquely positioned to aid the business in this regard, as it deals with risk, paradox and ambiguous situations every day.

When designing an innovation model, two major issues are important: selecting the strategy and guiding the evolution of organizational culture. These roles are the responsibility of senior management, and HR must be part of that group. The secondary focus is organizational learning, rewards and metrics. Additionally, conducting an innovation climate assessment will help to gauge employee perception of the firm's mentality regarding innovation (see Table 16.2).[9]

Table 16.2 Innovation Diagnostics

Strategy	▪ Strong strategic alignment between innovation initiatives and business strategy. ▪ Clear management support and widely understood innovation strategy. ▪ Well developed innovation platforms and clear understanding of customer needs.
Processes	▪ Visioning and idea generation processes. ▪ Effective idea screen process, fast innovation process and good process improvement. ▪ Strong project management discipline.
Resources	▪ Business and technology departments aligned, collaborating on innovation. ▪ Active staffing of people with nontraditional perspectives. ▪ Effective building of core competencies and partnerships to accomplish innovation needs.
Organization	▪ Effective leadership that supports innovation. ▪ An incentive system that rewards staff for innovation. ▪ Senior management responsibility for collaboration and innovation results.

Source: Adapted from Davila, T., Epstein, M. J., & Shelton, R. (2006). *Making innovation work: How to manage it, measure it, and profit from it.* Upper Saddle River, NJ: Wharton School Publishing.

Finally, success can be a large threat to innovation. Organizations at greatest risk are those that become complacent and conservative, with the goal to protect the core competencies that have led to success. For example, HR can become lax in examining the status of the company culture when performance is high. Additionally, cultural values that become a cultural dogma can threaten continued success, as in the well-known example of Toyota. To remain viable, the company challenged the long-held view of lifetime employment in Japan by changing to a strong performance-based climate with employee salaries based on capabilities rather than seniority. These changes were part of a major cultural shift in the company's HRM philosophy.[10]

HR as a Strategic Partner

The study *Creating People Advantage: How to Address HR Challenges Worldwide Through 2015* points to the HR professional as a strategic partner to enable the organization.[11] Kenneth W. Moore, president of Ken Moore Associates and a member of the SHRM Organizational Development Special Expertise Panel, reiterates this point, stating that "for HR to succeed as a value-added element of an organization, it must focus its efforts on keeping the company in business and growing the organization. HR professionals must first thoroughly understand the business that the company is in, and secondly, fully understand and master the complexities of human capital management. As an internal asset, HR must directly connect its work to satisfying the needs of the customers who buy the products or services, while also satisfying the needs of other stakeholders. Human resources must become a profitable and productive contributor to the organization, lest it be marginalized or outsourced." As such, it is essential to align with corporate strategy when designing and implementing creative initiatives, as highlighted by researchers Olivas-Luján and Florkowski in their 2008 article on human resource information and communication technologies (see Table 16.3).

Table 16.3 Ten Suggestions for Practice

1. Ensure the goal will fit with company strategy.
2. Create a business case with multiple justifications/advantages (e.g., cost reductions, efficiency savings, retention strategy, less overtime required).
3. A sense of urgency is frequently a pre-requirement to innovation.
4. Beware of innovating for innovation's sake.
5. As early as appropriate, identify and involve key users (not just senior managers) in the decision process.
6. Bandwagon arguments (i.e., "our competition is already doing it") may not be logical or rational, but can be very effective.
7. Prepare answers in advance of meeting with resistors.
8. Resist the urge to demand or expect 100 percent acceptance: keep the organizational goals and strategy as the priority.
9. The past matters: successful creative programs and policies pave the way for more radical innovations.
10. Tolerance of error is critical to foster an innovative organization.

Source: Adapted from Olivas-Luján, M.R. & Florkowski, G. (2008). Diffusion of HR-ICTs: An innovations perspective. In G. Martin, M. Reddington, & H. Alexander (Eds.), *Technology, outsourcing & transforming HR* (pp. 231-256). Oxford: Butterworth-Heinemann.

Innovation strategy must begin at the macro level. As pointed out in a 2008 article titled "The Role of HR in Organizational Development and Innovation," there are foundation areas where HR professionals must assume strategic and innovative roles, focusing on culture and designing approaches that align HR strategies with that culture. Specifically, HR's role is to provide leadership for innovation through the underlying principles of the company culture and the cultural philosophy.[12] HR can establish a strategy that will support the mission and the greater company innovation strategy. Several factors influence the selection of an innovation strategy. Internal factors include organizational mission and strategy, success of the current business model, organizational culture, technical capabilities and funding. External factors include best practices, the competition and rate of technological change.[13]

Finally, it is important to state that HR leaders can affect creativity through developing innovative solutions to the challenges and issues faced by their respective organizations. At the same time, they can play a role in creativity by examining and challenging the work that they do and how they do it in order to find new and better ways of accelerating organizational performance. The following sections offer some examples and case studies of traditional HR problems with creative suggestions and solutions.

Anticipating Change

Even in challenging economic times, skills shortages remain a reality. Thus, HR leaders must anticipate change to determine future workforce needs, examine different economic scenarios and find creative and innovative ways to address human capital requirements. A key area for change management is the organization's communication strategy. Recent SHRM research found that communications strategies have increased by 92 percent in the economic downturn. For example, HR and senior management teams use confidence-building communications to assure employees of their value in the organization.[14]

Many organizations are carefully examining their requirements for human capital. Approximately 53 percent of companies have expanded their workforce planning strategies and 38 percent have initiated workforce planning. Such initiatives include the analysis of critical positions to identify internal talent for development to fill specific positions and/or take on broader responsibilities. As a result, leadership and career development are gaining importance. In fact, leadership development initiatives have increased by 80 percent (see Figure 16.1).[15]

Unscheduled time off is yet another area where companies may reduce costs. A 2009 SHRM survey report, *Examining Paid Leave in the Workplace*, identifies a number of incentives that organizations with paid sick time and PTO plans use to minimize employee use of unplanned time out, lower costs and maintain productivity. Some of the most commonly offered incentives to curb unplanned absences include compensation for unused leave (36 percent), extra time off (21 percent), bonuses (19 percent), being allowed to carry over leave into the next year (8 percent) and gift certificates (5 percent).[16]

Developing and Retaining the Best Employees

Managing talent is a top HR "value-add" for business success. HR needs to strategically lead workforce planning, consider the implications of the company's future geographic footprint and implement programs that will forward talent development. The following mini-case study portrays an example of how a mid-size organization in the highly competitive marketplace of international banking changed its approach to talent management and focused on its strength—the corporate culture. Libby Anderson, MS, SPHR, president of EDA HR Services, a member of the SHRM Organizational Development Special Expertise Panel and a trainer for the bank's initiative, describes in her own words why the firm took a calculated risk and invested in a new corporate training university, when most companies are focusing on conserving resources.

Mini-Case Study: A New Corporate University

Libby Anderson: Recently, I worked with a local bank in Florida that wanted to preserve and nurture its valuable workplace culture, even in tough times, and thus decided to develop its corporate training university. The main focus was to substantially raise the bar on the level of professionalism of every employee. A corporate culture of high expectations and productivity had made the difference in maintaining and growing the bank's customer base, and now the goal was to be a world-class organization in the banking industry. With the establishment of a new corporate university, the bank set out to strategically and thoughtfully cultivate its internal talent. The two-day kick off workshop with supervisors and managers, who came from throughout Florida to attend the event, was such a success that the organization developed a one-day mandatory program for the entire workforce. This initiative, completed within just a few months, was an enormous investment in terms of management and employee time, requiring the use of specialized trainers in the HR field to accomplish the goal. Ultimately, the company's strong focus on professionalism—from etiquette and personal appearance to productivity and customer service—will result in a "five-star" reputation in the marketplace.

In many cases, organizations in the United States find it necessary to look beyond the domestic labor market to fill certain positions. Thus, talent management also warrants a brief discussion of foreign nationals in the U.S. employment market and the necessity for innovative approaches. However, in the current U.S. immigration climate, retaining non-U.S. talent can be difficult. John R. Wilson, president and CEO of

Figure 16.1 | Changes as a Response to Current Financial Challenges: Leadership and Career Development

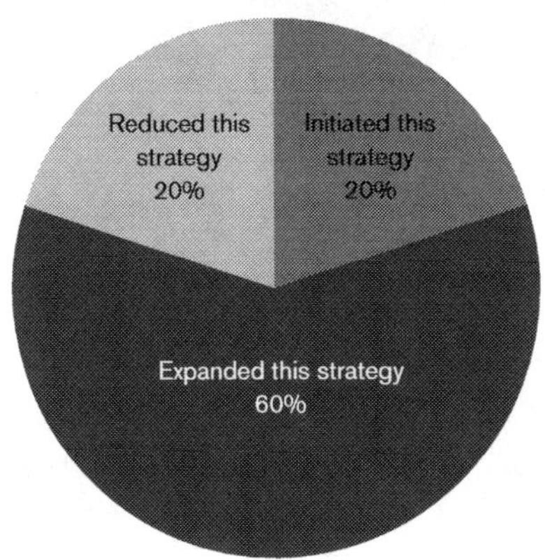

(n = 234)
*Leadership and career development initiatives in this study were defined as initiatives designed to develop a diverse generation of leaders from within.
Note: Respondents who indicated "not applicable" were excluded from this figure.
Source: SHRM 2009 Poll: Programs and Practices to Confront the Workplace Effects of the Downturn in the Economy

GoffWilson, P.A., and a member of the SHRM Global Special Expertise Panel, works closely with immigration issues in his law practice. He explains that the retention of key employees who are foreign nationals presents a variety of challenges during an economic downturn: "These employees were most often chosen by the employer as the best talent available, given unique skills they possess. The employer and the foreign national employee have now invested considerable resources for key positions. Unfortunately, many of these employees have not completed their immigration process and, as a result, must leave the United States due to the lack of available immigrant visas. The employer now finds itself scrambling to fill positions with lesser talent, oftentimes requiring the employer to outsource geographically to other countries." If immigration challenges occur, HR should develop contingency plans, where appropriate, by looking through a creative lens—for example, developing internal talent through mechanisms such as job sharing, internal training, succession planning and/or establishing knowledge management programs to share information in order to be better prepared for unexpected vacancies.

Employer brand and reputation are also directly related to the talent pipeline. A 2008 SHRM study found that 74 percent of HR professionals cite company reputation as critical for successful recruiting. HR professionals who work in talent management, benefits and compensation, employee relations, community outreach, knowledge management, and leadership development are engaged in tasks that ultimately have an impact on an organization's reputation. Taking innovative steps to improve and/or provide increased visibility of the company reputation through the employer brand—both within the organization and in the marketplace—is clearly one area where HR can creatively use the HR value proposition.[17]

Enhancing Employee Commitment

Employee commitment and engagement influence talent retention. Research has shown that employees with the highest levels of commitment perform 20 percent better and are 87 percent less likely to leave the organization.18 Not only does engagement have the potential to significantly affect employee retention, productivity and loyalty, it is also a key link to customer satisfaction, company reputation and overall stakeholder value.[19] Thus, finding creative ways to increase employee commitment is an HR imperative.

With today's changing demographics, the Millennial generation (Generation Y) is an important talent pool. Chapter 9 found that organizations that successfully attract the Millennial generation take a creative approach to adapting the workplace culture to meet the needs of this large segment of the workforce.[20] A 2008 survey by *Human Resource Executive* identified three primary factors important to this generation: (1) an employer with a sense of social responsibility that genuinely cares about the environment, (2) availability of the latest technology, and (3) work/life balance.[21] The following mini-case study shows how a U.S. company with traditional HRM policies and practices took a fresh approach to attract and keep new talent.

Mini-Case Study: Chesapeake Energy Corporation[22]

In the 1970s and 1980s, when high demand for oil declined, few young people wanted to work for energy companies. As a result, Chesapeake Energy had a gap of a generation in its workforce. With rapid growth in recent years, the company now actively seeks out young talent, but competition for young workers in this industry is fierce. To successfully attract and retain talent in the Millennial generation, the company focuses on being creative. Supervisors and managers—often Baby Boomers in their 50s—are trained to know what young workers want in the workplace. HR teaches managerial staff about what makes this generation different and unique, and offers recommendations on how to work with them. For example, how should a manager respond to a young employee who says that he or she is not being challenged? To demonstrate that the company is serious about using this talent pool to its fullest advantage, the organization has shifted how promotions are viewed. Young employees are now given responsibility early. If a younger employee is the best person for the position, he or she can be promoted instead of having to pay dues for many years. This shift is a clear stand to make the organization more attractive to the Millennial generation.

Managing Work/Life Balance

Work/life balance is an important factor for talent retention. In fact, the *2007-2008 Towers Perrin Global Workforce Study* cites work/life balance as one of the top five retention drivers worldwide.[23] One way to increase retention is to provide options to address work/life balance through various workplace policies and programs. The 2009 SHRM survey report *Examining Paid Leave in the Workplace* highlights a number of approaches to help employees balance their work and personal lives. For example, 45 percent of companies report offering paid floating holidays to their workers, 33 percent include paid personal leave, and 8 percent offer the option to purchase additional vacation leave.[24]

Flexible work arrangements (FWAs) are another way that organizations can help employees achieve work/life balance. SHRM research notes that such arrangements give employees greater control over where and when work gets done, allowing employees to optimize their work and life responsibilities. While U.S. organizations are not required to offer formal FWAs, this research found that such programs are beneficial for both employers and employees. For example, the quality of employees' personal/family life is positively affected, according to 68 percent of HR professionals, and retention of employees (89 percent) was reported to have been positively influenced by the implementation of FWAs. Thus, when HR and organizational leaders seek innovative opportunities to promote work/life balance, it is important to keep in mind that flexible work arrangements are well-received.[25]

Insights in the Global Arena

A paradigm shift is often at the forefront of innovation. Thus, global HR professionals must be aware of innovative trends and be open to trying new tactics. For example, managing globalization may require breaking with traditional ways of managing human capital to take full advantage of opportunities in new global markets. The following mini-case study presents such a scenario, where a shift in roles in a Chinese R&D operation will demand a shift in organizational culture and mindset.

Mini-Case Study: A Multinational Corporation in China

A company in the high-tech industry has an R&D operation in China, with hundreds of engineers. To date, these China-based R&D personnel have been focusing on adaptation of products developed outside of China to fit the needs of the Chinese marketplace. A remarkable characteristic of these employees—in contrast with the firm's R&D staff elsewhere in the world—is their youth. Their average age is in the late 20s, and many managers are under age 40. In general, they are well-educated, hard-working and very capable, but lack the experience of R&D staff in other parts of the world. In many cases, they tend to wait for direction rather than take initiative on their own, perhaps due to cultural factors such as deference to hierarchy and directives from the organization's headquarters.

Based on changes in the global business environment and the growing importance of the Chinese market, even during a time of financial crisis, the company has decided to make fundamental changes in the role of its R&D operation in China. Increasingly, the company has observed other businesses operating in China launching "first in China" products prior to introducing them in other regions. To be competitive, senior management has given this China R&D operation a new role: to search for these kinds of brand-new products and applications and to introduce them to other parts of the global organization.

To accomplish this task, the young Chinese R&D staff will be asked to move from a secondary product adaptation role to an integral role in the design and development of new products. In fact, since Chinese customers now have the potential of placing orders at sufficient volume, it is important to integrate their needs at the start of the design process rather than building applications more suited for other markets and then trying to adapt them to China. Therefore, the Chinese R&D employees will now be participating in global R&D teams working on the next generation of products.

Ernie Gundling, Ph.D., president of Aperian Global, consults with this multinational corporation. From a talent management standpoint, he notes that these changes will require a variety of forms of strategic partnership with HR and also will have significant implications: (1) Chinese employees will need to feel that they have official permission to take on different kinds of tasks and therefore will be watching closely to see how their actions—such as greater risk-taking—are rewarded or punished by their own managers, (2) R&D employees elsewhere in the world who are concerned about potential job loss will need to be convinced of the benefits of working more closely with their Chinese colleagues to facilitate effective knowledge transfer, and (3) engineers eager for career development are likely to be motivated by opportunities for more challenging and meaningful roles, which could be leveraged to improve retention in a very competitive talent market in China. As Dr. Gundling points out, "it will be important to provide language and cultural training in order for Chinese employees to participate effectively in global teams. Likewise, global team leaders will need to learn how to draw out the maximum contributions from their Chinese colleagues. Finally, there may be requirements for short-term or long-term expatriate assignments to and from China in order to better integrate key employees into global R&D operations." This mini-case study portrays an example of using talent quite differently than in the past, based on a new philosophy that requires significant cultural shifts in order to be successful.

In Closing

Never before have creativity and innovation in human resource management been so critical for sustainability and growth, particularly in tough economic times. Ultimately, as HR and organizational leaders seek out new ideas, willingness to take risks and try different approaches will be required for success.

Chapter 17

Career Development for HR Professionals

In today's work environment, the employee is ultimately responsible for his or her career development—the process by which individuals establish their current and future career objectives, assess their existing skills, knowledge or experience levels, and then implement an appropriate course of action to attain their desired career objectives.[1]

Although HR often provides career development opportunities to the overall workforce, HR professionals are also accountable for their own careers. Interestingly, the SHRM *2008 Managing Your HR Career* survey report found that nearly 75 percent of HR professionals began their careers in a business area other than HR.[2] Whether you are considering human resources as your first or next career or figuring out the next HR career move, career development is a vital part of career success. This article provides information and perspectives on what HR professionals, either new to HR or in the early years of their career, can do to leverage and promote their own career development for the future.

Pathways in HR

Many organizations have a human resource department. Since companies depend on employees for success in the marketplace, human resource management (HRM) is a critical function. HRM is defined as the formal structure within an organization responsible for all the decisions, strategies, factors, principles, operations, practices, functions, activities and methods related to the management of people.[3] Within HRM (commonly referred to as human resources or HR), there are three basic tracks:

- **Generalist:** An individual who possesses the capabilities to perform more than one diversified function rather than specializing in or having responsibility for one specific function.[4]
- **HR Specialist:** A term used to define an individual who has expertise and responsibility for a specific area or function within the field of human resources (e.g., compensation, benefits, employee relations).[5]
- **Executive:** The highest-ranking individual, or group of individuals, who has managerial or administrative authority for the business operations of the entire organization, business unit or function.[6]

Additionally, within HR, there are several areas of specialization (see Table 17.1). This list, although not exhaustive, provides the most common areas of HR (some areas are also known by other terms, as noted in brackets.) For students considering HR as a career, SHRM offers guidance in its new career resource, *Choose a Career. Choose HR* (To download a complete PDF of the brochure or request printed copies, visit the SHRM Student Programs web site.) Professionals interested in transitioning into HR will find that their expertise from another discipline can be beneficial. Individuals with experience in the following fields can use their expertise in an HR career: accounting (math data analysis, detail-orientation), sales (ability to access needs, influence people), marketing and communications (writing and presentation skills), information technology (programming, report writing, systems and software technology) and administrative (data entry, writing and customer service skills, scheduling/time management).[7] No matter the path that Career Development for HR Professionals leads to HR, all HR professionals will want to be knowledgeable about their respective career development plans.

Table 17.1 Specialization Areas in Human Resources

- Compensation and benefits (total rewards)
- Employee and labor relations
- Global human resource management
- Organizational and employee development (training)
- Safety and security (risk management)
- Staffing management (workplace planning/readiness, recruiting and retention)
- Workplace diversity

Looking Ahead

Before designing a career development plan, the key questions to consider are:

1. What skills are needed to be a successful HR professional?
2. What are your short- and long-term career goals?
3. What types of companies and work environments are best suited to your goals?
4. Where can you find good career advice?

While you may not have immediate answers for all of these questions, they provide an opening to begin the discussion about career development—at any career stage.

SHRM research indicates that the top most important factors for an individual to attain his or her next job in human resources are strategic/critical thinking, leadership and interpersonal communication skills (see Figure 17.1). Additionally, key business partner skills for HR include strategic planning, organizational design, change management, cross-functional experience and global understanding.[8] When assessing your skill base and development gaps, these points are important to keep in mind. Further, when seeking career advice, there are many options. According to the SHRM *2008 Managing Your HR Career* survey report, the most influential sources of HR career advice are supervisors/managers or other high-level professionals in a supervisory role, colleagues, mentors/coaches, HR professionals, professors and friends.[9] Clearly, to foster career development, there is a rich resource of professionals available to draw upon and network with in order to gain insight and gather feedback.

Additionally, whether you are new to the HR field, considering a move to another company or seeking to broaden or expand your HR experience, there are different roads to reach these goals. In particular, today's work environment offers many choices that have an impact on career development: geography, company size, industry, internal positions or external consulting. In terms of geography, different regions present various possibilities, such as lifestyle, cost of living, different climates, proximity to family, company size and industry focus.[10] For industry sectors, HR professionals should consider the types of services and products to which they are drawn. Another way to select an industry is to consider the "hot fields" where growth and opportunity are likely. Company size is another key factor. In today's global market, experience in a multi-billion-dollar global company is highly recommended. Some companies emphasize a friendly work atmosphere, with opportunities for creative and innovative projects. There are other choices to consider, such as whether to develop a career in a company with a well-known brand, such as Microsoft or Southwest Airlines, or work as a consultant in a specialized company, using skills such as speaking, writing and designing training materials.[11] To

Figure 17.1 | Top Most Important Factors in Attaining Next HR Job

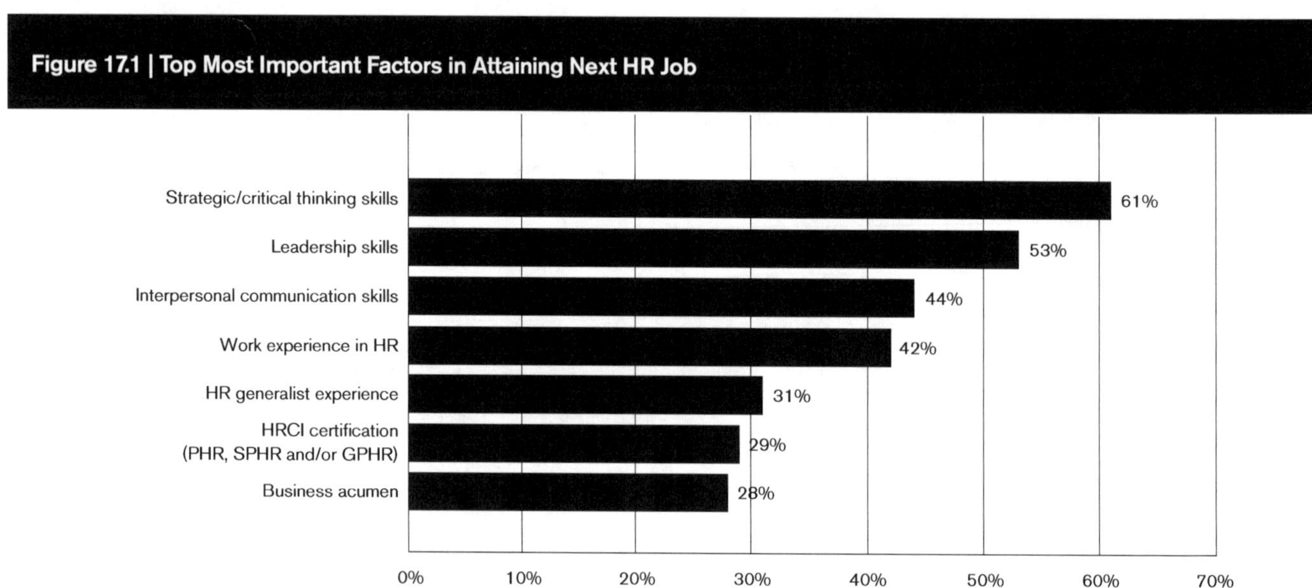

(n = 604)

Note: Data sorted in descending order. Percentages do not total 100% as respondents were allowed to select up to five choices.
Source: 2008 Managing Your HR Career: A Survey Report by the Society for Human Resource Management

gain new expertise and hone skills, thoughtful consideration of these many options plays a critical part in career development.

Make a Plan

To leverage the process of career development, career coaches highly recommend having a career plan. First, there are a number of factors to consider: (1) knowledge of what skills are essential or "nice to have;" (2) assessment of your own skill set and experience; (3) identification of skill/experience gaps; (4) possible avenues to fill gaps; and (5) a record of accomplishment. One way to approach this plan is by using time segments, such as three- to five-year increments. In fact, taking the next step may require planning as far as a year ahead.[12] At the same time, it is important to understand that having a plan does not necessarily mean all will move forward as you expect or anticipate. Being flexible allows for recognition of opportunities when they come along. Suggested action items to design a career plan are:[13]

1. Work with your manager to discuss core competencies and ways to expand your demonstration of them.
2. Work with your manager to develop an action plan for other developmental areas.
3. Request and/or volunteer for special projects to gain exposure and experience.
4. Become known for your work by building a portfolio of measurable accomplishments.
5. Actively support the achievements and success of your colleagues and staff and, by doing so, share in their success.

Figure 17.2 | HR Organizations—a Business Partner Model

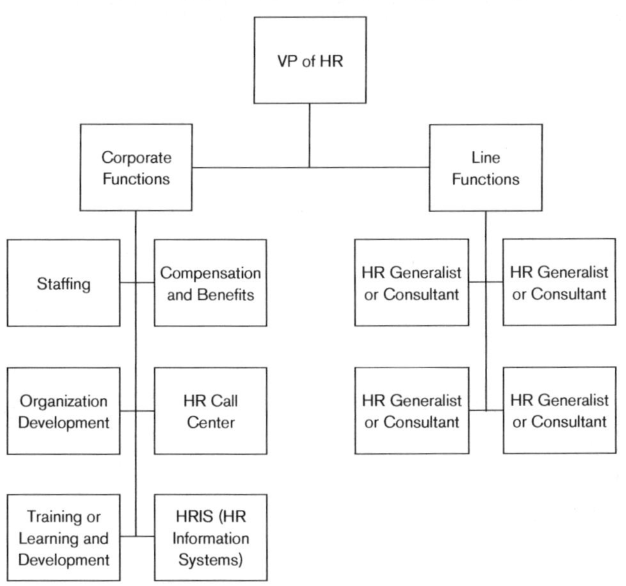

Source: Adapted from Palmer, P., & Finney, M. L. (2004). *The human resource professional's career guide: Building a position of strength.* San Francisco: John Wiley & Sons, Inc.

As highlighted in Figure 17.2, different HR functions within an HR organization require a variety of skill sets—from specialist to generalist to executive. Research shows that certain skills and experience are essential in order to attain the next HR job. The SHRM *2008 Managing Your HR Career* survey report identified the top "very important" factors as interpersonal communication skills, personal drive/ambition, reputation in the organization, strategic/critical thinking skills, leadership skills, work experience in HR and business acumen. The survey results also highlight the importance of having HR generalist experience, networking and risk management skills. In fact, four out of 10 respondents were in a generalist role, the most commonly reported function across job titles.[14]

However, the survey results also found that HR professionals can encounter obstacles in advancing their careers. In fact, these kinds of obstacles can also be seen in other professions, such as difficulty due to a lack of specific experience in different organizations, industries and sectors. Other obstacles cited include a lack of corporate HR strategy, business acumen, leadership skills, a mentor, formal HR education, academic degrees and certification. Additional obstacles are the lack of a clear HR career path, the size of the organization, and gender, racial and age-biased glass ceilings.[15]

Finally, another key factor in career planning is "the pace"—that is, how quickly you want to move forward on your career track. Different paces have advantages and disadvantages. For example, the advantages of the "fast route" are additional responsibility, more promotions and a quicker climb up the corporate ladder; a drawback is the loss of work/life balance (such as family time and/or non-work-related interests). The fast pace is not for everyone. Another option, "taking the scenic route," allows for family and outside interests as well as steady career progress. No one pace is right for everyone, so it is best to adopt a combination of both fast and more moderate paces, adjusting direction as needed.[16]

Find a Mentor/Career Coach

In the business world, formal mentoring programs are gaining attention as a vehicle to improve turnover, foster employee loyalty and provide training and development to talented employees. The informal mentoring relationship provides high-level coaching, opens doors to different networking opportunities and often results in a lasting professional friendship.[17] As highlighted in the Hay Group study of the world's best-in-class leaders, the top 20 of this group have their high-potential employees mentored by admired senior leaders.[18]

For the HR professional, the goal of the mentor or career coach is not merely to help attain another job. The greater purpose is to gain advice about working well with one's manager, improve performance, increase one's salary and grow with added responsibilities.[19] A career coach helps the HR professional develop strong working relationships, gain insights to reach the next level of responsibility and become an effective leader. In selecting a coach, it is important to ensure trust and respect. The HR professional will want to have personal chemistry with his or her coach and feel comfortable sharing weaknesses and strengths. To assist the HR professional to move beyond his or her comfort levels, a coach will use various formal assessment processes, such as the Myers-Briggs Type Indicator, interviews with colleagues or the 360-degree feedback tool.[20]

If the organization does not offer a mentoring program, the company may cover the cost of an outside coach. There are many ways to find a mentor/coach, such as by working with your manager, using your network and asking for recommendations at a professional HR chapter.[21] In fact, some chapters, such as the Northern Virginia SHRM Chapter, have formal mentoring programs. SHRM also offers a mentoring program (for more information, visit www.shrm.org).

Formal Education

In today's competitive environment, a college or university degree is essential for HR professionals. SHRM's research reveals that 85 percent of HR professionals have a college/university degree (associate's degree, bachelor's degree, master's degree, MBA, JD or doctorate). Of this group, 47 percent hold a bachelor's degree and 20 percent a master's degree. Additionally, about 64 percent of respondents received their highest degree in either business administration/management (35 percent) or human resources (29 percent).[22]

As discussed earlier, HR professionals must be knowledgeable about their field and be business literate. Therefore, when selecting a school, HR professionals will want to carefully consider a mix of HR and business courses. Some universities offer advanced executive programs for HR career development. SHRM has developed an HR curriculum, emphasizing that human resource management should be taught in a business context.[23] Increasingly, more schools and universities are adopting this approach. Information about these schools can be found on the Resources for HR Educators page of the SHRM web site and in SHRM Foundation's directory of graduate programs in HR management. For a sample listing of international universities, refer to Table 5 in the June 2007 issue of *SHRM Research Quarterly*, "HR and Business Education."

Professional Certification

Certification by a professional group is another way that HR professionals promote their knowledge, credibility and experience. A professional certification indicates that an individual has met the standards of a credentialing organization. Professional certification, which is indicated by specific initials after one's name (e.g., PHR, SPHR), not only provides recognition of one's accomplishments but also exhibits initiative to potential employers. The SHRM *2008 Managing Your HR Career* survey report found that 53 percent of respondents have one or more professional certification (e.g., PHR 55 percent, SPHR 32 percent and GPHR 4 percent).[24] SHRM's affiliate, the Human Resource Certification Institute (HRCI, www.hrci.org), develops and offers credentialing programs to validate mastery in the field of human resource management and to promote organizational effectiveness. At this time, HRCI offers three core certifications for HR professionals, as well as California state-specific certification:

- PHR® (Professional in Human Resources)
- SPHR® (Senior Professional in Human Resources)
- GPHR® (Global Professional in Human Resources)
- PHR-CA® and SPHR-CA® (PHR with state certification in California and SPHR with state certification in California).

Below are examples of other HR certifications from various organizations: CDA (Certified Diversity Recruiter), AIRS Human Capital Solutions: www.airsdirectory.com

- CEBS (Certified Employee Benefits Specialist), International Society of Certified Employee Benefits Specialists: www.iscebs.org
- CCP (Certified Compensation Professional), World at Work: www.worldatwork.org
- GMS (Global Mobility Specialist), Worldwide ERC: www.erc.org

HR Competencies

To be effective in new and/or different roles—and have a positive impact on organizational performance—HR professionals continually need to expand their competencies as individuals and professionals within organizational HR departments. Royal Dutch Shell, a global company with a core HR staff of

3,000 serving 112,000 employees in 40 countries, is an excellent example of a company that proactively promotes career development for its HR professionals. Shell conducts an annual global HR talent review, such as reviewing individual development plans, identifying future leaders and implementing succession plans. An online tool, HR Functional Excellence, also helps HR professionals manage their short-, medium- and long-term goals. In addition, Shell has identified the skills required for different job levels in its Leadership Competence Framework and Personal and Business Skills Competence Framework. These tools help HR staff better determine internal and external educational opportunities to increase their competencies.[25]

To assess their competency levels, HR professionals may refer to the *2007 Human Resource Competency Study*. While not focused on a particular specialization of HR, this model presents a broad spectrum of HR competencies. This global research project, conducted by the RBL Group and the Ross School at the University of Michigan, in conjunction with the Society for Human Resource Management and other parties, examined the business context and demographics that affect the HR profession and identified six essential HR competency domains. The study considered the roles played by HR professionals and, in particular, examined their ability to use knowledge.[26]

Outlined in Table 17.2 are the six HR competency domains: credible activist, operational executive, business ally, talent manager/organizational designer, culture and change steward, and strategy architect. In the business ally domain, for example, HR professionals contribute to the success of the organization by knowing the setting or social context in which the company operates, articulating the value proposition and leveraging business technology. In this area, HR professionals demonstrate that they know the business sections of the company (e.g., finance, marketing) and how the company makes money (i.e., the value chain of the business—the customers—and their reasons for buying the company's products/services).[27] By using this competency model, HR professionals can evaluate their strengths and identify areas in which they need to develop expertise to be an effective business partner (visit HR Competency Assessment Tools page on the SHRM web site).

Global Human Resources

As the pace and reach of globalization continue to increase, HR professionals should equip themselves with the skills and experiences to make strategic contributions. In fact, many companies now require time spent working and living in other major markets as a prerequisite to the C-suite. In a global environment, like other business professionals, HR professionals will interface with international staff, suppliers and government officials, all of whom will likely have different values, beliefs, assumptions and traditions. Therefore, HR professionals must continuously broaden their global business expertise, global mindset and global leadership skills.

Table 17.2 HR Competencies for Today and the Future

Relationships	**Credible Activist** is respected, admired, listened to and offers a point of view, takes a position and challenges assumptions by: ▪ Delivering results with integrity ▪ Sharing information ▪ Building relationship of trust ▪ Doing HR with an "attitude" (risk taking, influencing others, candidate observations)
Systems & Processes	**Operational Executive** administers the day-to-day work of managing people inside an organization by: ▪ Implementing workplace policies ▪ Advancing HR technology **Business Ally** contributes to the success of the business by: ▪ Interpreting social context ▪ Serving the value chain ▪ Articulating the value proposition ▪ Leveraging business technology
Organizational Capabilities	**Talent Manager/Organizational Designer** masters theory, research and practice in both talent management and organizational design by: ▪ Ensuring today's and tomorrow's talent ▪ Developing talent ▪ Shaping organization and communication ▪ Fostering communication ▪ Designing reward systems **Culture & Change Steward** recognizes, articulates and helps shape a company's culture by: ▪ Facilitating change ▪ Crafting culture ▪ Valuing culture ▪ Personalizing culture (helping employees find meaning in their work, managing work/life balance, encouraging innovation) **Strategy Architect** knows how to make the right change happen by: ▪ Sustaining strategic agility ▪ Engaging customers

Source: Adapted from The *2007 Human Resource Competency Study* conducted by the RBL Group and the Ross School of Business at the University of Michigan, in cooperation with regional partners: SHRM, IAE, IMI, AHRI, National HRD Network and Tsinghua University.

Yet, to achieve first-hand knowledge of a global business requires taking advantage of opportunities to learn, develop and gain a solid understanding of the pressing issues related to a global business. As Dr. Ernest Gundling, co-president of a management consulting firm and a member of the SHRM Staffing Management Special Expertise Panel, notes, "If we think five to 10 years into the future, global experience and expertise will only become a more crucial factor in succession planning and promotion discussions." He points out that while the traditional three- to five-year international assignment is the best way to immerse oneself in another culture, there are also other possible development opportunities, such as international business trips, short-term assignments, participating in or leading a global team and working for a leader with substantial global experience. Additional developmental opportunities include joining a business unit with a global portfolio, obtaining a global HR professional certification, gaining proficiency in a foreign language and hosting employees from abroad.

Further, in addition to essential leadership competencies, global HR leaders face unique challenges that require additional competencies. To clarify, a global leader is commonly defined as someone who cultivates business in a foreign market, sets business strategy at a global level and manages globally diverse and diffused teams.[28] Researchers have identified global leadership competencies that can contribute to success. For the HR professional working in a global environment, these global competencies—a global mindset, cross-cultural communication skills and respect for cultural diversity—are essential for success in the global workplace.[29] Morgan McCall and George Hollenback studied successful global leaders and developed a list of common competencies specific to the global leader (see Table 17.3).[30] HR practitioners can focus on these global leadership competencies to support their own professional development and thus better promote their organization's overall global business strategy.

Table 17.3 Global Executive Competencies

- Open-minded and flexible in thought and tactics
- Cultural interest and sensitivity
- Able to deal with complexity
- Resilient, resourceful, optimistic and energetic
- Honesty and integrity
- Stable personal life
- Value-added technical or business skills

Source: McCall, M., & Hollenbeck, G. (2002). *Developing global executives: The lessons of international experience.* Boston: Harvard Business School Publishing.

Other Developmental Opportunities

Additional opportunities for career development include volunteering in professional capacities, participating in professional HR associations and using focused professional development. Volunteering enhances career development and often has the dual advantage of giving back to the community. It offers the opportunity to build expertise, provide mentorship to others, gain leadership expertise and/or expand your network—while making a contribution. For example, by serving on a committee of a local charity event, an individual gives positive exposure to his or her company while supporting a worthy cause. When selecting where or how to volunteer, HR professionals should consider factors such as available personal time (versus family and work commitments), personal and professional interests and whether support would be needed from the company (e.g., activities held during the business day or business week, financial contributions, travel expenses).[31] Membership in professional associations offers opportunities to gain professional contacts, keep up to date with developments in the HR field, gain wider access to certification credits and become known in the HR community. SHRM, for example, has more than 575 local professional membership chapters where HR professionals come together to learn, grow and share information. The use of focused professional development is gaining momentum as a vehicle to address career development. For example, a recent study by the Hay Group found that the best companies for leaders encourage rotational job assignments, so that high-potential employees gain exposure cross-divisionally and/or functionally, as well as work abroad to gain international experience.[32]

What Do HR Jobs Pay?

When mapping out a career transition, relocation or a move to another industry—or aiming for a higher HR position—it is useful to have a clear understanding of remuneration. Many factors determine salary, such as demand, geographic region, company size, experience and education. HR professionals can gain a better sense of what companies pay by using an up-to-date database. One such database is the SHRM Compensation Data Center. In collaboration with Watson Wyatt Data Services, a recognized leader in global compensation surveys, the Center provides information on salaries, bonuses and other cash compensation for approximately 170 HR positions. Further, in addition to annual base pay, the various options of total rewards (e.g., salary, benefits, retirement plans, bonuses, stock options, vacation days) are important to keep in mind. The article titled "Incentive Pay Fuels HR Salaries" in the November 2007 issue of HR Magazine provides a broad perspective regarding HR compensation. For example, 2007 medium total cash compensation of common HR positions includes an HR assistant at $36,600 annual compensation, an employee training specialist at $55,500 and a human resources manager at $80,700.[33]

More Tips for Career Development

1. **Ask your family and friends.** Family members and friends can be a useful resource. It is helpful to learn what they think you are good at doing and what they see as your strengths and weaknesses.[34]

2. **Keep a career journal.** By keeping a detailed list of accomplishments (e.g., project descriptions with results/outcomes and corresponding metrics, company name, date, HR role/title, business focus), it is easier to update a resume and prepare for interviews. In the interview, you can then more easily talk about why certain decisions were made and what their impact was, how problems were solved, how a project was successfully completed and/or why a new initiative or process was established—and thus demonstrate strategic thinking and business acumen as well as your HR contributions to the organization.[35]

3. **Get advice from experts.** Based on their individual career experiences, members of the SHRM Organizational Development Special Expertise Panel provide advice to today's HR professionals:

What do you recommend for professionals new to HR in order to further their careers?

- "Read! *HR Magazine*, business periodicals, newspapers—to gain an understanding of HR competencies, the business and the environmental influences on the industry."
- "Remain relevant with shifting times: be active in the community by volunteering in leadership roles on nonprofit boards."
- "Learn how to read and understand your company's financial condition at all times—then link your work to those performance drivers."
- "Take an international assignment."
- "Invest time and money in your development."

What is the best advice you have ever received?

- "If someone offers you an opportunity to demonstrate your skills, embrace the opportunity with humility, grace and passion."
- "Develop business acumen, including business metrics."
- "Diversify your career development portfolio with stretch assignments."
- "Surround yourself with people who know things you do not, and that includes hiring people who may be smarter than you."
- "Discover what you are passionate about and find opportunities to do that."
- "I was out to change the world. My manager helped me understand that change does not happen overnight and that HR professionals need to be smart about the causes they pursue."

What suggestions can you offer HR professionals who want to move up the corporate ladder?

- "Be a generalist early in your career, make a mid-career move to specialist in one to three fields, and later in your career, select a specialty that you enjoy most or accept a top HR position."
- "Learn how your company operates, understand the industry and develop a rapport with the power brokers."
- "Deliberately choose career moves that will give breadth and depth to your portfolio."
- "Don't limit yourself to HR activities. Learn everything you can about the business you are in and focus your HR efforts on making other functions (e.g., operations, marketing) exceed their objectives."
- "Introduce yourself and volunteer, so that your skills become obvious to those around you."

Later in Life

Increasingly, older workers are extending their working years beyond the traditional age of retirement. Consequently, it is wise to begin to think now about what areas of work might be of interest later in life. After retiring from an HR career, there are many types of related jobs that would be appropriate for HR professionals. Options to consider include consultant, speaker, author, executive recruiter, teacher/college professor, corporate advisor or board member, and community or economic development volunteer.[36] As suggested in Table 17.4, being better prepared for future opportunities—now or later in life—means being a life-long learner.

Table 17.4 Prepare Yourself for the Future!
▪ Stay curious–be a life-long learner and embrace new opportunities.
▪ Give yourself the chance to try new things.
▪ Embrace failure–learn one thing from that experience.
▪ Seize opportunities to meet new people–especially people outside of your company.
▪ Explore unknown territories–new geographic locations.
▪ Give yourself time to think about the future.

Source: Adapted from Palmer, P., & Finney, M. L. (2004). *The human resource professional's career guide: Building a position of strength.* San Francisco: John Wiley & Sons, Inc.

Conclusion

As do all professional fields, human resource management has many facets of learning, expertise and levels of responsibility. Consequently, there are many opportunities to contribute to an organization. Career development in HR requires honest self-appraisal and thoughtful evaluation—along with feedback from others—to know what the next steps are to leverage the right opportunities. Therefore, to move forward at any career stage, taking stock of your career path and identifying possible career development opportunities is a smart move.

Endnotes

CHAPTER 1

[1] Kaye, B., & Jordan-Evans, S. (2003, August). Engaging talent. *Executive Excellence, 20, 8, 11.*

[2] Corporate Leadership Council. (2004). *Driving performance and retention through employee engagement.* Washington, DC: Corporate Executive Board.

[3] Ibid.

[4] SHRM Glossary of HR Terms, www.shrm.org.

[5] Society for Human Resource Management. (2006). *SHRM Special Expertise Panels 2006 trends report.* Alexandria, VA: Author.

[6] Casner-Lotto, J., & Barrington, L. (2006). *Are they really ready to work?* United States: The Conference Board, Corporate Voices for Working Families, Partnership for 21st Century Skills and Society for Human Resource Management.

[7] Konrad, A. M. (2006, March/April). Engaging employees through high-involvement work practices. *Ivey Business Journal Online, 1-6,* www.iveybusinessjournal.com.

[8] Ibid.

[9] Vance, R. J. (2006). *Effective practice guidelines: Employee engagement and commitment.* Alexandria, VA: SHRM Foundation.

[10] Crabtree, S. (2005, January 13). Engagement keeps the doctor away. *Gallup Management Journal,* http://gmj.gallup.com.

[11] Salanova, M., Agut, S., & María Peiró, J. (2005). Linking organizational resources and work engagement to employee and customer loyalty: The mediation of service climate. *Journal of Applied Psychology, 90, 6, 1217-1227.*

[12] Shaufeli, W., Salanova, M., González-Romá, V., & Bakkers, A. B. (2002). The measurement of engagement and burnout: A two sample confirmatory factor analytic approach. *Journal of Happiness Studies, 3, 71-92.*

[13] Corporate Leadership Council. (2004). *Driving performance and retention through employee engagement.* Washington, DC: Corporate Executive Board.

[14] Ibid.

[15] Families and Work Institute. (2004). *Generation & gender in the workplace.* New York: American Business Collaboration.

[16] Glen, C. (2006). Key skills retention and motivation: The war for talent still rages and retention is the high ground. *Industrial and Commercial Training, 38, 1, 37-46.*

[17] May, D. R., Gilson, R. L., & Harter, L. M. (2004). The psychological conditions of meaningfulness, safety and availability and the engagement of the human spirit at work. *Journal of Occupational and Organizational Psychology, 77, 11-37.*

[18] Kaye, B., & Jordan-Evans, S. (2003, August).

[19] Ramarajan, L., & Barsade, S. G. (2006, November). *What makes the job tough? The influence of organizational respect on burnout in the human services.* Philadelphia, PA: University of Pennsylvania.

[20] Kress, N. (2005, May). Engaging your employees through the power of communication. *Workspan, 48, 5, 26-32.*

[21] BlessingWhite. (2006). *Employee engagement report.* Princeton, NJ: Author.

[22] Corporate Leadership Council. (2004).

[23] Wright, P. M., Gardner, T. M., & Moynihan, L. M. (2003). The impact of HR practices on the performance of business units. *Human Resource Management Journal, 13, 3, 21-36.*

[24] Rieger, T., & Kamins, C. (2006, November 9). Are you failing to engage? *Gallup Management Journal.* Retrieved November 14, 2006, from http://gmj.gallup.com.

[25] Thackray, J. (2001, March 15). Feedback for real. *Gallup Management Journal.* Retrieved November 15, 2006, from http://gmj.gallup.com.

[26] Galinksy, E., Bond, J. T., Kim, S. S., Backon, L., Brownfield, E., & Sakai, K. (2005). *Overwork in America: When the way we work becomes too much.* New York: Families and Work Institute.

[27] Vance, R. J. (2006).

[28] Glen, C. (2006).

[29] Gil Saura, I., Berenquer Contrí, G., Cervera Taulet, A., & Moliner Velázquez, B. (2005). Relationships among customer orientation, service orientation and job satisfaction in

financial services. *International Journal of Service Industry Management, 16, 5, 497-526.*

[30] Branham, L. (2005). Planning to become an employer of choice. *Journal of Organizational Excellence, 24, 3, 57-68.*

[31] Society for Human Resource Management. (2006).

[32] Mercer HR Consulting. (2006, July). *Managing attraction and retention in China.* Retrieved October 26, 2006, from www.mercer.com.

[33] Towers Perrin. (2006, February). *Winning strategies for a global workforce.* Retrieved October 25, 2006, from www.towersperrin.com.

[34] Ibid.

[35] Galinksy, E., Salmond, K., Bond, J. T., Brumit Kropf, M., Moore, M., & Harrington, B. (2003). *Leaders in a global economy: A study of executive women and men.* New York: Families and Work Institute, Catalyst and the Center for Work & Family.

[36] Feeling good matters in the workplace. (2006, January 12). *Gallup Management Journal.*

[37] Corporate Leadership Council. (2004). *Driving performance and retention through employee engagement.* Washington, DC: Corporate Executive Board.

[38] BlessingWhite. (2006).

CHAPTER 2

[1] Dunn, J. (2006, Winter). Strategic human resources and strategic organization development: An alliance for the future? *Organization Development Journal, 24(4), 69-77.*

[2] SHRM Glossary of Human Resources Terms, www.shrm.org.

[3] Dunn, J. (2006, Winter).

[4] Yaeger, T., & Sorensen, P. (2006, Winter). Strategic organization development: Past to present. *Organization Development Journal, 24(4), 10-17.*

[5] McLean, G. N. (2006). *Organizational development: Principles, processes, performance.* San Francisco: Berrett-Koehler Publishers, Inc.

[6] Yaeger, T., & Sorensen, P. (2006, Winter).

[7] Jelinek, M. & Litterer, J. A. (1988). Why O.D. must become strategic. In W. A. Pasmore & R. W. Woodman (Eds.), *Research in Organizational Change and Development.* Greenwich, CT: JAI Press.

[8] Cummings, T., & Worley, C. (2005). *Organization development and change (8th ed.).* Mason, OH: Southwestern.

[9] Wirtenberg, J., Abrams, L., & Ott, C. (2004). Assessing the field of organization development. *The Journal of Applied Behavioral Science, 40(4), 465-480.*

[10] IBM Business Consulting Services. (2006, March). Majority of global CEOs plan fundamental change and expect new forms of innovation to drive growth, according to IBM study [Press Release]. Retrieved April 10, 2007, from www-03.ibm.com/press/us/en/pressrelease/19289.wss.

[11] Carol Rusaw, A. (2005/Winter, 2004/Fall). How downsizing affects organizational memory in government: Some implications for professional and organizational development. *Public Administration Quarterly, 28(3/4), 482-501.*

[12] McLean, G. N. (2006).

[13] Ibid.

[14] McLean, G. N., & McLean, L. D. (2001). If we can't define HRD in one country, how can we define it in an international context? *Human Resource International, 4 (3), 313-326.*

[15] Ibid.

[16] Rowland, H. (2007). Organizational development: The new buzz word. *Strategic Direction, 23(1), 3.*

[17] Henderson, G. M., & Provo, J. (2006, June). A new work ahead—are we ready? *Human Resource Development Review, 5(2), 274-278.*

[18] Beer, M., & Nohria, N. (2000). Resolving the tension between theories E and O of change. In M. Beer & N. Nohria (Eds.), *Breaking the code of change (pp. 1-33).* Boston: Harvard Business School Press.

[19] McWilliam, C. L., & Ward-Griffin, C. (2006). Implementing organizational change in health and social services. *Journal of Organizational Change Management, 19(2), 119-136.*

[20] Rossett, A. (1998). *First things fast: A handbook for performance analysis.* San Francisco: John Wiley & Sons, Inc.

[21] Worley, C. G., & Feyerherm, A. E. (2003). Reflections on the future of organization development. *Journal of Applied Behavioral Science, 39, 97-115.*

[22] McLean, G. N. (2006).

[23] Eisen, S. (2002). *A Delphi study of global trends, implications for managers, emerging intervention strategies, and future competencies in OD.* Retrieved from www.Sonoma.edu/programs/od/delphi/.

[24] Smith, I. W. (2004). Continuing professional development and workplace learning 6: HRD and organizational learning. *Learning Management, 25(1/2), 64+.*

[25] Cummings, T. G., & Worley, C. G. (2005).

[26] Mager, R., & Pipe, P. (1997). *Analyzing performance problems (3rd ed.).* Atlanta: CEP Press.

[27] McLean, G. N. (2006).

[28] Ibid.

[29] Ibid.

[30] Ibid.

[31] Kirkpatrick, D. L. (1998). *Evaluating training programs:*

The four levels (2nd ed.). San Francisco: Berrett-Koehler.

[32] Rowland, H. (2007).

[33] McLean, G. N. (2006).

[34] Yeager, T. F., Head, T. C., & Sorensen, P. F. (2006). *Global organization development: Managing unprecedented change.* Greenwich, CT: Information Age Publishing, Inc.

[35] McLean, G. N. (2006).

[36] Hofstede, G. (2001). *Culture's consequences (2nd ed.).* London: Sage.

[37] Yeager, T. F., Head, T. C., & Sorensen, P. F. (2006).

[38] McLean, G. N. (2006).

[39] Cummings, T. & Worley, C. (2001). *Organization development and change (7th ed.).* Cincinnati, OH: South Western College Publishing.

[40] Yeager, T. F., Head, T. C., & Sorensen, P. F. (2006).

[41] Ibid.

[42] Razi, N. (2006, Winter). Employing O.D. strategies in the globalization of HR. *Organization Development Journal, 24(4), 62-69.*

CHAPTER 3

[1] Groff, T. R., & Jones, T. P. (2003). *Introduction to knowledge management: KM in business.* New York: Butterworth Heinemann.

[2] The Boston Consulting Group, Inc., and the World Federation of Personnel Management Associations. (2008). *Creating people advantage: How to address HR challenges worldwide through 2015.* Boston: The Boston Consulting Group, Inc.

[3] Society for Human Resource Management. (2008, May). *2008 executive roundtable symposium on sustainability and human resource management strategy.* Alexandria: Author.

[4] Boudreau, J. W. (2003). Strategic knowledge measurement and management. In S. E. Jackson, M. A. Hitt & A. S. Denisi, (Eds.), *Managing knowledge for sustained competitive advantage: Designing strategies for effective human resource management (pp. 360 - 396).* San Francisco: Jossey-Bass.

[5] Hackett, B. (2000). *Beyond knowledge management: New ways to work and learn.* New York: The Conference Board.

[6] Society for Human Resource Management. (2008). Customized benchmarking service [unpublished data]: www.shrm.org/Research/benchmarks/Pages/default.aspx.

[7] Lepak, D. P., & Snell, S.A. (2003). Managing the human resource architecture for knowledge-based competition. In S. E. Jackson, M. A. Hitt & A. S. Denisi, (Eds.), *Managing knowledge for sustained competitive advantage: Designing strategies for effective human resource management (pp. 127-154).* San Francisco: Jossey-Bass.

[8] Groff, T. D., & Jones, T. P. (2003).

[9] Lewison, J. (2001, October). *Knowledge management* [SHRM white paper]. Retrieved February 13, 2009, from www.shrm.org

[10] Tetrick, L. E., & Da Silva, N. (2003). Assessing the culture and climate for organizational learning. In S. E. Jackson, M. A. Hitt & A. S. Denisi, (Eds.), *Managing knowledge for sustained competitive advantage: Designing strategies for effective human resource management (pp. 333-359).* San Francisco: Jossey-Bass.

[11] Coulson-Thomas, C. (2004). The knowledge entrepreneurship challenge: Moving on from knowledge sharing to knowledge creation and exploitation. *The Learning Organization, 11(1), 84+.*

[12] Hackett, B. (2000).

[13] Schramm, J. (2005). Learning to compete in a knowledge economy. *SHRM Workplace Visions, 3.*

[14] Maurer, S. D., Lee, T. W., and Mitchell, T. R. (2003). Retaining knowledge by retaining technical professionals: Implications of the unfolding turnover model and the job embeddedness construct, in Jackson, S. E., Hitt, M. A., & Denisi, A. S. (Eds.). *Managing knowledge for sustained competitive advantage: Designing strategies for effective human resource management (pp. 303-330).* San Francisco: Jossey-Bass.

[15] Levering, R., & Moskowitz, M. (2009, February 2). And the winners are... *Fortune, 159(2), 67-78.*

[16] Tampoe, M. (1996). Motivating knowledge workers: The challenge for the 1990s. In P.S. Myers, (Ed.), *Knowledge management and organizational design (pp. 179-189).* Boston: Butterworth-Heinemann.

[17] Kim, J., & King, J. (2004). Managing knowledge work: Specialization and collaboration of engineering problem-solving. *Journal of Knowledge Management, 8(2), 53+.*

[18] Wenger, E., McDermott, R. & Snyder, W. M. (2002). *Cultivating communities of practice: A guide to managing knowledge.* Boston: Harvard Business School Press.

[19] Archibald, D., & McDermott, R. (2008, November/December). Benchmarking the impact of communities of practices. *Knowledge Management Review, 11(5), 16-22.*

[20] Groff, T. D., & Jones, T. P. (2003).

[21] Society for Human Resource Management. (2008, April–June). The employer brand: A strategic tool to attract, recruit and retain talent. *Staffing Research, 2.*

[22] Day, D. V. (2007). *Developing leadership talent* [SHRM Foundation's Effective Practice Guidelines Series]. Alexandria, VA: SHRM Foundation.

[23] Society for Human Resource Management. (2009, April). *SHRM poll: Programs and practices to confront the workplace*

effects of a downturn in the economy. Retrieved from www.shrm.org/surveys.

[24] HR Policy Association. (2008). *2008 annual CHRO survey.* Retrieved February 11, 2009, from www.hrpolicy.org.

[25] AARP. (2005, December). *The business case for workers age 50+: Planning for tomorrow's talent needs in today's competitive environment.* Washington, DC: AARP & Towers Perrin.

[26] Lahaie, D. (2005). The impact of corporate memory loss: What happens with a senior executive leaves? *International Journal of Health Care Quality, 18(4/5), 35-48.*

[27] Piktialis, D., & Greenes, K. A. (2008). *Bridging the gaps: How to transfer knowledge in today's multigenerational workplace.* New York: The Conference Board.

[28] Watson Wyatt. (2008, October). *Workforce planning survey.* Retrieved February 11, 2009, from www.watsonwyatt.com.

[29] Society for Human Resource Management. (2009, February 1). *SHRM economic stimulus price winners and their case studies.* Retrieved from www.shrm.org.

[30] Gundling, E. (2003). *Working Globe-Smart: 12 people skills for doing business across borders.* Mountain View, CA: Davies-Black Publishing.

[31] Woodward, N. H. (2009, February 25). *Expats still essential, but recession changes their roles.* Retrieved March 10, 2009, from www.shrm.org.

[32] Inkpen, A. C. (2008, March/April). Managing knowledge transfer in international alliances. *Thunderbird International Business Review, 50(2), 77+.*

[33] Minbaeva, D. B., & Michailova, S. (2004). Knowledge transfer and expatriation in multinational corporations: The role of disseminative capacity. *Employee Relations, 26(6), 663+.*

[34] Hackett, B. (2000).

[35] Ibid.

CHAPTER 4

[1] Benedict, A. (2007, April). *SHRM 2007 change managements survey report.* Alexandria, VA: Society for Human Resource Management.

[2] SHRM Glossary of Human Resources Terms, www.shrm.org.

[3] Guy, G., & Beaman, K. (2005). *Effecting change in business enterprises: Current trends in change management.* New York: The Conference Board.

[4] Harvard Business School Press and Society for Human Resource Management. (2005). *The essentials of managing change and transition.* Alexandria, VA: Authors.

[5] Ibid.

[6] Guy, G., & Beaman, K. (2005).

[7] Harvard Business School Press and Society for Human Resource Management. (2005).

[8] Ibid.

[9] Benedict, A. (2007, April).

[10] Guy, G., & Beaman, K. (2005).

[11] Ibid.

[12] Lawler III, E., & Worley, C. G. (2006). *Built to change.* San Francisco: Jossey-Bass.

[13] Palmer, B. (2004). Overcoming resistance to change. *Quality Progress, 37(4), 35-40.*

[14] Armenakis, A. A., & Harris, S. G. (2002). Crafting a change message to create transformational readiness. *Journal of Organizational Change, 15(2), 169-184.*

[15] Harvard Business School Press and Society for Human Resource Management. (2005).

[16] Guy, G., & Beaman, K. (2005).

[17] Zaccaro, S. J., & Banks, D. (2004, Winter). Leader visioning and adaptability: Bridging the gap between research and practice on the ability to manage change. *Human Resource Management, 43(4), 367-380.*

[18] Neves, P., & Caetano, A. (2006, December). Social exchange processes in organizational change: The roles of trust and control. *Journal of Change Management, 6(4), 351-364.*

[19] Senge, P. M. (1990). *The fifth dimension: The art and practice of the learning organization.* New York: Doubleday.

[20] Kotter, J. P. (1996). *Leading change.* Boston: Harvard Business School Press.

[21] Zaccaro, S. J., & Banks, D. (2004, Winter).

[22] Benedict, A. (2007, April).

[23] Holden, D. (2007, May/June). The missing ingredient in organizational change. *Industrial Management, 49(3), 8-15.*

[24] Hughes, M. (2007, March). The tools and techniques of change management. *Journal of Change Management, 7(1), 37-49.*

[25] Harvard Business School Press and Society for Human Resource Management. (2005).

[26] Karp, T. (2005, March). Unpacking the mysteries of change: Mental modeling. *Journal of Change Management, 5(1), 87-97.*

[27] Harvard Business School Press and Society for Human Resource Management. (2005).

[28] Lawler, E. E., III. (2000). Pay system change: Lag, lead or both? In M. Beer & N. Northia (Eds.), *Breaking the code of change, pp. 323-336.* Boston: Harvard Business School Press.

[29] Harvard Business School Press and Society for Human Resource Management. (2005).

[30] Ibid.

[31] Bridges, W. (2003). *Managing transitions: Making the most*

of change (2nd ed.) Cambridge, MA: Da Capo Press.

[32] Harvard Business School Press and Society for Human Resource Management. (2005).

[33] Kriegel, R., & Brandt, D. (1996). *Sacred cows make the best burgers: Developing change-ready people and organizations.* New York: Warner Books.

[34] Benedict, A. (2007, April).

[35] Bareil, C., Savoie, A. & Meunier, S. (2007, March). Patterns of discomfort with organizational change. *Journal of Change Management, 7(1), 13-24.*

[36] Evans, P., Pucik, V., & Barsoux, J-L. (2002). *The global challenge. New York: McGraw-Hill Irwin.*

[37] Society for Human Resource Management. (2007, July 23). Starbucks adds HRO to menu. Retrieved July 23, 2007, from www.shrm.org/outsourcing/news.

[38] Brahy, S. (2006, Autumn). Six solution pillars for successful cultural integration of international M&As. *Journal of Organizational Excellence, 53-63.*

[39] Kelly, S. (2005, November/December). Entrusting HR to lead a major global transformation program. *Strategic HR Review, 5(1), 20-24.*

CHAPTER 5

[1] Presser, J. (2006, February). *Approaching a metric of human capital synergy* [SHRM white paper]. Retrieved June 10, 2006, from www.shrm.org.

[2] Huselid, M. (1995, June). The impact of human resource management practices on turnover, productivity and corporate financial performance. *Academy of Management Journal, 38, 3, 635+.*

[3] SHRM Glossary of HR Terms, www.shrm.org.

[4] Schneider, C. (2006, February 15). The new human-capital metrics. *CFO Magazine, 1+.*

[5] Gates, S. (2002). *Value at work: The risks and opportunities of human capital measurement and reporting.* New York: The Conference Board.

[6] Ulrich, D., & Brockbank, W. (2005). *The HR value proposition.* Boston: Harvard Business School Press.

[7] Gates, S. (2003). *Linking people to strategy: From top management support to line management buy-in.* New York: The Conference Board.

[8] Ulrich, D., & Brockbank, W. (2005).

[9] Becker, B. E., Huselid, M. A., & Ulrich, D. (2001). *The HR scorecard: Linking people, strategy and performance.* Boston: Harvard Business School Press.

[10] Lawler III, E. E., Boudreau, J. W., & Mohrman, S. A. (2006). *Achieving strategic excellence: An assessment of human resource organizations.* Palo Alto, CA: Stanford University Press.

[11] Gates, S. (2002).

[12] Ibid.

[13] Dooney, J., & Smith, N. (2005). *SHRM human capital benchmarking study: 2005 executive summary.* Alexandria, VA: Society for Human Resource Management.

[14] Gates, S. (2002).

[15] HayGroup. (2005, February). *What makes the most admired companies great?* Retrieved May 4, 2006, from www.haygroup.com.

[16] Becker, B. E., Huselid, M. A., & Ulrich, D. (2001).

[17] Denton, D. K. (2006, March). Measuring relevant things. *Performance Improvement, 45, 3, 33–38.*

[18] Ibid.

[19] Schneider, C. (2006, February 15).

[20] Becker, B. E., Huselid, M. A., & Ulrich, D. (2001).

[21] Ibid.

[22] Esen, E. (2006, June). *2006 job satisfaction survey report.* Alexandria, VA: Society for Human Resource Management.

[23] Watson Wyatt and Human Resource Planning Society. (2006, April). *The human capital ROI study.* Retrieved May 4, 2006, from www.watsonwyatt.com.

[24] The Gallup Organization. (1998). *Employee engagement = Business success.* Retrieved March 7, 2006, from www.bcpublicservica.ca.

[25] Schramm, J. (2006, April). HR technology competencies: New roles for HR professionals. *SHRM Research Quarterly, 1.*

[26] Collison, J. (2005, March). *2005 HR technology survey report.* Alexandria, VA: Society for Human Resource Management.

[27] Lawler III, E. E., Boudreau, J. W., & Mohrman, S. A. (2006).

[28] Dooney, J., & Smith, N. (2006). *SHRM human capital benchmarking study: 2006 executive summary.* Retrieved June 29, 2006, from www.shrm.org.

[29] HayGroup. (2006, April). Leading the global organization: Structure, process, and people as the keys to success. *Hay Group Insight Selections, 11, 1–4.*

[30] Watson Wyatt Worldwide. (2005). *Maximizing the return on your human capital investment: The 2005 Watson Wyatt human capital index report.* Washington, D.C.: Author.

[31] Sparrow, P., Brewster, C., & Harris, H. (2004). *Globalizing human resource management.* London: Routledge.

[32] GMAC Relocation Services. (2006). *Global relocation trends 2005 survey report.* Woodridge, IL: Author.

[33] Society for Human Resource Management. (2005, November). *Measuring the success of a repatriation program* [SHRM Case Study]. Retrieved May 9, 2006, from www.

shrm.org/hrresources/casestudies_published/GlobalHR.asp.

CHAPTER 6

[1] Lawler, III, E. E. (2005, Summer). From human resource management to organizational effectiveness. *Human Resource Management*, 44, 2, 165-169.

[2] SHRM Glossary of HR Terms, www.shrm.org.

[3] AberdeenGroup Inc./Human Capital Institute. (2005). *Retaining talent: Retention and succession in the corporate workforce*. Boston: Author.

[4] Morton, L. (2004, January). *Integrated and integrative talent management: A strategic HR framework*. New York: The Conference Board.

[5] Fegley, S. (2006, January). *2006 talent management survey report*. Alexandria, VA: Society for Human Resource Management.

[6] Morton, L. (2005). *Talent management value imperatives: Strategies for execution*. New York: The Conference Board.

[7] Towers Perrin. (2003). *Working today: Understanding what drives employee engagement*. Retrieved February 14, 2006, from www.towersperrin.com.

[8] Tucker, E., Kao, T., & Verma, N. (2005). *Next-generation talent management: Insights on how workforce trends are changing the face of talent management*. Retrieved January 26, 2006, from www.hewitt.com.

[9] Morton, L. (2005).

[10] Dell, D., & Hickey, J. (2002). *Sustaining the talent quest*. New York: The Conference Board.

[11] Collison, J. (2005, June). *2005 future of the U.S. labor pool survey report*. Alexandria, VA: Society for Human Resource Management.

[12] Morton, L. (2005).

[13] IBM Corporation. (2005). *The capability with: The global human capital study 2005*. Retrieved January 12, 2006, from www.ibm.com.

[14] Morton, L. (2005).

[15] Fegley, S. (2006, January).

[16] Dell, D., & Hickey, J. (2002).

[17] Corporate Leadership Council. (2003). *High-impact succession management: From succession planning to strategic executive talent management*. Retrieved January 27, 2006, from www.executiveboard.com.

[18] Walker, J. W., & LaRocco, J. M. (2002). Perspectives: Talent pools: The best and the rest. *HR. Human Resource Planning*, 25, 3, 12-15.

[19] Corporate Leadership Council. (2004). *Driving performance and retention through employee engagement*. Retrieved January 27, 2006, from www.executiveboard.com.

[20] The Gallup Organization. (1998). *Employee engagement = business success*. Retrieved March 7, 2006, from www.bcpublicservica.ca.

[21] Burke, M. E. (2005, March). *2005 reward programs and incentive compensation survey report*. Alexandria, VA: Society for Human Resource Management.

[22] Towers Perrin. (2003).

[23] Dell, D., & Hickey, J. (2002).

[24] Fegley, S. (2006, January).

[25] Throop, M. (2005). *Fueling the talent engine: Finding and keeping high performers, a case study of Yahoo! Inc.* Alexandria, VA: SHRM Foundation.

[26] Tucker, E., Kao, T., & Verma, N. (2005).

[27] Watson Wyatt. (2005). *Maximizing the return on your human capital investment: The 2005 human capital index report*. Retrieved March 6, 2006, from www.watsonwyatt.com.

[28] Fegley, S. (2006, June). *2006 succession planning survey report*. Alexandria, VA: Society for Human Resource Management.

[29] Cohn, J. M., Khurana, R., & Reeves, L. (2005, October). Growing talent as if your business depended on it. *Harvard Business Review*, 83, 10, 62-70.

[30] Fegley, S. (2006, January).

[31] Cohn, J. M., Khurana, R., & Reeves, L. (2005, October). Growing talent as if your business depended on it. *Harvard Business Review*, 83, 10, 62-70.

[32] Huselid, M. A., Becker, B.E., & Beatty, R. W. (2005). *The workforce scorecard: Managing human capital to execute strategy*. Boston: Harvard Business School Press.

[33] Morton, L. (2005).

[34] Ibid.

[35] Accenture. (2004). *The high-performance workforce study 2004*. Retrieved January 31, 2006, from www.accenture.com.

[36] Schweyer, A. (2004). *Talent management systems: Best practices in technology solutions for recruitment, retention and workforce planning*. Canada: John Wiley & Sons Canada, Ltd.

[37] Manpower. (2006, February). *Talent shortage survey: Global results*. Retrieved February 21, 2006, from www.manpower.com.

[38] Kuptsch, C., & Pang, E. F. (Eds.) (2006, January). *Competing for global talent*. Retrieved January 30, 2006, from www.ilo.org.

[39] Building Engineering & Science Talent/BEST. (2004). *The talent imperative: Meeting America Section 1s challenge in science and engineering*, ASAP. San Diego, CA: Author.

[40] Gandossy, R., & Kao, T. (2004). *Channels to anywhere: The supply chain for global content.* Retrieved January 26, 2006, from www.hewitt.com.

[41] Industrial Relations Counselors, Inc. (2004). IRC survey of global talent management practices. Retrieved January 12, 2006, from www.orcinc.com.

[42] Tucker, E., Kao, T., & Verma, N. (2005).

[43] Morton, L. (2005).

[44] Deloitte. (2005). *2005 talent management strategies survey.* Retrieved February 8, 2006, from www.deloitte.com.

[45] Brakeley, H., Cheese, P., & Clinton, D. (2004). *The high-performance workforce study 2004.* Retrieved January 13, 2006, from www.accenture.com.

[46] Industrial Relations Counselors, Inc. (2004). *IRC Survey of global talent management practices.* Retrieved March 6, 2006, from www.orcinc.com.

[47] Towers Perrin. (2002, September). *Talent management powers performance at leading companies.* Retrieved January 23, 2006, from www.towersperrin.com.

[48] Tucker, E., Kao, T., & Verma, N. (2005).

CHAPTER 7

[1] Murray, S. (2003). *Diversity makes a difference.* Retrieved February 22, 2005, from www.allianzgroup.com.

[2] Judy, R. W., & D'Amico, C. (1997). *Workforce 2020: Work and workers in the 21st century.* Indianapolis, IN: Hudson Institute.

[3] SHRM Glossary of HR Terms, www.shrm.org.

[4] Jayne, M. E. A., & Dipboye, R. L. (2004, Winter). Leveraging diversity to improve business performance: Research findings and recommendations for organizations. *Human Resource Management*, 43, 4, 409-424.

[5] Thomas, D. A., & Ely, R. J. (2002). Making differences matter: A new paradigm for managing diversity. Retrieved March 15, 2005, from *Harvard Business Online*, www.hbsp.harvard.edu.

[6] Gardenswartz, L., Rowe, A., Digh, D., & Bennett, M. F. (2003). *The global diversity desk reference: Managing an international workforce.* San Francisco: John Wiley & Sons, Inc.

[7] Hart, M. A. (1997). Managing diversity for sustained competitiveness. New York: The Conference Board.

[8] Carr-Ruffino, N. (1999). *Diversity success strategies.* Boston: Butterworth-Heinemann.

[9] Hart, M. A. (1997).

[10] Ibid.

[11] Martino, J. (1999). Diversity: An imperative for business success. New York: The Conference Board.

[12] Society for Human Resource Management. (2001). Impact of diversity initiatives on the bottom line. Alexandria, VA: Author.

[13] Richard, O. C., & Johnson. N. B. (2001, Summer). Understanding the impact of human resource diversity practices on firm performance. *Journal of Managerial Issues*, 13, 2, 177-196.

[14] Lockwood, N. R. (2004, December). Corporate social responsibility: HR's leadership role. *SHRM Research Quarterly*, 4.

[15] Cole, Y. (2004, June/July). Top 10 companies for diversity. *DiversityInc* Top, 3, 3, 56-96.

[16] Humphreys, J. M. (2004, August). The multicultural economy 2004: America's minority buying power. Georgia Business and Economic Conditions, 63, 3, 1-12.

[17] Cole, Y. (2004, June/July).

[18] Martino, J. (1999).

[19] Schramm, J. (2004). SHRM 2004-2005 workplace forecast: A strategic outlook. Alexandria, VA: Society for Human Resource Management.

[20] Hubbard, E. E. (2004). *The diversity scorecard: Evaluating the impact of diversity on organizational performance.* Burlington, MA: Elsevier Butterworth-Heinemann.

[21] Ibid.

[22] Ibid.

[23] Matton, J. N., & Hernandez, C. M. (2004, August). A new study identifies the "makes and breaks" of diversity initiatives. *Journal of Organizational Excellence*, 23, 4, 47-58.

[24] Hart, M. A. (1997).

[25] Cole, Y. (2004, June/July).

[26] Carr-Ruffino, N. (1999).

[27] Business for Social Responsibility. Board diversity. Retrieved March 4, 2005, from www.bsr.org.

[28] Catalyst. (2003). 2003 Catalyst census of women board of directors. Retrieved March 7, 2005, from www.catalystwomen.org/knowledge/titles/files/fact/Snapshotpercent202004.pdf.

[29] The Conference Board. (1999). Board diversity in U.S. corporations. New York: Author.

[30] Richard, O. C., & Johnson, N. B. (2001, Summer).

[31] Collison, J. (2003, June). SHRM/NOWCC/CED older workers survey. Alexandria, VA: Society for Human Resource Management.

[32] Towers Perrin HR Services. (2004, October). The coming talent crisis: Is your organization ready? Retrieved March 21, 2005, from www.towers.com.

[33] Hewitt Associates. (n.d.). The workforce is changing: Is your organization? Retrieved March 21, 2005, from www.hewitt.com.

[34] Hewitt Associates. (2004, February). Preparing the workforce of tomorrow. Retrieved February 10, 2005, from www.hewitt.com.

[35] Cole, Y. (2004, June/July).

[36] Burke, M. E. (2004, June). SHRM 2004 benefits survey report. Alexandria, VA: Society for Human Resource Management.

[37] Lengnick-Hall, M. L., Gaunt, Ph., & Collison, J. (2003, April). Employer incentives for hiring individuals with disabilities. Alexandria, VA: Society for Human Resource Management.

[38] Grant, B. Z., & Kleiner, B. H. (1997). Managing diversity in the workplace. Equal Opportunities International, 16, 3, 26-33.

[39] Hewitt Associates. (2004, February).

[40] Ibid.

[41] Hubbard, E. E. (2004).

[42] Ibid.

[43] Matton, J. N., & Hernandez, C. M. (2004, August).

[44] National Urban League. (2004, June). Diversity practices that work: The American worker speaks. New York: Author.

[45] Kochan, T., Bezrukova, K., Ely, R., Jackson, S., Joshi, A., Jen, K., et al. (2002, October). The effects of diversity on business performance: Report of the Diversity Research Network. Building Opportunities for Leadership Development Initiative, Alfred P. Sloan Foundation and the Society for Human Resource Management.

[46] Catalyst. (2004). Connecting corporate performance and gender diversity. New York: Author.

[47] European Commission. (2000, June 28). Communication from the Commission to the Council, the European Parliament, the Economic and Social Committee and the Committee of the Regions: Social policy agenda. Brussels: Author.

[48] European Commission. (2004). Equality and non-discrimination—annual report 2004. Brussels: Author.

[49] European Commission. (2005). Report from the Commission to the Council, the European Parliament, the European Economic and Social Committee and the Committee of the Regions on equality between men and women, 2005. Brussels: Author.

[50] Singh, V., & Point, S. (2004, August). Promoting diversity management: New challenges and new responses by top companies across Europe. Management Focus [Cranfield School of Management, www.cranfield.ac.uk/som/research/centres/cdwbl].

CHAPTER 8

[1] Bodley, J. H. (1999). *Cultural anthropology: Tribes, states, and the global system (3rd edition).* United Kingdom: Mayfield Publishing Company.

[2] Society for Human Resource Management. (n.d.). Glossary of HR Terms. Retrieved May 14, 2008, from www.shrm.org.

[3] Society for Human Resource Management. (2007). *The 2007-2008 workplace trends list.* Alexandria, VA: Author.

[4] Society for Human Resource Management. (2008). *Workplace forecast.* Alexandria, VA: Author.

[5] Gelfand, M. J., Erez, M., & Aycan, Z. (2007). Cross-cultural organizational behavior. *Annual Review of Psychology, 58, 479-514.*

[6] Alon, I., & Higgins, J. M. (2005, November/December). Global leadership success through emotional and cultural intelligence. *Business Horizons, 48(6), 501+.*

[7] Hall, E. T. (1964). *The silent language.* Greenwich, CT: Fawcett.

[8] Hofstede, G. (1980). *Culture's consequences: International differences in work-related values.* Newbury Park, CA: Sage.

[9] Trompenaars, F. (1993). *Riding the waves of culture: Understanding cultural diversity in business.* London: Nicholas Brealey.

[10] Varner, I., & Beamer, L. (2005). *Intercultural communication in the global workplace* (3rd ed.). London: McGraw-Hill Irwin.

[11] Ting-Toomey, S. (Ed.). (1994). *The challenge of facework: Cross-cultural and interpersonal issues.* Albany, NY: State University of New York Press.

[12] Trompenaars, F., & Hampden-Turner, C. (1998). *Riding the waves of culture: Understanding diversity in global business, 2nd edition.* New York: McGraw-Hill.

[13] Ibid.

[14] Ibid.

[15] Ibid.

[16] Ibid.

[17] Tosti, D. T. (2002). Global fluency. In K. Beaman (Ed.), *Boundaryless HR: Human capital management in the global economy (pp. 109-119).* Austin, TX: Rector Duncan & Associates, Inc.

[18] Varner, I., & Beamer, L. (2005).

[19] Martin, J. S., & Chaney, L. H. (2006). *Global business etiquette: A guide to international communication and customs.* Westport, CT: Praeger Publishers.

[20] Zhu, Y., Nel, P., & Bhat, R. (2006). A cross cultural study of communication strategies for building business relationships. *Cross Cultural Management, 6(3), 319-341.*

[21] Ibid, p. 339.

[22] Carter, L. (2005). *Best practices in leading the global workforce: How the best global companies ensure success throughout their workforce.* Burlington, MA: Linkage.

[23] Storti, C. (2007). *Speaking of India: Bridging the communication gap when working with Indians.* Boston: Intercultural Press.

[24] Carobolante, L. (2005, October). International English: A new global tool. *Mobility, 64-80.*

[25] Kim, T-Y, & Leung, K. (2007). Forming and reacting to overall fairness: A cross-cultural perspective. *Organizational Behavior and Human Decision Processes, 104, 83-95.*

[26] Lam, S. K., Schaubroeck, J., & Aryee, S. (2002, February). Relationship between organizational justice and employee work outcomes: A cross-national study. *Journal of Organizational Behavior, 23, 1-18.*

[27] Level Playing Field Institute. (2007, January). *The corporate leavers study: The cost of employee turnover due solely to unfairness in the workplace.* San Francisco: Author.

[28] From ADLER, *International Dimensions of Organizational Behavior, 5E,* © 2008 South-Western, a part of Cengage Learning, Inc.

[29] Moran, R. T., Harris, P. R., & Stripp, W. G. (1993). *Developing the global organization: Strategies for human resource professionals.* London: Gulf Publishing Company.

[30] Claus, L. (2008). Employee performance management in MNCs: Reconciling the need for global integration and local responsiveness. *European J. International Management, 2(2), 132-152.*

[31] Harris, P. R., & Moran, R. T. (1996). *Managing cultural differences,* 4th edition. Houston, TX: Gulf.

[32] Aycan, Z. (2005, July). The interplay between cultural and institutional/structural contingencies in human resource management practices. *The International Journal of Human Resource Management, 16(7), 1083-1119.*

[33] Milliman, J., Taylor, S., & Czaplewski, A. J. (2002). Cross-cultural performance feedback in multinational enterprises: Opportunity for organizational learning. *HR. Human Resource Planning, 25(3), 29-44.*

[34] Ibid.

[35] Ibid.

[36] Ibid.

[37] Papalexandris, N., & Panayotopoulou, L. (2004). Exploring the mutual interaction of societal culture and human resource management practices: Evidence from 19 countries. *Employee Relations, 26(5), 495-509.*

[38] Society for Human Resource Management. (2008). *Workplace forecast.* Alexandria, VA: Author.

[39] Rosen, R., Digh, P., Singer, M., & Phillips, C. (2000). *Global literacies: Lessons on business leadership and national cultures.* New York: Simon & Schuster.

[40] Gupta, A. K., Govindarajan, V., & Wang, H. (2008). *The quest for global dominance: Transforming global presence into global competitive advantage* (2nd edition). San Francisco: John Wiley & Sons, Inc.

[41] Evans, P., Pucik, V., & Barsoux, J-L. (2002). *The global challenge: Frameworks for international human resource management.* New York: McGraw-Hill Irwin.

[42] Gupta, A. K., Govindarajan, V., & Wang, H. (2008).

[43] Aycan, A. (2005, July). The interplay between cultural and institutional/structural contingencies and institutional/structural contingencies in human resource management practices. *The International Journal of Human Resource Management, 16(7), 1083-1119.*

[44] Aycan, A., & Fikret-Pasa, S. (2003). Career choices, job selection criteria, and leadership preferences in a transitional nation: The case of Turkey. *Journal of Career Development, 30(2), 129-144.*

[45] Inkson, K., Khapova, S. N., & Parker, P. (2007). Careers in cross-cultural perspective. *Career Development International, 12(1), 5+.*

[46] Lirio, P., Lituchy, T. R., Ines Monserrat, S., Olivas-Lujan, M. R., Duffy, J. A., Fox, S., et al. (2007). Exploring career-life success and family social support of successful women in Canada, Argentina and Mexico. *Career Development International, 12(1), 28-50.*

[47] Khapova, S. N. (2007). Dynamics of western career attributes in the Russian context. *Career Development International, 12(1), 68+.*

[48] Song, L. J., & Werbel, J. D. (2007). Guanxi as impetus? Career exploration in China and the United States. *Career Development International, 12(1), 51-67.*

CHAPTER 9

[1] Judy, R. W., & D'Amico, C. (1997). *Workforce 2020: Work and workers in the 21st century.* Indianapolis, IN: Hudson Institute, Inc.

[2] Society for Human Resource Management. (2008). *Workplace forecast.* Alexandria, VA: Author.

[3] Eyerman, R., & Turner, B. S. (1998). Outline of a theory of generations. *European Journal of Social Theory, 1, 91-106.*

[4] Kupperschmidt, B. R. (2000). Multigeneration employees: strategies for effective management. *The Health Care Manager, 19, 65-76.*

[5] Schewe, C. D., & Evans, S. M. (2000). Market segmentation by cohorts: The value and validity of cohorts in America and abroad. *Journal of Marketing Management, 16, 129-142.*

[6] AARP. (2007). *Leading a multigenerational workforce.*

Washington, DC: Author.

7 Glass, A. (2007). Understanding generational differences for competitive success. *Industrial and Commercial Training, 39(2), 98+.*

8 Ibid.

9 Arsenault, P. M. (2004). Validating generational differences: A legitimate diversity and leadership issue. Leadership & Organization Development, 25(1/2), 124+.

10 Author compilation from several sources: AARP. (2007). *Leading a multigenerational workforce.* Washington, DC: Author. Sabatini Fraone, J., Hartmann, D., & McNally, K. (2008). *The multigenerational workforce: Management implications and strategies for collaboration* [Executive Briefing Series]. Boston: Boston College Center for Work & Family. Zemke, R., Raines, C., & Filipczak, B. (2000). *Generations at work: Managing the clash of veterans, boomers, Xers and nexters in your workplace.* New York: American Management Association.

11 AARP. (2007).

12 Deal, J. J. (2007). *Retiring the generation gap: How employees young and old can find common ground.* San Francisco: Jossey-Bass and the Center for Creative Leadership.

13 Whitacre, T. (2007, December). Managing a multigenerational workforce. *Quality Progress, 40(1), 67.*

14 Tucker, E., Kao, T., & Verma, N. (2005, July/August). Next-generation talent management: Insights on how workforce trends are changing the face of talent management. *Business Credit, 107(7), 20-28.*

15 Passel, J. S., & Cohn, D. (2008, February 11). *U.S. population projections: 2005 – 2050.* Washington, DC: PewResearchCenter.

16 Author compilation from several sources: Johnston, W. B., & Packer, A. H. (1987). *Workforce 2000: Work and workers for the twenty-first century.* Indianapolis, IN: Hudson Institute, Inc. Judy, R. W., & D'Amico, C. (1997). *Workforce 2020: Work and workers in the 21st century.* Indianapolis, IN: Hudson Institute, Inc.

17 Johnson, E. (2008, November). 2008 SHRM human capital leadership awards – Finalists – Competitive workforce award. [*HR Magazine*] Alexandria, VA: Society for Human Resource Management.

18 Guss, E., & Miller, M. C. (2008, October). *Ethics and generational differences: Interplay between values and ethical business decision* [SHRM white paper]. Retrieved from www.shrm.org.

19 Ibid.

20 Deal, J. J. (2007).

21 Martin, C. A. (2005). From high maintenance to high productivity: What managers need to know about Generation Y. *Industrial and Commercial Training, 37(1), 39-45.*

22 Flander, S. (2008, April). Millennial magnets. *Human Resource Executive, 22-29.*

23 Ibid.

24 Glass, A. (2007).

25 Westerman, J. W., & Yamamura, J. H. (2007). Generational preferences for work environment fit: Effects on employee outcomes. *Career Development International, 12(2), 150+.*

26 Beutell, N. J., & Wittig-German, U. (2008). Work-family conflict and work-family synergy for generation X, baby boomers, and matures: Generational differences, predictors and satisfaction outcomes. *Journal of Managerial Psychology, 23(5), 507-523.*

27 Harrington, B. (2008). *The work-life evolution study.* Boston: Boston College Center for Work & Family.

28 Tucker, E., Kao, T., & Verma, N. (2005, July/August).

29 Sabatini Fraone, J., Hartmann, D., & McNally, K. (2008). *The multigenerational workforce: Management implications and strategies for collaboration* [Executive Briefing Series]. Boston: Boston College Center for Work & Family.

30 AARP. (2007).

31 Author compilation from two sources: Jenkins, J. (2008, Winter). Strategies for managing talent in a multigenerational workforce. *Employment Relations Today, 34(4), 19-26. AARP. (2007). Leading a multigenerational workforce.* Washington, DC: Author.

32 Sabatini Fraone, J., Hartmann, D., & McNally, K. (2008).

33 Salt, B. (2008, September). *The global skills convergence: Issues and ideas for the management of an international workforce.* Australia: KPMG International.

34 D'Amato, A., & Herzfeldt, R. (2008). Learning orientation, organizational commitment and talent retention across generations: A study of European managers. *Journal of Managerial Psychology, 23(8), 929-953.*

35 Burke, M. E. (2004, August). *Generational differences survey report.* Alexandria, VA: Society for Human Resource Management.

36 Crumpacker, M., & Crumpacker, J. M. (2007, Winter). Succession planning and generational stereotypes: Should HR consider age-based values and attitudes a relevant factor or a passing fad? *Public Personnel Management, 36(4), 349-370.*

37 Jenkins, J. (2008, Winter). Strategies for managing talent in a multigenerational workforce. *Employment Relations Today, 34(4), 19-26.*

38 AARP. (2008, August). AARP best employers for workers over 50 program. Retrieved November 17, 2008, from www.aarp.org.

CHAPTER 10

[1] Pucik, V. (2005). Global HR as competitive advantage: Are we ready? In M. Losey, S. Meisinger & D. Ulrich (Eds.), *The future of human resource management: 64 thought leaders explore the critical HR issues of today and tomorrow (pp. 370-377).* Hoboken, NJ: John Wiley & Sons, Inc.

[2] Tosti, D. I. (2002). Global fluency. In K. V., Beaman (Ed.), *Boundaryless HR: Human capital management in the global economy (pp. 109 -119).* Austin, TX: IHRIM Press Book.

[3] Towers Perrin. (2005). *Winning strategies for a global workforce: Attracting, retaining and engaging employees for competitive advantage.* Retrieved May 17, 2010, from www.towerswatson.com.

[4] McKinsey & Company. (2010, May). *Five forces reshaping the global economy: McKinsey global survey results.* Retrieved May 12, 2010, from www.mckinseyquarterly.com.

[5] Evans, P., Pucik, V., & Barsoux, J-L. (2002). *The global challenge: Frameworks for international human resource management.* New York: McGraw-Hill Irwin.

[6] Pucik, V. (2005).

[7] Society for Human Resource Management. (2010). *What senior HR leaders need to know: Perspectives from the United States, Canada, India, the Middle East and North Africa.* Alexandria, VA: Author.

[8] Lombardo, M. M., & Eichinger, R. W. (2004). *FYI for your improvement,* 4th ed. Greensboro, NC: Center for Creative Leadership.

[9] Alon, I., & Higgins, J. M. (2005, November/December). Global leadership success through emotional and cultural intelligence. *Business Horizons, 48(6), 501+.*

[10] See Chapter 8.

[11] Pucik, V. (2005).

[12] Gundling, E. (2003). *Working globe smart: 12 people skills for doing business across borders.* Mountain View, CA: Davies-Black Publishing.

[13] Society for Human Resource Management. (2010). Successfully transitioning to a virtual organization: Challenges, impact and technology. *SHRM Research Quarterly, 2.*

[14] Schullion, H., & Collings, D. G. (2006). *Global staffing.* London: Routledge.

[15] Briscoe, D. R., Schuler, R. S., & Claus, L. (2009). *International human resource management: Policies and practices for multinational enterprises,* 3rd edition. New York: Routledge.

[16] Ibid.

[17] Brookfield Global Relocation Services. (2010). *Global relocation trends: 2010 survey report.* Woodridge, IL: Author.

[18] Ibid.

[19] Ibid.

[20] Marx, E. (2001). *Breaking through culture shock: What you need to succeed in international business, 2nd ed.* London: Nicholas Brealey Publishing.

[21] Ibid.

[22] Towers Watson. (2010). *The shape of the emerging "deal": Insights from Towers Watson's 2010 global workforce study.* Retrieved May 12, 2010, from www.towerswatson.com/assets/pdf/global-workforce-study/TWGWS_Exec_Summary.pdf.

[23] Ibid.

[24] Brookfield Global Relocation Services. (2010).

[25] Briscoe, D. R., Schuler, R. S., & Claus, L. (2009).

[26] The Interchange Institute. (2008). *Voices from the road: The personal and family side of international assignments.* Retrieved May 20, 2010, from www.interchangeinstitute.org.

[27] The Interchange Institute. (2008). *Voices from home: The personal and family side of international assignments.* Retrieved May 20, 2010, from www.interchangeinstitute.org.

[28] Claus, L., & International SOS. (2009). *Duty of care of employers for protecting international employees, their dependents and international business travelers.* Trevose, PA: International SOS.

[29] Leki, R. S. (2009). *Travel wise: How to be safe, savvy and secure abroad.* Boston: Intercultural Press.

[30] Storti, C. (2001). *The art of coming home.* Yarmouth, ME: Intercultural Press.

[31] Brookfield Global Relocation Services. (2010).

[32] Ibid.

CHAPTER 11

[1] HayGroup. (2005). *What makes great leaders: Rethinking the route to effective leadership.* Retrieved July 17, 2006, from www.haygroup.com.

[2] Martin, A., & Ernst, C. (2005). Leadership, learning and human resource management: Exploring leadership in times of paradox and complexity. *Corporate Governance, 5, 3, 82-95.*

[3] Fegley, S. (2006, September). *SHRM 2006 strategic HR management survey report.* Alexandria, VA: Society for Human Resource Management.

[4] SHRM Glossary of HR Terms, www.shrm.org.

[5] Watson Wyatt. (2003). Leadership: The critical key to financial success. *Drake Business Review, 1, 1, 21-25.*

[6] Hernez-Broome, G., & Hughes, R. L. (2004). Leadership

development: Past, present and future. *HR. Human Resource Planning, 27, 1, 24-33.*

[7] Schein, L. (2005). *The business value of leadership development.* New York: The Conference Board.

[8] Bilimoria, D., & Godwin, L. (2005). Engaging people's passion: Leadership for the new century. In R. S. Rims & S. A. Quatro (Eds.), *Leadership: Succeeding in the private, public and not-for-profit sectors.* New York: M.E. Sharpe.

[9] Kotter, J. P. (1990). *A force for change: How leadership differs from management.* New York: The Free Press.

[10] Doh, J. P. (2003). Can leadership be taught? Perspectives from management educators. *Academy of Management Learning & Education, 2, 1, 54-68.*

[11] Avolio, B. J. (2005). *Leadership development in balance: MADE/Born.* Mahwah, NJ: Lawrence Erlbaum Associates.

[12] Martin, A., & Ernst, C. (2005).

[13] Crosbie, R. (2005). Learning the soft skills of leadership. *Industrial and Commercial Training, 37, 1, 45-51.*

[14] Avolio, B. J., & Gardner, W. L. (2005, June). Authentic leadership development: Getting to the root of positive forms of leadership. *Leadership Quarterly, 16, 3, 315+.*

[15] Barrett, A., & Beeson, J. (2002). *Developing business leaders for 2010.* New York: The Conference Board.

[16] Pollitt, D. (2005). Leadership succession planning "affects commercial success." *Human Resource Management International Digest, 13, 1, 36-39.*

[17] Avolio, B. J. (2005).

[18] Burke, R. J. (2006). Why leaders fail: Exploring the darkside. *International Journal of Manpower, 27, 1, 91+.*

[19] Garonzik, R., Nethersell, G., & Spreier, S. (2006, Winter). Navigating through the new leadership landscape. *Leader to Leader, 30-39.*

[20] Weiss, D., & Molinaro, V. (2006). Integrated leadership development. *Industrial and Commercial Training, 38, 1, 3-12.*

[21] Ibid.

[22] Who's next in line: Succession management planning and leadership development go hand in hand. (2004). *Strategic Direction, 20, 6, 30+.*

[23] SHRM Glossary of HR Terms, www.shrm.org.

[24] Kur, E., & Bunning, R. (2002). Assuring corporate leadership for the future. *The Journal of Management Development, 21, 9/10, 761-780.*

[25] Berchelman, D. K. (2005, Fall). Succession planning. *The Journal for Quality and Participation, 28, 3, 11-13.*

[26] Fegley, S. (2006). *SHRM 2006 succession planning survey report.* Alexandria, VA: Society for Human Resource Management.

[27] Berchelman, D. K. (2005, Fall).

[28] Holstein, W. J. (2005, November). Best companies for leaders. *Chief Executive, 213, 24-30.*

[29] Esen, E., & Collison, J. (2005). *SHRM/Catalyst employee development survey report.* Alexandria, VA: Society for Human Resource Management.

[30] Conger, J. A., & Fulmer, R. M. (2003, December). Developing your leadership pipeline. *Harvard Business Review, 81, 12, 76-84.*

[31] McCarty Kilian, C., Hukai, D., & McCarty, C. E. (2005). Building diversity in the pipeline to corporate leadership. *The Journal of Management Development, 24, 1/2, 155-169.*

[32] Hernez-Broome, G., & Hughes, R. L. (2004).

[33] Paton, R., Taylor, S., & Storey, J. (2004). Corporate university and leadership development. In *Leadership organizations: Current issues and key trends.* New York: Routledge.

[34] Ibid.

[35] Yeo, R. K. (2006). Developing tomorrow's leaders: Why their world views of today matter? *Industrial and Commercial Training, 38, 2, 63-69.*

[36] Ulrich, D., & Smallwood, N. (2003, April). *Why the bottom line ISN'T: How to build value through people and organizations.* Hoboken, NJ: John Wiley & Sons.

[37] Esen, E., & Collison, J. (2005).

[38] Kaplan, R. S., & Norton, D. P. (1996). *The balanced scorecard.* Boston: Harvard Business Review.

[39] Schein, L., & Kramer, R. J. (2005). *The business value of leadership development.* New York: The Conference Board.

[40] Pollitt, D. (2005).

[41] Rosen, R., Digh, P., Singer, M., & Phillips, C. (2000). *Global literacies: Lessons on business leadership and national cultures.* New York: Simon & Schuster.

[42] Evans, P., Pucik, V., & Barsoux, J-L. (2002). *The global challenges: Frameworks for international human resource management.* New York: McGraw-Hill Companies, Inc.

[43] Alon, I., & Higgins, J. M. (2005, November/December). Global leadership success through emotional and cultural intelligences. *Business Horizons, 48, 6, 501+.*

[44] Kramer, R. J. (2005). *Developing global leaders: Enhancing competencies and accelerating the expatriate experience.* New York: The Conference Board.

[45] Bell, A. N. (2006). *Leadership development in Asia-Pacific: Identifying and developing leaders for growth.* New York: The Conference Board.

[46] Martin, A., & Ernst, C. (2005).

[47] HayGroup. (2005).

[48] Pollitt, D. (2005).

[49] Hewitt. (2005). *How the top 20 companies grow great leaders.* Retrieved August 2, 2006, from www.hewitt.com.

[50] Hernez-Broome, G., & Hughes, R. L. (2004).

CHAPTER 12

[1] SHRM Glossary of HR Terms: www.shrm.org.

[2] Daniel, T. A., & Metcalf, G. S. (2005, May 1). *The science of motivation* [SHRM white paper]. Retrieved from www.shrm.org/Research/Articles/Articles/Pages/CMS_012666.aspx.

[3] Stanley, T. L. (2008, March). A motivated workplace is a marvelous sight. *SuperVision, 59/3, 5-9.*

[4] Lawler, E. E. III. (2003). *Treat people right! How organizations and individuals can propel each other into a virtuous spiral of success.* San Francisco: John Wiley & Sons, Inc.

[5] Knowledge@Wharton. (2010, February 17). Putting a face to a name: The art of motivating employees. Retrieved February 18, 2010, from http://knowledge.wharton.upenn.edu/article.cfm?articleid=2436.

[6] Ibid.

[7] Blanchard, K., & Shula, D. (2001). *The little book of coaching: Motivating people to be winners.* New York: HarperCollins Publishers, Inc.

[8] Bloomberg BusinessWeek.com/Hay Group. (2010, February). 2009 best companies for leadership. Retrieved February 24, 2010, from www.haygroup.com/ww/best_companies/index.aspx?id=156.

[9] Ibid.

[10] Dewhurst, S. (2009, April/May). How to regain your motivation for work. *Strategic Communication Management, 13/3, 14.*

[11] Ibid.

[12] Santamour, B., (2009, March). Inspired staff can see you through hard times. *Hospitals & Health Networks, 83/3, 10.*

[13] Ibid.

[14] Daniel, T. A., & Metcalf, G. S. (2005, May 1).

[15] Wilson, I., & Madsen, S. R. (2008, April). The influence of Maslow's humanistic views on employee's motivation to learn. *Journal of Applied Management and Entrepreneurship, 13/2, 46-63.*

[16] Overton, L. (2009, February). Delivering business results. *E.learning Age, 6-9.*

[17] Latham, G. P. (2007). *Work motivation: History, theory, research, and practice.* Thousand Oaks, CA: Sage Publications, Inc.

[18] Goleman, D., Boyatzis, R., & McKee, A. (2002). *Primal leadership: Realizing the power of emotional intelligence.* Boston: Harvard Business School Press.

[19] Luthans, F., Youssef, C. M., & Avolio, B. J. (2007). *Psychological capital: Developing the human capital edge.* New York: Oxford University Press.

[20] Pink, D. H. (2009). *Drive: The surprising truth about what motivates us.* New York: Riverhead Books.

[21] Dent, F., & Holton, V. (2009, November). Employee engagement and motivation. *Training Journal, 37.*

[22] Nohria, N., Groysberg, B., & Lee, L-E. (2008, July-August). Employee motivation: A powerful new model. *Harvard Business Review, 86/7-8, 78-84.*

[23] Ibid.

[24] Ibid.

[25] Society for Human Resource Management. (2009). *2009 employee benefits: A survey report by SHRM.* Alexandria, VA: Author.

[26] Society for Human Resource Management. (2009). The multigenerational workforce: Opportunity for competitive success. *SHRM Research Quarterly, 1.*

[27] Marson, C. (2005). *Motivating the "what's in it for me?" workforce: Managing across the generational divide.* Charlotte, NC: Marston Communications.

[28] Accenture. (2010, February 10). Young people in China and India are reshaping corporate information technologies. Retrieved March 3, 2010, from http://newsroom.accenture.com/article_display.cfm?article_id=4937.

CHAPTER 13

[1] Blair, B. E., & Kochan, T. (2000). *The new relationship: Human capital in the American corporation.* Washington, DC: Brookings Institution Press.

[2] Kaplan, R., & Norton, D. (2001). *The strategy-focused organization: How balanced scorecard companies thrive in the new business environment.* Boston: Harvard Business School Press.

[3] Lawler, E., & McDermott, M. (2003). Current performance management practices. *WorldatWork Journal, 12, 2, 49-60.*

[4] Kotter, J., & Heskett, J. (1992). *Corporate culture and performance.* New York: The Free Press.

[5] Becker, B., Huselid, M., & Ulrich, D., (2001). *The HR scorecard: Linking people, strategy, and performance.* Boston: Harvard Business School Press.

[6] Lawler, E., & McDermott, M. (2003).

[7] *Working today: Understanding what drives employee engagement—The 2003 Towers Perrin talent report.* Towers Perrin. Retrieved December 19, 2003, from www.towers.com/towers/webcache/towers/United_States/publications/Reports/Talent_Report_2003/Talent_2003.pdf

[8] Stark, M. (2002). Five years of insight into the world's most admired companies. *Journal of Organizational Excellence, 22, 1, 3-12.*

[9] Lawler, E., & McDermott, M. (2003).

10 Lawler, E. (2000). *Rewarding excellence.* San Francisco: Jossey-Bass Publishers.

CHAPTER 14

1 O'Neill, T. 1 A., Lewis, R. J., & Hambley, L. A. (2008). Leading virtual teams – potential problems and simple solutions. In J. Nemiro, M. Beyerlein, L. Bradley, & S. Beyerlein (Eds.), *The handbook of high-performance virtual teams: A toolkit for collaborating across boundaries (pp. 59-83).* San Francisco: Jossey-Bass.

2 Fisher, K., & Fisher, D. (2001). *The distance manager: A hands-on guide to managing off-site employees and virtual teams. New York: McGraw-Hill.*

3 Ibid.

4 Lockwood, N. R. (2004, August). *SHRM Briefly Stated: Team series part III: Global virtual teams.* Retrieved from www.shrm.org.

5 Ibid.

CHAPTER 15

1 Business Roundtable—Institute for Corporate Ethics. (2009). *The dynamics of public trust in business—Emerging opportunities for leaders.* Retrieved July 16, 2009, from www.corporate-ethics.org.

2 Society for Human Resource Management & the Ethics Resource Center. (2008, June). *The ethics landscape in American business.* Alexandria, VA: Authors.

3 Weaver, G. R. (1993). Corporate codes of ethics: Purpose, process and content issues. *Business and Society, 32(1), 44-58.*

4 Weaver, G.R., Treviño, L. K., & Cochran, P. (1999). Corporate ethics programs as control systems: Influence of executive commitment and environmental factors. *Academy of Management Journal, 42 (1); 41-57.*

5 Ibid.

6 Tyler, T., Dienhart, J., & Thomas, T. (2008, Winter). The ethical commitment to compliance: Building value-based cultures. *California Management Review, 50(2), 31-51.*

7 Ethics Resource Center. (2009, November). *2009 National Business Ethics Survey. Retrieved from www.ethics.org.*

8 Treviño, L. K., & Weaver, G. R. (2003). *Managing ethics in business organizations.* Stanford, CA: Stanford University Press.

9 Society for Human Resource Management & the Ethics Resource Center. (2008, June).

10 Ethics Resource Center. (2006). *Critical elements of an organizational ethical culture.* Retrieved September 25, 2009, from www.ethics.org/resource/criticalelements-organizational-ethicalculture.

11 Berenbeim, R. E., & Dubinsky, J. E. (2008, January). Working at the intersection of human resources and business ethics: The need for collaboration. *Executive Action series* [The Conference Board], 2–9.

12 Guss, E., & Miller, M. C. (2008, October). *Ethics and generational differences: Interplay between values and ethical business decisions* [white paper]. Retrieved from www.shrm.org.

13 Deal, J. J. (2007). *Retiring the generation gap: How employees young and old can find common ground.* San Francisco: Jossey-Bass and the Center for Creative Leadership.

14 Society for Human Resource Management. (2008, July). *Volunteerism: Moving up on the strategic agenda.* Alexandria, VA: Author.

15 Deloitte. (2008). *2007 volunteer IMPACT survey.* Retrieved September 10, 2009, from www.deloitte.com.

16 De Colle, S., & Werhane, P. H. (2007, Spring). Moral motivation across ethical theories: What can we learn for designing corporate ethics programs? *Journal of Business Ethics, 81, 751-764.*

17 Urbany, J.E., Reynolds, T.J., & Phillips, J. M. (2008, Summer). How to make values count in everyday decisions. *MITSloan Management Review.* Retrieved July 16, 2009, from www.sloanreview.mit.edu.

18 Society for Human Resource Management & the Ethics Resource Center. (2008, June).

19 Ethics Resource Center. (2009, November).

20 Tyler, T., Dienhart, J., & Thomas, T. (2008, Winter).

CHAPTER 16

1 The Boston Consulting Group, Inc., and the World Federation of Personnel Management Associations. (2008). *Creating people advantage: How to address HR challenges worldwide through 2015.* Boston: The Boston Consulting Group, Inc.

2 DeGraff, J., & Lawrence, K. A. (2002). *Creativity at work: Developing the right practices to make innovation happen.* San Francisco: John Wiley & Sons, Inc.

3 Thakok, A. V. (2000). *Becoming a better value creator: How to improve the company's bottom line—and your own.* San Francisco: Jossey-Bass, Inc.

4 Ibid.

5 Michalko, M. (2001). *Cracking creativity: The secrets of creative genius.* Berkeley, CA: Ten Speed Press.

6 Society for Human Resource Management. (2009). Leveraging HR and knowledge management in a challenging economy. *SHRM Quarterly, 4.*

7 Barrington, L., Foster, G. D., van Ark, B., & Woock, C. (2009, May). *Innovation and U.S. competitiveness.* New

York: The Conference Board.

[8] Ibid.

[9] Davila, T., Epstein, M. J., & Shelton, R. (2006).*Making innovation work: How to manage it, measure it, and profit from it.* Upper Saddle River, NJ: Wharton School Publishing.

[10] Ibid.

[11] The Boston Consulting Group, Inc., and the World Federation of Personnel Management Associations. (2008).

[12] Rees, R. T. (2007, Winter). The role of HR in organizational development and innovation. *Employment Relations, 33(4), 29-34.*

[13] Davila, T., Epstein, M. J., & Shelton, R. (2006).*Making innovation work: How to manage it, measure it, and profit from it.* Upper Saddle River, NJ: Wharton School Publishing.

[14] Society for Human Resource Management. (2009, February 17). *SHRM poll: Programs and practices to confront the workplace effects of the downturn in the economy.* Retrieved from www.shrm.org/surveys.

[15] Ibid.

[16] Society for Human Resource Management. (2009, May). *Examining paid leave in the workplace: Helping your organization attract and retain talented employees.* Retrieved from www.shrm.org/surveys.

[17] Society for Human Resource Management. (2008, April-June). The employer brand: A strategic tool to attract, recruit and retain talent. *SHRM Staffing Research, 2.*

[18] Corporate Leadership Council. (2004). *Driving performance and retention through employee engagement.* Washington, DC: Corporate Executive Board.

[19] See Chapter 1.

[20] See Chapter 9.

[21] Flander, S. (2008, April). Millennial magnets. *Human Resource Executive, 22-29.*

[22] Ibid.

[23] Towers Perrin. (2008). *2007-2008 Towers Perrin global workforce study.* Retrieved June 6, 2009, from www.towersperrin.com.

[24] Society for Human Resource Management. (2009, April). *Examining paid leave in the workplace: Helping your organization attract and retain talented employees.* Retrieved from www.shrm.org/surveys.

[25] Society for Human Resource Management. (2009, July). *Workplace flexibility in the 21st century: Meeting the needs of the changing workforce.* Alexandria, VA: Author.

CHAPTER 17

[1] Society for Human Resource Management. (2008). *SHRM glossary of human resources terms.* Retrieved February 13, 2008, from www.shrm.org/hrresources/hrglossary.

[2] Society for Human Resource Management. (2008, February). *2008 managing your HR career.* Alexandria, VA: Author.

[3] Society for Human Resource Management. (2008).

[4] Ibid.

[5] Ibid.

[6] Ibid.

[7] Palmer, P., & Finney, M. L. (2004). *The human resource professional's career guide: Building a position of strength.* San Francisco: John Wiley & Sons, Inc.

[8] Lawler, III, E. E., Boudreau, J. W., & Albers Mohrman, S. (2006). *Achieving strategic excellence: An assessment of human resource organizations.* Stanford, CA: Stanford Business Books.

[9] Society for Human Resource Management. (2008, February).

[10] Palmer, P., & Finney, M. L. (2004). *The human resource professional's career guide: Building a position of strength.* San Francisco: John Wiley & Sons, Inc.

[11] Ibid.

[12] Ibid.

[13] Robb, D. (2006, June). Higher performance. *HR Magazine, 51(6), 135-142.*

[14] Society for Human Resource Management. (2008, February).

[15] Ibid.

[16] Palmer, P., & Finney, M. L. (2004).

[17] Lockwood, N. R. (2004, August). *Formal and informal mentoring.* [SHRM Briefly Stated Mentoring Series]. Retrieved on February 4, 2008, from www.shrm.org.

[18] Hay Group. (2008). Preparing for your future: Best companies for leaders. Hay Group webinar, January 2008, www.haygroup.com.

[19] Miller, G. (2001). *The career coach: Winning strategies for getting ahead in today's job market.* New York: Doubleday.

[20] Grensing-Pophal, L. (2007, February). Coaching HR. *HR Magazine, 52(2), 95-99.*

[21] Ibid.

[22] Society for Human Resource Management. (2008, February).

[23] Society for Human Resource Management. (2006). *SHRM human resource curriculum guidebook and templates.* Alexandria, VA: Author.

[24] Ibid.

[25] Robb, D. (2006, June).

[26] *The 2007 Human Resource Competency Study conducted by the RBL Group and the Ross School of Business at the University of Michigan, in cooperation with regional partners: SHRM, IAE, IMI, AHRI, National HRD Network and Tsinghua University.*

[27] Ibid.

[28] Caligiui, P. (2006). Developing global leaders. *Human Resource Management Review, 16, 219-228.*

[29] Rosen, R., Digh, P., Singer, M. & Phillips, C. (2000). *Global literacies: Lessons on business leadership and national cultures.* New York: Simon & Schuster.

[30] McCall, M., & Hollenbeck, G. (2002). *Developing global executives: The lessons of international experience.* Boston: Harvard Business School Publishing.

[31] Poore, C. A. (2001). *Building your career portfolio.* Franklin Lakes, NJ: Career Press.

[32] Hay Group Limited. (2008). Preparing for your future: Best companies for leaders. Hay Group webinar, January 2008, www.haygroup.com.

[33] Dooney, J., & Esen, E. (2007, November). Incentive pay fuels HR salaries. *HR Magazine, 52(11), 35-43.*

[34] Miller, G. (2001). *The career coach: Winning strategies for getting ahead in today's job market.* New York: Doubleday.

[35] Palmer, P., & Finney, M. L. (2004).

[36] Ibid.

Index

Additional SHRM-Published Books

Assessing External Job Candidates
By Jean M. Phillips and Stanley M. Gully

Assessing Internal Job Candidates
By Jean M. Phillips and Stanley M. Gully

Becoming the Evidence-Based Manager: Making the Science of Management Work for You
By Gary P. Latham

Corporate India and HR Management: Creating Talent Pipelines, Leadership Competencies, and Human Resources
By Society for Human Resource Management

The Cultural Fit Factor: Creating an Employment Brand That Attracts, Retains, and Repels the Right Employees
By Lizz Pellet

The EQ Interview: Finding Employees with High Emotional Intelligence
By Adele B. Lynn

Evaluating Human Resources Programs: A 6-Phase Approach for Optimizing Performance
By Jack Edwards, John C. Scott, and Nambury S. Raju

HR and the New Hispanic Workforce: A Comprehensive Guide to Cultivating and Leveraging Employee Success
By Louis Nevaer and Vaso Perimenis Ekstein

HR Competencies: Mastery at the Intersection of People and Business
By Dave Ulrich, Wayne Brockbank, Dani Johnson, Kurt Sandholtz, and Jon Younger

Human Resource Transformation: Demonstrating Strategic Leadership in the Face of Future Trends
By William J. Rothwell, Robert K. Prescott, and Maria W. Taylor

Igniting Gen B & Gen V: The New Rules of Engagement for Boomers, Veterans, and Other Long-Termers on the Job
By Nancy S. Ahlrichs

Investing in What Matters: Linking Employees to Business Outcomes
By Scott P. Mondore and Shane S. Douthitt

Leading with Your Heart: Diversity and *Ganas* for Inspired Inclusion
By Cari M. Dominguez and Jude Sotherlund

Managing Diversity: A Complete Desk Reference & Planning Guide
By Lee Gardenswartz and Anita Rowe

Never Get Lost Again: Navigating Your HR Career
By Nancy E. Glube and Phyllis G. Hartman

Performance Consulting: A Practical Guide for HR and Learning Professionals
By Dana Gaines Robinson and James C. Robinson

Reinventing Talent Management: How to Maximize Performance in the New Marketplace
By William A. Schiemann

Rethinking Retention in Good Times and Bad: Breakthrough Ideas for Keeping Your Best Workers
By Richard P. Finnegan

Smart Policies for Workplace Technologies: Email, Blogs, Cell Phones and More
By Lisa Guerin

Staffing Forecasting and Planning
By Jean M. Phillips and Stanley M. Gully

Staffing to Support Business Strategy
By Jean M. Phillips and Stanley M. Gully

Stop Bullying at Work: Strategies and Tools for HR and Legal Professionals
By Teresa A. Daniel

Strategic Staffing: A Comprehensive System for Effective Workforce Planning
By Thomas P. Bechet